I am so blessed and honoured to be asked by the author to endorse her book, Secret: Fame or Failure 107 Women of the Bible.

Dorothy is not only my friend, but also one of my spiritual daughters, and it is such a blessing to see what God is doing in her life in the production of this book. Get ready to be blessed.

This book provides deep provocative insight of so many women mentioned in the bible. Their stories come from a different perspective providing such valuable source of hope, inspiration, and encouragement. It is a must-read for all women; highly recommended for those women who struggle with daily challenges, those women whose lives are mundane and uninteresting, and those who need to make sense of life issues. This book will raise your profile to be your best for God.

The theme conveyed from cover to cover highlights that no experience in life goes to waste, even when one cannot identify with the true essence or meaning of their experience. Every person and every situation is driven by God-ordained purpose. The author has laid the foundation by setting forth the experiences of 107 women of the bible, showing how their lives and circumstances can teach us how to depend on God and how to be strong and not give up.

May God richly bless and encourage you as you glean from the pages.

WRITTEN BY REV. CYNTHIA. M. JACK whose pastoral ministry spans more than four decades. Her wisdom and experience in the field of ministry has been used over the years to build the kingdom of God by teaching adults and children. Through her ministry as pastor, teacher and lecturer in theology she has had a global impact. Rev. Jack continues her service in the kingdom also as a life coach and mentor.

Secret: Fame or Failure 107 Women of the Bible—*A very interesting, mind-blowing, and informative read. I enjoyed this book so much: it was refreshing, inspiring, and gives readers a new concept.*

T0327952

I have been a Christian for two decades and I am truly amazed at the greatness of the women in this book. I have learnt so much of their character, courage, strength and faith. Some women faced a lot of adversities and disadvantages, yet they overcame their battles and challenges. Some of them I didn't remember the names, but they made a difference. The simplicity of those women's faith move mountains. Today as Christian women, we can draw strength, courage and overcome in the same way.

The author has brought creativity to a new level, mixing excerpts from the most famous book in the world (the Bible) with modern-day reality.

I love it. It's a must-read.

HAZEL BROWNE – HEALTH PROFESSIONAL MANAGER AND CHRISTIAN LEADER (UK)

The Secret to Fame *and success and/or Failure and destruction can be found in the number one bestseller of all time, the bible; our "Basic Instructions Before Leaving Earth." However, the way we interpret and unravel these secrets will define our destiny. This book decipher these secrets in an innovative way and in some instances with humour and very cryptic messages. After reading the bible for more than forty years of my life and hearing hundreds of sermons on some of these characters, the meaning and relevance of the lives and circumstances of these women are now more prominent. I am able to compare many of my experiences with numerous bible characters in this book. On the other hand, I can view some of these women as mentors and examples.*

Personally, I am amazed. My knowledge from the hundreds of sermons heard and bible literature read never tallied that there were so many women in the bible. To be honest I have always heard about a handful, possibly around twenty-five, so it is great to know that after all these years I am discovering stories and learning about many great women who have been overlooked. This is a holistic and comprehensive look at women of the bible. Good, bad, or indifferent, they all had a purpose.

My knowledge of the biblical account of the first woman, Eve, is that she was naked until she sinned. I never thought that she went to fellowship (church) daily with Adam and God was most present, but she was in the nude. I never thought she got married in the most simplistic bridal wear, naked. Apart from learning about so many wonderful women I have never heard about, I am gaining wisdom on those that I have been familiar with.

I love the book and recommend it to all women and their families. I guarantee that there is so much to discover. It is impossible to read this book without unraveling biblical truths.

What's amazing to me is everything that happened in the beginning with Adam and Eve still resonate today. Eve was beautiful, loving, gracious, powerful, and extraordinarily influential. It was easy for her to think that she was more knowledgeable. In today's society women have a lot of influence over men. I often wonder what the world would be like today if Eve did not make that tragic and fatal decision. This book was very informative, insightful, inspirational, intriguing, and thought-provoking. An interesting read and I highly recommend.

LOIS KAREN HARRIS - MILLER, CHRISTIAN TEACHER AND COUNSELOR, WIFE, MOTHER (USA)

SECRET:
FAME OR FAILURE

SECRET:
FAME OR FAILURE

107 Women of the Bible

Dorothy Johnson

ELM HILL

A Division of
HarperCollins Christian Publishing

www.elmhillbooks.com

Secret: Fame or Failure
107 Women of the Bible

Published in Nashville, Tennessee, by Elm Hill, an imprint of Thomas Nelson. Elm Hill and Thomas Nelson are registered trademarks of HarperCollins Christian Publishing, Inc.

Elm Hill titles may be purchased in bulk for educational, business, fund-raising, or sales promotional use. For information, please e-mail SpecialMarkets@ ThomasNelson.com.

New King James Version of the Bible and Blazing Glory Holy Bible were the text used for the preparation of this book.

Library of Congress Cataloging-in-Publication Data

Library of Congress Control Number: 2018951382

ISBN 978-1-595558459 (Paperback)
ISBN 978-1-595558480 (Hardbound)
ISBN 978-1-595557933 (eBook)

Acknowledgement and Appreciation

Foremost, I want to express my gratitude to Almighty God for His strength, wisdom, and divine revelation as I penned my first book. It has been an extraordinary journey of faith and wisdom.

Special thanks and acknowledgement to my dear mother, whose faithful life and service to God spans sixty years. Mum, you impacted my life in incredible ways and taught me the ways of God both in word and deeds. I salute you, Mum.

Thanks to my dear husband Colin for his love, commitment, and support in creating an environment of understanding as I worked arduously to produce this book.

A few years ago I was in Florida when I began writing. I was deeply touched and encouraged as Chandra at age five sat with me, having her mother's laptop to commence her book also. Thanks, Chandra. I look forward to reading your book.

Thanks, Brenique, my twelve-year-old niece who only found out that I was writing this book a few months ago. Your words were inspiring.

Thanks to my brothers, their wives, children, and their grandchildren for their love and support.

To all my friends, church brethren, and ex-colleagues who reminded me that they are waiting to read the book. Thank you.

Special thank you, Theastarr, my God daughter even though we are in different parts of the world. You were always in my living room thanks to modern technology. You made such an indelible contribution to secure an excellent finish.

To all those who inspired me to a finished product, IT IS HERE FINALLY!

Introduction

Controversy on gender roles and gender stereotype is unavoidable; this has been around for millennia. It is paradoxical, many of the concepts governing women in society are not made by women. This huge problem is presented in some societies as selective termination of pregnancies of female infants. In other societies, girls are unfairly disadvantaged and are deprived educationally, whereas in some cultures girls become childhood brides with no choice in the matter.

Sad but true, in some cultural settings women are equal to a commodity or a product used by consumers. Bias among women can present itself as less remuneration than their male counterpart for the same job. Among religious groups, although women and men received the same theological training, women were not recognised in the same manner as men. They were not granted similar opportunities among the hierarchy within the clergy, nor were given similar roles or titles. This gap existed for countless decades it is only in recent times that women have been given greater recognition and access to promotion within the clergy. This list of prejudices against women is in no way exhaustive. These inequalities and many more are the real challenges women face in their efforts to be who they are meant to be.

Amidst these disparities many women have excelled in various facets of our society—in fashion, music, comedy, sports, art and culture, religion, education, social justice, and politics just to mention a few. They have been recognised for their contribution both nationally and globally. Women like *Queen Elizabeth II, the late Margaret Thatcher, Oprah Winfrey, Michelle Obama, the late Mother Theresa, Malala Yousafzai (Nobel Peace Prize winner), Hilary Clinton, and Theresa May* fit into this category. Public recognition of women was not always the norm and even today in some cultures, women cannot attain to a sphere of affluence or influence. Highest accolade and commendation are in order to Queen Victoria II and Queen Elizabeth II for their role in the monarchy, spanning a period of over one hundred twenty years. They are the two longest reigning monarchs in British history, taking them where **no man has been before**.

Arguably women have always been a stabilising factor in society past and present. They have influenced the state, military, economy, nations, politics, and the spiritual climate. However, it is with much regret that some of these vital contributions have been silenced and buried. These achievements deserve to be celebrated as some emerged amidst unprecedented struggle.

Among the galleries of ancient literature, there is no writing as unique as the bible, showcasing its female characters within an exclusively male-dominant culture. These women were not included in the population statistics of their times according to Exod. 12:37 and Matt. 14:21, 15:38, nor were they the main teachers of the word of God though they knew the God of the word. How did they do it? Their success was based on principles. Such principles can still be applied to twenty-first century thinking and living, since failure and success are deeply embedded in principles and habits. The best of these women were trailblazers for freedom of thought and action, contributing to the present high status of womanhood.

Upon careful examination of the holy book (the bible), women like Esther, Ruth, Mary the mother of Jesus, and Hannah are commended for their positive impact. On the other hand, what lessons can be learnt from women like Eve? She was part of the original sin and through her disobedience the entire human race plunged into spiritual darkness. Sapphira who colluded with her husband in wrongdoing, as a result they both died at the church altar. Jezebel, who agreed with her husband to covet their neighbour's garden as their own; after doing so she sent a death threat to the prophet of God.

Many fundamental lessons can be learnt from both groups since their actions are governed by principles. These principles are constant and always produce results. We can learn how to govern our lives from those who defied logic, conquered and subdued nations. These actions forced them to obtain supernatural favours. They lived and communicated future realities as if they had already occurred. It is of even greater consolation that these heroines influenced their nations in an era when it is alleged that some Jewish men prayed daily *thanking God, they were not classified in any of these categories, a Gentile, a dog, and a woman.* However, their success derived from application of the right principle, coupled with the right attitude and action.

As you embark upon reading this book, remember that some of the female characters are women who lived and existed in real time, while some are figurative or metaphorical figures. Some women carried full and complete identity with names and addresses, while others were known only by where they lived, many others by the circumstances they found themselves in, or by the names of their husband or children. Those known by their son's name have greatness conferred on them by the sons they produced. These women at some time in their lives were pregnant with greatness, cradled greatness, and allowed greatness to suckle at their breasts. On the other hand, some women's greatness must be recognised through their husband, since behind every great man stands a greater woman.

Secret: Fame or Failure is informative, exciting, dynamic, and creative, bringing many of the popular bible stories alive. It is a great tool for studying the lives of outstanding Christian women. This unique publication enhances the knowledge of scholars who have studied the bible for many years. It is compact with divine revelation and teaching, linking the lives of ancient women with those alive today. It is the writer's hope that every reader will be impacted by one or more of the characters within this book, whose life stood out bringing about permanent change in ancient times.

FOREWORD

M ost Christians like to boast that their favourite book is the Bible. However, let's be real, how many of us actually understand it? The King James Version—hmmmm, all those 'eths' at the end of words. What can we do but pray that the Holy Spirit interprets the words on the pages for us? I mean scripture is *God-breathed*... I grew up in Church where many times my mind drew blanks as I listened to the preacher speak so eloquently about what he studied from God's word. Years later I found myself sitting in Bible school with the same thought, *"What are these people speaking about?"*

I remember that first day after my theology class, I prayed and asked the Holy Spirit to interpret everything I read. This practice continued until the day I graduated. At times I thought reading the Bible was tedious because I didn't understand what was written. As an avid reader and author, I know the importance of research, and oh my, did I have (and continuously have) to research the Bible. Concordances, dictionaries, articles, books, and good ol' internet search engines help me with my studies of the Bible. Of course my main interpreter is the Author of authors Himself, The Creator of the Universe: God.

Months ago, Mrs. Dorothy Johnson, aka *my godmother*, asked me to embark upon a journey with her—to help her edit her very first book. The word *honoured* is an understatement of how I felt. As the owner of Empress Royále Publishing, I had the pleasure of having my godmother as my first client.

Secret: Fame or Failure isn't your ordinary Bible study aid. I've seen many of those over the years. This book takes creativity to a whole new level—the author brings to life over 100 powerful women mentioned in the Bible. I'm sure many of us haven't even heard one quarter of the names mentioned.

The difference between this book and others that I've read, is the author's ability to highlight women of the Bible, both good and bad. While other books may seek to place emphasis on lessons that one can learn from the 'good' women of the Bible, *Secret* expose the impact of women whether negative or positive.

Dorothy Johnson is not only qualified in the field of biblical teaching and medicine, but she also exemplifies what it means to be a woman, a Proverbs 31 woman. Her life is an open book and she is straightforward. Not only is she interested in the lives of young people, but her passion for helping us to understand God's truth shines forth in the way she communicates. She has been my godmother for over twenty-nine years and I have always found it easy to speak with her.

Coming from Trinidad and Tobago, I am happy to be part of this ground breaking work. Dorothy is a proud Tobagonian who represent the smaller of the twin island with dignity.

Dorothy is well-travelled and has experienced life in various ways that are not known to many. Her annual ministry report to her family and prayer partners highlights the work that she does with women, leaders and young people. Over the years, I have seen pictures and heard the testimonies from the people she has impacted.

From the raw tone of the accounts, *Secrets* is a book you wouldn't want to put down. As a Christian, leader, and teacher of biblical truths, I've gleaned many insights from Dorothy's writing. It is not your typical **dos and don'ts** of the Bible, but something fresh, as presented in the section called **Modern-Day Reality**. Her writing is biblical, experiential, entertaining, stimulating, but all in all relevant to modern-day Christians.

Secret is a book you could use as a study aid for your Bible reading. It's not only for women's ministries or youth groups, but for anyone who want to understand the essential qualities of what it takes to be a woman, shape society, and impact legacy.

SPREAD THE WORD. THE SECRET IS OUT.

— Theastarr 'Empress' Valerie
Royalty, author, teacher, missionary
Owner of Empress Royále Publishing

CONTENTS

CHAPTER 1

EVE

(Genesis 2:21–25; 3:1–24; 4:1–26)

She was the perfect bride: no trail, no veil, simply naked.
How romantic!

The beginning seems the right place to start. The earth had experienced an invasion of astonishing beauty for the first time. So as not to alarm the man, he was completely anesthetised so she could be created. God took one of his ribs and mixed the rib with precious elements of love, graciousness, beauty, power of influence, then out came the most astonishing beauty the world has known. The man was created from the raw material, earth. But she was made from the refined product; her name was *Eve*.

God stood a little distance from the scene as Adam awoke. His eyes dazzled, he froze and stood speechless, then he muttered, 'Chemistry fantastic, mathematics spot on, one plus one is still one.'

God moved this woman down the aisle of the garden called Eden. God performed the first ever wedding ceremony. What a Father—Giver.

She was the perfect bride: no trail, no veil, simply naked. In fact she was the first bride ever; what a romantic moment this must have been.

Adam yelled, '*WOW, she is part of me, she came out of me.* **I will call her woman, or I will call her, "WOW, I am complete," or "WOW, MAN this is all good."**

Adam, who was also naked, made his wedding vows while introducing himself. He found it very easy to make that commitment for life to the woman he fell in love with, even if he had only seen her a few minutes earlier. There is certainly a notion of love at first sight.

Adam knew he had kissed singleness goodbye. A naked man took a naked woman, under the open canopy of heaven in the presence of a Holy God, to become his wife in the most beautiful garden. This was purity and perfection, and must be the most romantic union ever. None before like it, and certainly none after to be its equal; it was first class and all that follows will be unequivocal. Just imagine: no rivalry, no adultery, no polygamy; they both had eyes for each other only.

Before Adam met his mate he looked at all the animals and realised there was no companion for him, none to communicate with him in a way that could touch his heart and meet all his intimate desires.

God made a man in His divine image and deposited in him all that man needed to relate upwards to God his Creator. He was also able to relate on his level to the woman God created from him, for him.

It is not good for neither the man nor the woman to go solo.
(GENESIS 2:18, PARAPHRASED)

As Eve wandered alone to explore, she met a serpent who chatted with her and persuaded her to indulge (Genesis 3:1–4). This creature stood up on Eve's level, paying her compliments, boosting her ego.

Eve did not realise that these compliments were superficial since the serpent's intention was covert. The serpent was not interested in her beauty, or her sweet sounding voice, neither was he interested in her well-proportioned physique. The serpent's plan was one of deception and to win over her pure mind to his wicked ways of thinking. Satan always uses a medium that is appealing. Before the technological era, he used a spectacular, upright-walking and talking serpent.

This genius of a serpent was a master advertiser of *forbidden substances*. Sometimes you look at an advertisement and ask, what does this have to do with the product? You are right, what does a serpent have to do with forbidden fruits?

Fruits, fruits what a treat,
Only sweet when you eat
Open your eyes,
Makes you smarter
Simple, wiser, happier and better,
Just have it,
Instant result, guaranteed.

Eve then glided across the garden and met her naked husband in the middle of the flower bed. Adam thought it was one of those romantic moments since he had experienced many of those moments before. His eyes were fixed on her, as she had both hands hidden behind her back. Eve said, *'Darling close your eyes, I have something for you.'* She then bit the fruit and held it in her mouth, and asked Adam to open his eyes. Adam was so captivated and weakened by love, he bit the fruit from Eve's mouth.

Eve's downfall came as she walked in solitude, took advice from her enemy, and acted on the enemy's advice. She made major life and death decisions without consulting her husband. She went from living in paradise and enjoying the pleasure of a sinless world to living in a sinful world. Her experience was diverse and without parallel but I am sure she prefers the former.

Adam met with his Creator daily; imagine having a worship service in the middle of the garden with God. No dress code for 'church': they came just as they were naked. He never read a book but he called all the animals by their names as we know them today. Up until that moment he was totally obedient to God. However, there came a moment in his life when he did not think about God. Adam was completely covered by her love so he refused to have his wife fall into temptation alone. Her influence was extraordinary.

Eve's act of disobedience was not that which the Creator desired; it encompassed revolt and rebellion, which resulted in severe consequences. Her actions changed the entire course and destiny of the universe and humanity. God desired obedience; this was their test of obedience. Sadly the couple failed the obedience test. As a result of their disobedience, the entire universe spiralled out of control, reaping a harvest of destruction and disaster from then to now.

Eve's action caused a negative impact on earth, which continued through her offspring and the entire human race. Her first son became increasingly jealous of his innocent younger brother, which resulted in the very first murder on planet Earth.

Eve as the only woman who met God personally, must also be credited for the powerful influence she exerted on her man. She was beautiful, romantic, and created companionship and intimacy. She was a teacher of how to love. If she had exercised her power of influence and acted in obedience, then the whole of creation would be in eternal paradise here on earth.

The principle, however, remains the same: a woman can create an oasis of love for her husband and have him reciprocate that love. Eve knew that any love given away will multiply and return in greater proportion and propensity. It is rather intrinsic within human nature to wander away from what seems too elementary or what some refer to as outdated. This was not only a problem in Eve's time, but the current generation suffers with the same tendencies. The underlying principle is that someone or something is influencing you and you are influencing someone else. The serpent influenced Eve who influenced her husband Adam. This episode could have had a happy ending if the power of the most influential, who is God, was residing within this original pair.

Questions for consideration:

1. Would Eve have acted differently if she knew that all of humanity depended on her decision?
2. Would she disobey if she knew that it would cost Jesus His life?
3. Would she have communicated with the serpent or chosen to run away if she knew that sin, death, and pain would be the consequences?
4. Would she have sacrificed eternal happiness, peace, joy and love, which would have followed her obedience?

Eve's act of disobedience had both global and lasting repercussion through many generations for thousands of years. Sometimes we find ourselves in a similar position like Eve. We know that obedience is the right way, but we sometimes justify ourselves into disobedience.

The consequences of our obedience or disobedience have not changed. The influences in our lives affect the choices and decision-making processes. The outcomes can be either positive or negative. Like Eve, our actions and deeds do not end at the point of committing; the outcome continues through generations, either as a welcoming or unwelcoming reality.

Modern-Day Reality: Eternal destiny is gained or lost in a moment.

CHAPTER 2

ADAH

(Genesis 4:19–23)

Greatness was birthed and cradled in her arms;
from her womb came creativity and ingenuity.

Living in a polygamous marriage was her biggest challenge. Marriage was competitive since her husband loved one wife more than the other. She dressed herself elegantly and always looked her best; she consciously worked hard to be the better of the two wives. Adah stood out. She was the wife of Lamech. In the process of time she became pregnant and gave birth to sons, on two separate occasions. Her sons had a normal Jewish upbringing, they knew about God's work in creation and His ability to sustain lives. The first was called Jabal; he was creative and ingenious, without a blueprint, he was the first man in history to make a tent.

After his timely invention most Israelites lived in tents, moving from place to place like nomads. Abraham and his family lived in tents. Adah had a second son who was an intellectual. Her second son Jubal took all the excessive bits from the tent construction, odds and ends of materials, went off in his tent and became an inventor. He created a string and wind instrument. His mother and brother heard the unusual sweet sound and were drawn to Jubal's tent. Jubal had unknowingly commenced the music industry by inventing the harp and the flute. Every music band, group, or individual singer owes their achievement to Jubal, the originator. He discovered how to change moods from low to high through the powerful effect of music. Jubal was a gifted son and was willing to experiment in an industry that never existed before. He was able to play these instruments and to teach others. The flute and the harp are the primary musical instruments, and all other musical instruments were derived from these.

Her husband Lamech was wealthy and worked in the field. He owned lands and cattle, the legacy of his family wealth. One day he had a quarrel with one of his workers, and the worker took an instrument and lashed out at him. Hurt and angry, Lamech hit the worker in the head, causing his death.

Lamech came home calling his two wives to a family meeting. He told Adah and her rival he was harsh in punishing one of the workers who hurt him. Lamech told them, he killed a worker and God will punish him severely. Adah supported her husband even though she knew he would be punished by God.

Lamech family's history would be recorded in the modern-day *Guinness World Records* since his father (her father-in-law) was the oldest man who ever lived on earth (just thirty-one years short of his one thousandth birthday). Mystery surrounds this family also as Lamech's grandfather mysteriously disappeared into heaven; he never died.

Her greatness can be endorsed, because of the great sons, she nurtured. Her greatness was birthed and cradled in her arms; from her womb came creativity and ingenuity. The tent-making industry and the music industry have its origins within her home.

Modern-Day Reality: Inventive and creative minds are in the house.

CHAPTER 3

MRS. NOAH

(Genesis 6:18–22; 7:1–24; 8:1–22; 9:1–17;
1 Peter 3:20; 2 Peter 2:5)

Noah would not have achieved his goals with
a wife who murmured and complained.

E vil! Evil! Evil! It was inescapable as the earth was populated, the people were involved in every abominable deed the world ever knew. Wickedness was widespread; among the thousands of families who existed there was only one family who believed in God and followed His teachings. Noah and his family were found to be godly people, willing to obey God's instruction. Therefore God asked Noah to build a very large boat, bigger than the *Titanic*. Noah and his wife were a few hundred years old and had lived more than half of their lives.

Though the Bible never recorded her name, there was a Mrs. Noah. She along with her husband and their three boys Shem, Ham, and Japheth lived in a grossly corrupted land. People hated each other, crimes were on the increase, and their thoughts and actions were perpetually evil. God was fed up with the blatant violence and decided to wipe out all the corrupt people.

God had a strategic plan to bring about this destruction so that the land would be clean. God gave Noah all the measurements and the unique design for the boat. Noah took a few years to build this boat. He got help from his wife, sons, and their wives. All the other people he knew came and looked at the structure of the boat, and laughed as they thought it was ludicrous. None of them had seen rain before. They mocked at the thought that rain would come and this very large boat would float on the water. Noah and his family remained committed.

*Mrs. Noah gave her husband full support as he nailed every piece of wood together to make this big boat. She also nailed the wood and handed him the tools and the materials that he needed. She encouraged Noah from the onset and there were moments of celebrations as the ark began to take shape. This construction took over sixty years, yet she and her family never doubted. They were optimistic and full of faith. Noah would not have achieved his goals with a wife who murmured and complained. He would not have realised his target if he had to divert his energies and deal with distraction. Mrs. Noah was completely engrossed in the **call**. She was not excluded, though she was prepared to remain in the background and not be recognised.*

Wow! The finale came, big celebration as the boat was completed. God instructed the family; her husband as the head of the family took her and their sons along with their daughters-in-law into the boat.

She witnessed all the wild animals arriving as couples, male and female, into the big boat. Some animals were quicker on their feet so they arrived early. When the tortoises arrived, they knew that all the animals were in; this was spectacular. God then shut the door.

These animals had one week to adjust to the new environment. Then it rained nonstop for six long weeks. Water covered the earth like a sea, it took five months before they could see any sign of life on the earth. The water finally subsided and just eight people, including Mrs. Noah, came out of the boat and started a new life. There was no more evil or violence on the earth. The colourful arch in the sky known as the rainbow appeared for the first time. The rainbow told the story of the great flood, it was also a reminder that the earth will never be destroyed by water again.

Although the biblical account never mentioned her by first name, she knew about faithfulness and loyalty to God and her husband. She knew about her role as a partner in business, a visionary. She had faith in God and her husband to envisage a finished product even before the ark was constructed. She anticipated a flood when she never saw one drop of rain fall in her life. She believed the wild animals could be tamed and would respond to God's voice. She also saw that men who were more intelligent than the animals would reason themselves out of God's simple command. She felt devastated and powerless at the demise of her fellow human beings.

She lived through three different periods in her life—a time of evil, a period of judgement, and a time when there was a recreation of human existence. She had a very distinct role in history, as her first-born Shem was the ancestor of the Jewish race through which Christ Jesus came.

Modern-Day Reality: It is important to remain faithful and committed even when there is little or no recognition.

CHAPTER 4

JOCHEBED: MOSES' MOTHER

(Exodus 2:1–10; 6:20; Numbers 26:59–61;
Hebrews 11:23)

From her womb came two of the greatest leaders in Jewish history.

Married to her nephew (this was not considered to be incestuous at that time), she was pregnant at the time of the biggest baby boom among the Israelites who were living in Egypt as slaves. Jochebed along with her husband Amram came from the tribe of Levi, a priestly lineage. She gave birth to a son at a time when the king commanded that all the boys should be thrown into the river Nile to drown. With maternal love for her special son, she did not want him thrown into the river, so she implemented a way of saving his life. She hid him anywhere in the house where she felt he would be safe. It was a miracle that she was able to do this for three months. In the midst of all the emotional turbulence, she also managed to get the baby to cry less often and with a soft pitch voice.

Time was running out and Jochebed knew she could no longer keep the baby in her house. Her husband told her if the king's wicked men found out, they would kill both mother and son. Her options became increasingly slim. Moses' mother was very optimistic and knew that God had chosen him to fulfill a special assignment.

In the third month of her son's life, she came up with a plan. She created a special basket with reeds and tar to keep the basket buoyant and waterproof. Placing the baby in the basket, she took him to the edge of the river and left him there. Her emotions were very high that day as it hurt to leave her child in a basket on the river, tied to a tree. The woman knew that God promised to look after her son. Her daughter was placed a few yards away as a watchman.

The river Nile was a popular place for bathing even for royals. When the daughter of the king, the princess, came by to bathe, she saw the basket and sent her servant to fetch it. She was amazed by the unusual discovery in it, a baby boy. Moses was floating in the same river, his contemporaries lost their lives by drowning. Many mothers were heartbroken, as life seemed worthless. These women knew that their sons were robbed of their destinies. Many of these boys could have become the next king, prime minister, or leader in Israel. However, Jochebed was not willing to abort her son's destiny; she was willing to risk her life for her son by disobeying the king's command.

Jochebed knew:

- *her son was born with a purpose.*
- *she had to act by faith despite the king's command.*
- *that she can trust in God to save her son's life. She let go of her son and let God do the impossible.*

God granted her favour and she experienced a miracle that day. She was now enrolled in the palace's payroll as an employee to raise her own son. She was allowed to keep her son while other babies from among the Israelites were dying. She was raising a prince, since Moses was now **adopted** *by the princess as her son.*

She hid her son for three months from an evil demise perpetrated by the wicked king of Egypt. By faith she disobeyed the king's order and was one of the four women mentioned in the hall of faith and fame in the book of Hebrews. Jochebed was married to her nephew Amram, who was her brother's son.

Her boys were used by God in unusual ways to deliver God's people from oppression and bondage.

From her womb came two of the greatest leaders in Jewish history. One of her sons wrote the first five books of the Bible, he recorded an accurate account of the events even though he was not present. Creation occurred hundreds of years before his birth, yet he compiled an accurate account. Her next son Aaron was the first high priest over Israel.

Jochebed was intelligent and creative. Her hands crafted a waterproof basket woven to keep her baby safe, a semi replica of which is still used in the modern day for a baby's first bed. She was ingenious, rationalising that her son would be safe in the river frequented by the king's soldiers, who were instructed to drown the Israelite baby boys in the same river. The act of leaving her baby on the banks of the river was equivalent to completely giving him away. Indeed it was an act of faith, a statement that she could not take care of him any longer, but God could.

Modern-Day Reality: It takes extraordinary actions to get extraordinary results.

CHAPTER 5

SHIPHRAH AND PUAH: THE MIDWIVES

(Exodus 1:15–22)

*They were willing to risk their lives to save the
lives of the children they had delivered.*

They were a special race selected by God to show the other nations who He is. The divine blessing made their lives productive even when they lived in Egypt under the authority of its king. God's people were slaves in Egypt. Israelite women were very fertile as their nation experienced a baby boom and population explosion, which infuriated the king.

The king gave the matter some serious thought. He concluded that the Israelites were stronger, more powerful, and they would soon out-number the Egyptians. So he devised a plan to control the population by eradicating the babies.

Shiphrah and Puah were excellent Egyptian midwives who had delivered thousands of babies. The king called an emergency conference with Shiphrah and Puah, promising them a big salary increase if they agreed to carry out his command. They were expected to continue to deliver the babies for the Israelite women. Upon delivery of the baby, they were to quickly check the baby's gender. All male babies were to be killed.

They felt what the king required was heartless and uncouth, and decided they were not going to obey the king. Obeying the king meant violating God's word. The midwives made a decision, sacrificing their career and their lives to save the lives of thousands of male babies.

The king realised there were lots of Israelite baby boys alive after his conference with the midwives. This made the king very angry. He ordered an emergency meeting with these two midwives. God gave these two midwives wisdom to answer the king. They told him that the Israelite women had precipitated labour; before the midwives could get ready, the babies were born 'kicking and screaming.' Egyptian women were different and had longer labours.

*The king was furious and asked **all** the people in Egypt to snatch all the male babies from the Israelite women and throw them in the Nile River so that the babies would drown. Much to the distress of the Israelite women, hundreds of Israelite mothers lost their babies this way.*

Shiphrah and Puah were godly, professional Egyptian women who stood up against an ungodly king. They were willing to risk their lives to save the lives of the children they had delivered. Their obligation was first to God and then to the parents of these children. They could not obey an ungodly king. Love and compassion reigned in their hearts and they chose to obey a higher law, the law of God. When the entire city of Egypt did not stand up against the command of the king to destroy the lives of these babies, these two midwives did. They were the midwives who delivered Moses and helped to preserve his life by giving his mother a few tips. They won the Nobel Peace Prize in their day.

Modern-Day Reality: The law of God is greater than that of a king.

CHAPTER 6

Princess/the Pharaoh's Daughter

(Exodus 2:1–10)

*She saved the life of one baby, whose mother failed to
comply with the order of the king.*

One summer afternoon as she strolled casually along the banks of the river Nile, her encounter was more than that which she had bargained for. Her father the king commanded that all the Hebrew baby boys should be killed. The frustrated king felt insecure over the population explosion among the Hebrews, realising he would be defeated, if they went to war. The pharaoh's daughter, the princess, was fascinated and stood in amazement as she saw a strange sight, a basket floating on the river Nile. She sent her servant to fetch the basket; she opened it and was completely flabbergasted and numb by a baby's cry. She was emotional and could not withhold the tears as it trickled down her face; however, she did not feel powerless. She knew that this was a desperate measure from a Hebrew woman to save the life of this baby; the princess then vetoed the king's command. She spared this baby boy. Is it possible that the princess was powerful as her father the pharaoh and could have saved the lives of many more babies? She saved the life of one baby, whose mother failed to comply with the order of the king.

The baby's sister was hiding from full view, caring for her brother from a distance. She came running from behind the grass and immediately engaged in conversation with the princess. She knew exactly what to say, recommending help to look after the baby. The little girl ran home to tell her mother the great news: the princess found the baby and wanted a babysitter. While this was happening, the princess named the baby **Moses***, as she found him on the water.*

At a time when other mothers lost their son. Jochebed got a salary from the princess to care for her three month old son. She took care of him until she weaned him. Then Moses was taken to the palace. His mother, a Hebrew, gave up all rights to her baby so that he could be raised by the pharaoh's household as a prince.

*The pharaoh's daughter recognised what it meant to be a daughter of the king; she was happy to challenge her father's decision and save the life of this special baby. There was conflict and division within the pharaoh's household, between the law of the pharaoh '***to kill the babies***' and the law of God '***to save lives.***'*

*The pharaoh's daughter was godly and chose the law of God for this little boy. She could not tell what his future would be like. She had no idea that one day he would confront her father so that an entire nation would be free from slavery. She could not see the disaster that would happen in Egypt as the pharaoh defied God's law, chasing after the Israelites (***led by Moses***) to his own fatality.*

She played a pivotal role in raising a Hebrew child who grew up to be one of the most outstanding leaders in Israel. Growing up in the pharaoh's house meant Moses was well equipped to confront the pharaoh to free God's people. Moses also had the best education in Egypt and was mightily used by God as the one receiving the law of God, from the hands of God, on a mountain.

Her real name was not mentioned in Moses' account of his childhood; however, her actions were. She was brave and influential; she was intelligent and quite knowledgeable of her rights as a daughter of the king. Even though the Egyptian 'did not serve God', she knew that God had the final authority over her own father, the king.

Modern-Day Reality: Daughters of a king live a life of entitlement and privilege.

CHAPTER 7

ZIPPORAH

(Exodus 2:21–22; 4:18–26; 18:1–27; Genesis 17:9–14;
1 Chronicles 1:32–33; Numbers 12:1; 20:1; 33:38–39;
Deuteronomy 10:6)

Zipporah taught them loyalty, integrity and obedience.

D aughters in Israel tended the flock in the absence of sons. These women were expected to perform a predominantly male-orientated task. They had to combat grave hostility from male chauvinists as they watered the flock. The men were unkind, unfriendly, and uncaring; they prevented the women from watering the animals at the well. Watering the flock was a lengthy, burdensome exercise since the women had to deal with men who chased them away. They complained every day to their fathers about the hostility of these unsympathetic men.

On one particular day, as the seven sisters went to water their flock, the men came to chase them away. Moses, an Israelite, had just arrived in Midian; he went to the well to 'hang out.' He was shocked as he witnessed these Midianite men abusing the women. Moses defended the women from their adversaries, taking over the task of watering the flock, sending the women home in quick time. Seemingly it took seven women to do the job of one man.

Their father noticed how quickly the girls had returned home from watering the flock, the task accomplished in record-breaking time. The young ladies related to Jethro (Reuel), their father, what had happened. They had received help from an Israelite man called Moses. Jethro asked them where the Israelite was. Moses was then invited to their home for a meal; he agreed to stay with them. Moses fell in love with Zipporah and married her. Zipporah obviously was the eldest daughter. In those times, the eldest daughter got married before the younger. She became pregnant and had a son who was called Gershom. These women were relieved from tending the flock, since Moses continued the task he volunteered to do, on the day he first arrived in Midian.

*Zipporah and her husband Moses served Jethro for some years then God asked them to move to another city. In obedience to God's command, Moses took his wife and son and moved out. As they were on their way, God appeared to Moses and was about to destroy his life. Zipporah knew God was angry with Moses because he failed to meet God's requirement. God commanded that the male infant should be **circumcised**. Zipporah, in a moment of rage, took a sharp stone and cut away the foreskin of their son Gershom. She threw the tissue of flesh at Moses' feet and called him a **bloody man**. This quick action saved Moses' life that day from the wrath of God.*

*Zipporah gave birth to her second son, Eliezer, whose name meant **God has helped me and delivered me from the sword of the pharaoh**. In the process of time, Moses made numerous appearances before the Pharaoh. God used him to perform signs and wonders to capture*

Pharaoh's attention. Pharaoh held God's people hostage in Egypt, refusing to let them go. Zipporah and her sons returned to Midian. They missed the miraculous exodus with the parting of the Red Sea. Zipporah was greatly influenced by her father, who felt Moses was overambitious, so he did not support him. Jethro no doubt thought Moses was too radical and out of his mind to stand before the pharaoh advocating for the Israelites.

Jethro was a priest from Median, a descendant of Abraham from his second wife Keturah, who were enemies of the Israelites, God's chosen people.

Zipporah and her two sons lived for an extended period of time with her father. Moses was happy with her decision to remain with her father, because of the opposition. This also meant Moses would not spend time to ease the tension, but he was able to concentrate on his mission without distractions.

Moses' success in leadership intrigued Jethro and was a prerequisite for his visit. Zipporah's father heard much about his son-in-law's success and wanted to witness it firsthand. On his visit, he brought Zipporah and her sons back to Moses. Jethro observed Moses in his role as a judge, a job that demanded all his time. Jethro knew this would result in Moses' inability to govern effectively, so he advised Moses to choose competent men to help him judge the people. Moses then appointed seventy (70) devoted leaders.

Many writers have attempted to reveal the true identity of Moses' wife Zipporah, one school of thought was his siblings Aaron and Miriam were displeased with his choice, so they revolted against Moses.

It is believed that Moses' marriage to Zipporah, an Ethiopian, took place before he fled to Midian, abandoning her.

This view seems unlikely since Moses was forty years old and most Jewish men were married later in life.

The timing of this event became questionable; if Moses was married to the Ethiopian woman and fled, leaving her behind, then it seems ludicrous that Miriam and Aaron would murmur about a wife who was not in Moses' life at that time.

Another thought is that Moses' first wife Zipporah died and Moses remarried an Ethiopian woman. Another view that seems inconsistent since Zipporah's death was not mentioned in scripture when *all* of Moses' other relatives' deaths were mentioned. (Numbers 20:1, 33:38–39; Deuteronomy 10:6, 32:50)

It must be noted that God did not punish Moses for his choice of marrying an Ethiopian. However, it seems more likely that since Midian bordered Ethiopia, it could have been referred to as Ethiopia.

Zipporah, a descendant of Abraham, was mentioned as Semitic; therefore, there was no valid reason for Moses' siblings to object to her.

Other scholars argued that Miriam and Aaron's real objection was Moses taking advice from Jethro and not including them in the chosen seventy (70). They could have also felt insecure that Moses' son, a mixed heritage male, could be appointed as his successor.

Their murmuring evoked God's wrath, which made Miriam a leper. She did not only object to Moses' wife or the woman Moses married, but she undermined his leadership and authority over Israel.

Zipporah was an example to her six sisters and taught them loyalty, integrity, obedience, and how to defend themselves against ungodly men. She was the wife of God's spokesman, the meekest man who ever lived. God used her husband Moses to bring freedom to His people from Egypt's oppression. She must be acknowledged for her quick actions of circumcising her firstborn son. She understood God's covenant relationship and blessings. Her wisdom must be valued in

handling discontentment and rifts with her in-laws as she lived peace-
ably among them.

Modern-Day Reality: God elevates us to a place of honour.

CHAPTER 8

MIRIAM

(Exodus 2:4–8; 15:20–21;
Numbers 12:1–16; 20:1)

Miriam commenced a song and dance.
The first record of women's freedom in Jewish history.

She was a babysitter at seven years old, taking care of her baby brother who was in a basket floating on the river Nile. The king had commanded that all boys from the Israelite families should be thrown into the river. Miriam was intelligent as she stood by the river a short distance from the basket, hiding herself in the bushes. She was very observant and her mother entrusted the care of her baby brother into her hands.

Miriam saw two women approaching the river as though they were going to take a bath. She then realised they were gazing in the direction of the basket as they talked. Fear came upon her as she watched one of the women walk over to the basket and pick it up. The women, though in a state of shock, smiled when they discovered the baby in the basket and proceeded to stop him from crying. Her little feet were heard running from the bushes; she spoke to the ladies. Miriam then found out that one of the ladies was the daughter of the king of Egypt. Miriam thought that the princess was getting attached to the baby, so she innocently asked 'would you like a babysitter to look after the baby?' The princess thought this was a brilliant idea, Miriam then ran home to call her mother. Miriam's mother was enlisted on the palace payroll and paid a monthly salary to take care of her own son, until he was old enough to live in the palace.

When Moses was grown, he became the man whom God used to deliver Israel from Egypt.

Miriam:

- *knew God's power was working through her brothers as they performed great miracles.*
- *was the first woman mentioned in scripture as a prophetess.*

As the children of Israel left Egypt, they walked through the Red Sea miraculously. However the Egyptians drowned when they attempted to pursue. Miriam gathered all the Israelite women and commenced a song and dance with the timbrel in thanksgiving. This was the first record of women's freedom in Jewish history.

God's people lived in tents as they journeyed to the Promised Land. As time passed, Miriam relinquished her elder-sister protective role as she became overly jealous of her brother Moses. She joined with her brother Aaron as they criticised Moses' ability to lead. This was sibling rivalry as the duo spoke against Moses. They felt that Moses behaved pompously and thought that only he could hear from God. Surely God could use them too, they often thought.

God:

- *was angry with Miriam and Aaron and confronted them outside their tent.*
- *told them that Moses was chosen to speak for Him.*
- *also told them that they should be afraid to speak evil of God's servant.*

Miriam became a leper, her skin as white as snow. Aaron asked Moses for forgiveness for himself and his sister. It is quite possible that Miriam, as the senior figure here, was expected to show greater wisdom and maturity and lead her junior brother by her example, which she did not. To whom much is given, much is expected. She was expected to lead by example because she was older and more experienced. She was expected to think differently and not entertain evil thoughts. Another reason that Aaron was spared of leprosy could be due to his priestly role. God is sovereign and chose to deal with Aaron differently. It could be because of God's covenant with Aaron and his descendants to be a priestly tribe, since priests could not have defect or disease. He was the one who declared a leprous person cleansed, therefore God spared him of leprosy. It could also be that Aaron promptly asked God for forgiveness, God forgave him and spared his life. When Aaron also asked his brother Moses for forgiveness, Moses prayed to God to heal his sister Miriam and she was healed. The custom was, leprous people must stay away from the public for seven days, then show themselves to the priest who will declare that they are clean, before they can go back into the public. After seven days, Miriam rejoined the team of Israelites who had not moved from Hazelroth.

Miriam was a powerful woman and the sister of two of the greatest world leaders. She knew the plan that God had for His people as she spoke with her brothers. However, she was the instigator of revolt and rebellion against God's leader and his authority. Aaron agreed with her, they both were defiant; as a result she became a leper. Miriam did not live to an old age, was never married, neither did she have children. She never came close to the Promised Land since she died and was buried en route in Kadesh. It is important to guard your heart against rebellion, revolt, and being defiant.

Modern-Day Reality: Trendsetter, instigator. Those who are given much are also expected to produce much.

CHAPTER 9

ELISHEBA/ELIZABETH

(Exodus 6:23; Leviticus 10:1–7; Numbers 3:1–4, 32;
20:28; 26:60–65; 27:18–23; 1 Chronicles 6:3–4,
48–50, 57; Matthew 1:4)

Surrounded by priests throughout her entire life.
Her father, husband, and four sons were all priests of God.

A chaotic period, the entire nation under siege, she lived in an era when the nation of Israel was held hostage by the king of Egypt. Elisheba saw the miracles in Egypt as the pharaoh hardened his heart against God.

Elisheba:

- left Egypt walking with all the Israelites through the Red Sea.
- saw the pharaoh's army pursuing them drown in the Red Sea.
- was among the congregation of Israel when Moses went into the mount and overstayed.

The people mourned and complained incessantly. In his frustration, her husband Aaron discussed his inadequacy to lead the people in the interim. They had further discussions and decided to get the people involved.

All the people quickly brought their gold jewelry voluntarily and together they created a golden calf. It became the object of their worship and a replacement for the true and Living God. Their ungodly act of creating this idol evoked the wrath of God against them. Moses heard the sound of jubilation as he returned from the mountain and wondered what was happening among the people. In his anger he threw the tablets with the law of God to the ground smashing them when he saw what his brother did in his absence.

God mercifully spared Aaron and his family, as the Commandment was not yet given. Elisheba and her family were mightily used by God as her sons ministered before the Lord as priests. Her influence spread to her descendants throughout history, since five generations later the second king of Israel, King David, emerged from her lineage.

Elisheba was:

- *the daughter of the priest Amminadab and sister to Nahshon.*
- *married to Aaron (first high priest),was Moses' sister-in-law.*
- *the mother of Nadab, Abihu, Eleazar, and Ithamar.*
- *surrounded by priests throughout her entire life. Her father, husband, and four sons were all priests of God.*

Her husband Aaron was an excellent leader from the Tribe of Levi, the priestly tribe. Her husband and their four sons became the leading priests in Israel. The priests and their ancestors worked in the temple and never went to war. They were financially sustained from lands and gifts given to them from the other tribes. Elisheba and her husband along with their sons lived in the city of Hebron. The city was a safe place since citizens fled to it for safety when their lives were threatened. Under Jewish custom, when a person unintentionally hurts another person, to avoid retaliation the offender can run to the city for safety and the priest will judge the matter and save his life.

Aaron's special duties were ministering to the people, burning sacrifices on the altar and offering sacrifices for sin. Aaron and his sons were the only people allowed into the Holy Place, and subsequent priests were selected to the priestly office only from descendants of Levi. As a high priest, Aaron was the only person who could enter into the Most Holy Place. This is a type of Christ, the only one worthy to enter into the Most Holy Place. Christ not only entered in the Most Holy Place, but He tore the veil so that all of us can enter into His Holiness.

Elisheba's life was not only prestigious as the wife and mother of priests, she had heart-rending moments. Her two eldest sons went into the temple to burn incense and did not act in obedience to God. As a result, both of them died while offering their sacrifice. However, her joy was realised when her third son Eleazer, was chosen by God after the death of her husband. He became the chief priest over the people, and every priest after came from her lineage. She must be credited as the mother of these three major groups of biblical heroes and stalwarts—prophet, priest, and king.

Her father Amninadab was mentioned in the genealogy of Jesus Christ, in the gospel's account of Matthew.

Modern-Day Reality: Great recognition for work behind the scenes.

CHAPTER 10

MRS. JOB

(Job 1:1–42:16)

It must not be forgotten that she was a part of the family's loss and pain.
She lost children just as much as her husband.

God made a claim on her husband that he was the only man who thought, spoke and lived right. When God sees your husband as **Mr. Perfect**, this must be an extraordinary honour. To be the wife of such a great man must also be unique. The couple had a great marriage, producing ten of the most beautiful children in their times. Job and his wife loved God, and taught their children about honouring God and sacrificing as a form of worship to God.

The couple's wealth consisted of 7,000 sheep, 3,000 camels, 1,000 oxen, and 1,000 donkeys. They had hundreds of servants to help them in the field. They owned houses and many acres of land.

The children:

- *all came together and decided to have regular parties and spend time at each other's houses.*
- *went to their first planned party at the eldest brother's house and the evening started out as a great time together.*
- *shared great memories.*

Mrs. Job played an active role with her husband in praying and offering sacrifices for each of their children. While all this was happening, Satan was having a conversation with God about Job's integrity. Satan described Job as mean and materialistic, and did not care about God. God asked Satan to show HIM the evidence. God gave Satan permission to prove his point.

Within a few hours, the Jobs had lost almost everything. Thieves took the donkeys and the oxen, and killed the servants. Only one servant was left alive to report the bad news. Another group of thieves also took the camels and killed the servants, and one servant was left alive to tell the bad news. There was a thunderstorm and lightning killed the 7,000 sheep, along with many of the servants. The servants who were left alive came one after the other to report to the Jobs what had happened. Even while all this was happening, still another servant came to report that there were gale-force winds at 150 miles per hour. The wind destroyed the eldest son's house where the party was taking place, and all ten children were dead. They were astonished by their loss, numbed by pain, and shocked by distress and grief; this was one of the saddest days in the lives of the couple. The weeks and months following were characterised by sorrow, depression, languish, ceaseless tears, mental and emotional lows. There was no pharmaceutical cure for their pain. However, they found the strength to pull themselves through the pain by comforting and strengthening one another.

Satan, the heartless enemy, felt he did not really do a good job and still had Job as his target. So he went back to God, complaining about Job.

God:

- *boasted about Job to Satan.*
- *told Satan that Job was perfect and Job loved HIM with all his heart.*
- *again gave Satan permission to hurt Job.*

So Job was covered in sores all over his body. The sores were leaking everywhere. Job was in a complicated position as he found walking, sitting, standing, and lying down were painful.

Mrs. Job:

- *knew the pains of losing her children and seeing her husband suffer.*
- *suffered emotional pain for which there was no cure while her husband suffered physical pains.*
- *came to a point in her life where she could not take her husband's suffering any more.*
- *had been there all the time and was supportive, but this time she lost the plot.*
- *thought no human being should be alive in this condition.*
- *wanted euthanasia.*
- *told Job to curse God and commit suicide, or she could assist him in dying.*

Job:

- *looked at her with his painful mouth and sore tongue, rebuking her immediately.*
- *told her that God was not there to give them good things all the time.*
- *said that they would be tested to see if they were just interested in goods and not God.*

She repented, dressed the sores, and joined Job in worship. This period was also marked by lonesomeness as all their family friends were nowhere to be seen in their bitter trial. There was no one to console them and share their burdens. God remembered the Jobs; when the trial period was over, they started a family again. God honoured Mrs. Job and He gave her the grace to conceive and have children again. Mrs. Job became pregnant and within a few years she had another ten children. They got double the amount of livestock and servants. They had 14,000 sheep, 6,000 camels, 2,000 oxen, and 2,000 donkeys. Their three daughters Jeminah, Keziah, and Keren-Happuch were the most beautiful women in the city.

Mrs. Job has been mentioned by preachers on numerous occasions only as one who advised her husband to curse God and die. It must not be forgotten that she was part of the family's loss and pain. She lost children just as much as her husband. She also experienced joy and jubilation at the restoration of their children and their wealth.

The Jobs' story made headline news as reporters were queuing to interview them. Their lives were amazing and no story like theirs was ever recorded in history. Theirs was a story that attracted international attention.

Job was the most popular man in his time. He was wealthy and he dispersed all of his wealth to his seven sons, making them reputable in the land. After such a period of depression and negativity, Job lived a further one hundred and forty (140) years and he was able to play with his grandchildren, great-grandchildren, and great-great-grandchildren. It is quite possible that Mrs. Job spent all those years with Job, or even outlived him.

Modern-Day Reality: God's grace is sufficient when you err; never remain in error.

CHAPTER 11

MRS. LOT

(Genesis 11:27–32; 13:1–11; 14:12; 16; 19:1–38; 2 Peter 2:6–9)

She was destroyed for turning away from serving God and for serving all the material wealth she had acquired.

Fascinated by rural perimeters, they finally set their eyes on the city; this was the fulfillment of all their dreams. They bid good-bye to Uncle Abraham and were determined to live life to the max. The people of Sodom were pleasure-seekers, revelers and loved the late nights. Lot's godly influence failed to infiltrate into the lives of those living in Sodom. It was surprising that after many years and in spite of the deviation around them, their lives could not be any happier. The people in the city became more corrupted and evil. God saw that the wickedness was getting out of hand and decided that He would destroy the city. He sent His angel to take Lot and his family out of the city because he was a righteous man (2 Peter 2:7–8). They did not realise the predicament they were in, as the destruction of their city became imminent. They hurried out of the city and managed to get to Zoar. God destroyed Sodom and Gomorrah with fire.

Lot's wife:

- *took her mind down memory lane as she thought about the impetuous life she lived in Sodom.*
- *wept as she saw her possessions reduced to ashes.*
- *could not believe that God would do something like that.*
- *had become an idolater.*
- *her heart was in the wrong place, craving wrong things.*
- *forgot that God had warned her to be careful, that these things would turn her heart away from Him.*
- *did not spare a thought about the people who were perishing in Sodom and Gomorrah.*
- *did not think that she would have been dead if she was still inside the city.*

All her possessions mattered more—her modern gadgets had much more importance than her own life and the life of all the people in Sodom and Gomorrah. She was overly materialistic and could not appreciate being alive without her worldly possessions.

*She became as a **pillar of salt**, and that area became a monument. Salt is soluble and would normally dissolve in water, but salt solidifies, creating a pillar. In the Old Testament, in addition to flavour and preserve, salt caused barrenness so that area was officially declared unfruitful, barren or uninhabitable (Deuteronomy 29:23).*

Those who saw the monument knew that:

1. *It was a sign of God's wrath.*
2. *Nothing would ever grow there.*
3. *It represented Lot's wife, her idolatry, and anger against God.*

Mrs. Lot would never know what happened to her daughters after she became a pillar of salt. Her daughters lived evil lives also. They made their father drunk and had sex with him, starting a family. She never knew she was the grandmother of two ungodly races, the Moabites and the Ammonites (Genesis19:34–38). This might be an indication that they did not leave a great legacy behind, as parents. They failed to raise their daughters in the fear of God. However, the account written in the book of Ruth, noted that she was a descendant of Moab, and Jesus was her offspring.

Lot's wife taught us that we must not allow our belief to be diluted, as it can become completely lost. She never allowed God to lead her to a safe haven. She was unsuccessful as she tried to serve two masters at the same time. The scripture assures us we cannot serve two masters at one time, as either we love one and hate the other. She was destroyed for turning away from serving God and for serving all the material wealth she had acquired. We are commanded to *serve one God, the true and Living God, and beside Him there is no other.*

We must never forget the mercies and favour of God who never deals with us as we deserve. He is faithful and compassionate, and His unfailing love will graft us into His Divine sphere when we go astray.

Modern-Day Reality: With choices come responsibility and consequences.

CHAPTER 12

MILCAH

(Genesis 11:27–32; 22:20–24; 24:15–16)

She had no reservation marrying someone who was twice her age...

Incestuous would be the description of this family through the eyes of our modern society. In the time of Milcah, it was the norm to marry within one's own family. Her biological father Haran died at a young age, leaving three young children behind. Paternal rights in Israel meant that the nearest male relative must take the guardianship of his deceased brother's children. Nahor, the eldest brother of the deceased, took Milcah and cared for her. Milcah grew up in her uncle's house as 'his daughter'. However, when Milcah was legally entitled to be married, her uncle Nahor married her. The law was not yet given in Israel and it was not unlawful to marry one's niece at that time. She was part of one family; her uncle Abraham was also her brother-in-law. Haran though deceased was not only her father, but he was also her brother-in-law since she was married to Nahor, her uncle. Her two siblings were Lot and Iscah. After the death of their father, her brother Lot was looked after by their uncle Abraham.

Milcah was a young bride and her husband was much older than she was. She had no reservation in her heart about marrying someone who was twice her age and she had no choice about who she married. Her marriage to Nahor produced eight sons. Their names were Uz, Buz, Kemuel, Kesed, Hazo, Pildash, Jidlaph, and Bethuel.

Isaac was Milcah's first cousin; they were children of two brothers Abraham and Haran. Isaac was also the nephew of her husband Nahor. He was married to her granddaughter Rebekah. Therefore her descendants were the twelve sons of Jacob. They were her great-grandsons.

Milcah:

- was the sister-in-law of Abraham, a man of faith and wealth.
- was surrounded by giants of faith and lived in a time when God's revelation in the earth is progressive.
- learnt about worshipping God and constructing an altar to sacrifice to the only true God.

She was influenced by godliness in the earth and ultimate sacrifice to God. She knew about the judgment of God and how the wicked were punished in the earth for their rebellion and for worshipping false gods.

Modern-Day Reality: We can influence and impact legacy in a godly manner.

CHAPTER 13

Sarai/Sarah

(Genesis 16:1–16; 17:1–27; 18:1–15; 20:1–18;
21:1–33; 22:1–24; 23:1–20; 25:10;
Galatians 3:29; 4:1–31; Hebrews 11:11)

God changed Sarai's name to Sarah, meaning princess.

It sounds preposterous, paternity at age ninety-nine with his wife having maternal rights at age ninety, first-time mother. They thought everyone would make them a laughing stock. They waited twenty-five years for the promise of this baby to become a reality, and even when the promise was given they were already past the time to have children. They knew they were not hallucinating; it was God speaking to them, since they knew God's voice as He had spoken to them numerous times before. Abram found it beyond belief that at age seventy-five God would promise him many children more than the amount of people in the population in his time.

Sarai was married to a great man of God, a man of faith. God asked them to migrate to another city.

Sarai and Abram:

- *did not have a hotel reservation, an address, or the name of a person they were going to stay with, but they obeyed. Leaving everything behind, they travelled to a strange land.*
- *had their moments of uncertainties but they knew God sent them.*
- *were also promised a baby, but eleven years later the couple was still childless.*
- *thought the time for the fulfillment of the promise was over. So they decided to allow their servant to have a child for Abram.*

The servant became pregnant and this did not solve the problem; it created more hostility and a stressful environment. Sarai was jealous and angry. However, it was too late to revert, so she had to manage the situation and live with the consequences of their actions. It was certainly not what God had intended.

*Sarai and her husband were blessed by God while living among their enemies. Abram was ninety-nine years old and still did not have the child that was promised. God told Abram from that day his name shall be Abraham. God changed Sarai's name to Sarah, meaning princess. God promised the couple a son named Isaac. In the Hebraic language, the word that means to **laugh** sound likes Isaac.*

Sarah:

- *was ninety and postmenopausal when three angels turned up to announce the birth of Isaac.*
- *found the idea ludicrous and she could not stop herself from laughing.*

Sarah and Abraham entertained the angels, treating them kindly.

Even in her old age, Sarah epitomised beauty; the king of Gerer wanted her to 'add to his collection of wives'. Abraham knew Sarah was very attractive so he thought the people would kill him and take Sarah. He lied, telling them she was his sister. The King took Sarah to his house. That night the Lord spoke to the king to return Sarah to her husband or he would be a dead man by the next day. The king was sorry for what he had done; he returned Sarah to her husband and he gave Abraham and Sarah a complimentary gift for his evil deeds. He begged Abraham for forgiveness and God healed all the women in his house, as they were barren because of Sarah.

Sarah became pregnant at ninety years old and had her first child. She did not have preconceptual care, nor was she fully prepared for motherhood. The pregnancy was uneventful and she gave birth on her ninety-first birthday. She called her son Isaac. Both Sarah and Abraham taught Isaac the ways of God. Isaac was circumcised and knew about worshipping God and offering sacrifices.

Isaac knew:

- *that a lamb without spot must be slain on the altar to honour God.*

- *God's people must serve Him the way He requested of them, as no other way would do.*
- *about tithing, as his father Abraham was the first to pay tithes to Melchizedek.*

Her son Isaac was referred to as the son of promise, the son of the free woman, which was a type of Christ. Isaac was also referred to as a type of Christ, as his father Abraham in obedience to God took him to Mount Moriah to offer him as a sacrifice. God interceded as Abraham was about to kill his son. God directed Abraham to a ram for the sacrifice. This was signposting us to Christ, the Lamb of God slain from before the world began.

Sarah was undoubtedly the oldest first-time pregnant woman (primigravida) in Bible times. She lived another thirty-six years after the birth of Isaac. She could be one of the only women in scriptures with recorded detailed account of her age at death and her burial.

The chronicle in Hebrews acknowledged Sarah among the few women receiving tribute for their faith in the hall of fame. By faith Sarai was strengthened to become pregnant and to go through labour and delivery when she was postmenopausal. Her body was rejuvenated to that of a woman sixty to seventy years younger. She was able to cope with nursing a baby and caring for an energetic toddler even in her nineties. This was possible because she knew that God was faithful to His promise.

Modern-Day Reality: Faith in God makes the impossible possible.

CHAPTER 14

HAGAR

(Genesis 16:1–16; 21:9–21; 25:12–18;
Galatians 4:1–31)

What was intended to solve the problem
became an even bigger problem...

Born into a civilized Egypt known for its wealth, power, and fame, Hagar's profession did not reflect this. She was head of the female servants in the house of her mistress Sarai and her master Abram. They were a Jewish couple. God promised Abram at age seventy-five (75), he will become a father, and that his children would be innumerable just as the stars in the sky. They went for a bit of advice from fertility experts in their days but Sarai did not conceive. Many years had passed, time was running out, and they were tired of waiting for a child. In those times it was culturally acceptable that if a woman could not have a child, her servant would have a child for her mistress. Servants were their mistress and master's property. Sarai and Abram had a discussion and thought God could only mean that the servant would have the baby, as it was impossible for Sarai to become pregnant. They were confident that allowing Hagar to have a child with Abram was the right thing to do. Sarai broke the news to Hagar and she welcomed it. As it was customary, Hagar was waiting for the moment. She believed having a baby for her master would give her a degree of recognition and status.

Abram had sexual relations with Hagar and she became pregnant. Hagar's attitude changed immediately. She was elated and thought she should be promoted in her master's house. She felt she deserved to be the mistress, not the maid. What was intended to solve the problem became an even bigger problem, creating lots of tension and ill feeling in Abram's house. Sarai became jealous, wanting Hagar to miscarry the baby, giving her strenuous tasks. Sarai became increasingly unkind to her servant Hagar.

*Hagar felt she would not allow Sarai to ill-treat her anymore, so one night when everybody was asleep, Hagar absconded. She had no friends or family around and did not know where to go, so she went in the country in an open field. Finally, she came to a small river and sat there. Far from being a safe haven, this field was the home of wild animals. Yet, she was prepared to risk her life and the life of her unborn baby. God knew her exact location and sent an angel to visit her. Hagar, shaken by the angelic encounter, froze and became speechless, it never dawned on her that she was significant. The angel comforted and reassured her. The message from God was precise. However, it was not what Hagar wanted to hear: **go back to your master's house and submit to Sarai.***

The angel was accurate in revealing the sex of her baby as well as the name. Reluctantly Hagar returned and submitted herself to Sarai, and a few months later she had a son, calling him Ishmael as the angel predicted. Hagar and Ishmael spent a further thirteen years in 'their master' Abram's house. In their private conversations, Hagar and her son Ishmael spoke about Sarai in a derogatory manner. Sarai was a first-time mother at age ninety-one, when she gave birth to Isaac. It is possible that she found motherhood tiring and demanding. She was infuriated when she saw the teenager Ishmael laughing and mocking her. Sarai knew she could not live with Hagar and her son any longer; she told her husband to get rid of Hagar and her son.

Hagar and her son were referred to in the New Testament as the bondwoman, which tends towards slavery and bondage, a type of the law. The scripture says that we must **put away the bondage and take on the free man who is a type of Christ**. The bondwoman and her son (the Mosaic Covenant) will contend with the free woman and her son (Christ and the New Covenant). Therefore, to prevent contest and contention, we must get rid of the bondwoman and her son and take on the free woman and her son.

The bondwoman and her son is Hagar and Ishmael, referred to as Moses and the law; under this dispensation, the Jews were expected **to do and live**. They found themselves inadequate, as not one of them could meet the requirements.

The free woman and her son are Sarai and Isaac, being referred to in the New Testament as Christ and the cross. Under this dispensation, the body of Christ/the church of the Living God is expected **to live and do**. Christ the sinless one was the only person to successfully uphold the law. Therefore, we cannot succeed in upholding the law unless we allow Christ to do it through us and for us; hence Christ is greater than the law. Even today only Christ can successfully keep the law of God. In order to keep God's law we must come to Christ the perfect One. He will live that life in us.

Hagar was faithful in her service to her master and mistress; however, in her displeasure she wandered off as she felt it would result in her being at peace. God's angel spoke with Hagar, who discovered she had made the wrong decision; she repented and returned to her master's house, then submitted to the lordship within it.

Modern-Day Reality: God has made divine provision; if you wander off course, come back.

CHAPTER 15

BASEMATH

(Genesis 26:34–35; 36:1–9, 13, 17)

… exposed to many heroes of faith yet not influenced.

S he was married to a man who lost out on his prestigious inheritance though he was positioned by birth to receive this wealth.
She was the wife of Esau, who was the grandson of Abraham. She was
the daughter of Elon and Ishmael. Her father was Ishmael, the son of
Abraham, with his slave girl Hagar. It was quite a common practice in
Israel to intermarry. Basemath was from the Hittite nation, a people
alienated from God. She was not the only wife of Esau since he was
also married to Judith, another Hittite woman. Basemath and her husband Esau had a son called Reuel. Her grandchildren were Nahath,
Zerah, Shammah, and Mizzah. Esau was the firstborn and entitled to
the covenant blessing. He lost his covenant blessing as he sold it for a
bowl of hot soup. His disobedience led him further away from God,
and he became the father of the Edomites who were enemies of God.
Basemath and Esau lived in the mountains of the land of Edom, the

land to which Esau fled as his wealth increased and the land could no longer facilitate his flock and his brother's.

The Edomites were the enemies of God and His people, the Israelites. Esau's twin brother Jacob became the father of the twelve tribes of Israel. These two brothers were extremely diverse in purpose and destiny. Jacob was a child of promise and his descendants inherited that promise; even Christ came out of his lineage. Esau was the son who lost the divine blessings and the curse visited his descendants after him. Basemath had no choice into which family she would be born. Her grandmother was Hagar and her father was Ishmael. Ishmael was not the son of promise/the free man, which was a type of Christ. Ishmael was the son of the bondwoman Hagar, whereas Isaac was the son of the free woman Sarah; he was the son of promise.

She had double negative family trait being a Hittite by birth, and the wife of one who lost the promise. Her husband commenced the nation of the Edomites, one of the nations that did not receive God's promise and blessings. Basemath was surrounded with greatness as her grandfather Abraham was the epitome of faith, yet she and her father Ishmael were not influenced by such great faith. They were absorbed by the fact that by birth they were not selected as the chosen one who will dispense the family blessings. They did not realise that by faith they can inherit a blessing that was not originally allocated to them, as Rahab discovered. They were contented to stay where they were and become jealous of Isaac, through whom God blessed the families on earth.

Even though she was the niece of Isaac, his brother Ishmael's daughter, she joined with many of the women who despised Rebekah and Isaac. Her example was not admirable since her actions were fuelled by jealousy. She yearned for the prosperity she saw in Isaac and his wife Rebekah. Basemath did not secure covenant blessings by birth;

she lived her life without godly influence and the knowledge that she could secured a covenant relationship with God and His people by her faith, as her grandfather Abraham did. She spent her entire life being 'fertilised and watered' by negativity when she was exposed to many heroes of faith whose lives displayed the blessing that preceded faith. Sadly her lifestyle was not worth emulating, although she had many positive influences around her.

Modern-Day Reality: Surrounded by greatness, but not impacted by it.

CHAPTER 16

Rebekah

(Genesis 24:1–67; 25:20–34; 26:1–35;
27:1–46; Romans 9:11–13)

Every member in the family agreed that Rebekah
must go with the men and marry Isaac.

Under Jewish customs, one of the major paternal rites was choosing a wife for his son. Her father-in-law to be, was a centenarian when his wife gave birth to their son. They did many extraordinary things in their lives. However, parenting a child at one hundred years old was the greatest challenge for Abraham and his wife Sarah. In spite of this humongous challenge, they successfully raised Isaac until he was grown. They trained him in the ways of God; he became strong in his faith. When Isaac was grown, his father wanted a wife for him from the Israelite nation, not from the other ungodly nations. Abraham wanted Isaac's wife to be a member of his father's household. He made a covenant with his chief servant, sending him to his hometown to bring back a wife for his son. The servant had mixed emotions—both honoured and petrified because his master trusted him to find the right woman for Isaac. The servant awoke and loaded the camels then headed off to Haran (present-day Turkey).

Abraham's servant travelled to Haran, navigating his journey as he went. There were moments of apprehension on the journey since he had no idea who Abraham's relatives were.

*He arrived at Haran and decided to wait at the well, since the entire village would go there for water. The servant concluded that all the eligible maidens would visit the well. He prayed to God, saying, '**Lord, the girl I speak to, if she is willing to do more than is asked of her, she will be the one**.' Many beautiful girls came to the well while the nervous servant perched on his camel, which was kneeling close to the mouth of the water source. The servant asked a few of the young ladies who came to the well for a drink, and they gave him a drink only. He knew they were not the woman he was in search of.*

He was not discouraged even though the process was longer than he anticipated.

*A few hours later, a young woman with exceptional demeanour came by. **Aha!** She looked like the **one**. He asked her for a drink of water for himself and all his servants. The young lady kindly offered the men a drink then she offered to get water for the camels, too. Abraham's servant was completely blown away as this young woman's action exceeded his expectations. He was certain that she was the girl he was looking for, to marry Isaac.*

The servant was beaming with excitement as he felt the mission was accomplished. He jumped off the camel, hugged the young woman, and gave the engagement ring and bracelet to her without asking her name or familial background. In those times marriages occurred among relatives.

Knowing that her family history was crucial, the servant then questioned the young woman and found out she was the granddaughter of Abraham's brother, and her name was Rebekah. She was a virgin and a shepherdess. Rebekah and her family were quite hospitable, accommodating the men overnight. The men related the purpose of their visit and how they felt God had prospered their trip. Every member in the family agreed that Rebekah must go with the men and marry Isaac. They blessed Rebekah for that moment and for the future also. They also blessed her children, who were not yet born. Rebekah was willing to go and meet the man she would marry.

The men set out with Rebekah to take her to the land of Canaan. Upon their approach, the mood was set as it was Rebekah's most memorable day. God and nature joined in the jubilation; the sun was gliding gracefully into the horizon. In the fields not too far away Rebekah glanced from the corners of her eyes. She saw the most handsome man she had ever seen. Secretly she hoped and prayed, "Lord let him be the one," so she put a veil over her face. She enquired who the young man was and found out, it was Isaac. Rebekah's beauty stunned Isaac, and he knew she was the woman for him. He fell in love with her instantly. Isaac was elated with the servant's choice. He took Rebekah to his tent to be his wife. Later on, as they journeyed Rebekah became the subject of envy; Isaac, fearing for his life, told her admirer that she was his sister. His admirer took Rebekah with the intention of marrying her. God revealed to this admirer that she was married, so he became very fearful of God's wrath and decided to return Rebekah to her husband immediately.

As most young brides, Rebekah had a happy and blissful first year of marriage. Her worst nightmare was realised when she found out that she could not have a child. Rebekah pretended to be happy as years of infertility followed. She knew culturally what would happen next:

her husband would take one of the female servants and have children with her. Instead Isaac prayed, asking God to take the barrenness away from Rebekah. God answered his prayers and not long after Rebekah became pregnant. It is incomprehensible, even with a stretch of the imagination to grasp what it was like to be pregnant without having a proper diagnosis of pregnancy. In the absence of pregnancy tests and ultrasound scans, Rebekah felt awful and she asked God why she felt that way. God responded to her request: informing her, that she was pregnant with twins. From within the womb these boys were not amicable; they were constantly at war. It was even more evidenced at their birth, when twin two (2) grabbed his brother's feet as they were born. Their struggles did not end there, even though they were the first twins in the world.

Rebekah and Isaac's parenting skills were subjected to scrutiny since there was parental preference coupled with partiality, as Isaac loved Esau and Rebecca loved Jacob. Esau the firstborn was a skillful hunter, while his brother Jacob enjoyed the luxury and comfort of his tent. The disparity between them led to insurmountable tensions in the home as the boys frequently quarrelled and fought. Their displeasure for each other escalated when Jacob stole his brother's rights and privileges. He deceived his father by pretending to be Esau, taking his blessings. Esau then resented Jacob, pursuing him to take his life. Rebekah had a special love for Jacob; she quickly sent him away to live with her relatives. He left home very despondent and went to live with his uncle Laban.

Rebekah was knowledgeable about the culture of her times and was not intimidated by a group of men at the well. She could relate to them and was relevant. She knew kindness and sacrifice, the type of generosity that secured her honour and unprecedented favour.

Modern-Day Reality: It is always honourable to go the extra mile.

CHAPTER 17

DEBORAH 1

(Genesis 24:59; 35:8)

… quite gifted in childcare and still energetic in old age.

S he lived her entire life devoted and committed to her masters and mistresses. Her deep love for children secured her a job in childcare and she became Rebekah's babysitter in the house of Laban, Rebekah's father. Deborah cared for Rebekah as her own child, nursing and helping her through childhood illnesses and all her milestones. Rebekah was always a happy child who had a deep love for Deborah, her nanny. They played together, visiting the fields and spending time exploring through the forest and mountains.

Rebekah grew into a fine young lady and when the time came for her to get married, she was chosen by Abraham's servants as the wife for Isaac, Abraham's son. This servant travelled for hundreds of miles in search of a wife for his master's son. Deborah was nervous as she thought her job in Laban's household had come to an abrupt end. Rebekah's love for Deborah was so strong that she decided that one person she would not leave behind was Deborah her nurse. Deborah was overjoyed when told she will accompany Rebekah to her new home. She was happy to continue serving Rebekah and took a long journey into a foreign land to care for Rebekah's children, who were not yet born. She was sent by her master Laban in faith to look after Rebekah's children. However, Rebekah was barren and could not conceive. Deborah was 'unemployed' since there was no baby to care for. Deborah was faithful and stayed with her mistress through difficulties and setbacks. She became part of the family and had no contact with her own biological relations. Deborah was now very senior, but she was quite gifted in childcare, and was still energetic in her old age.

God blessed Rebekah's womb so she conceived and gave birth to the first twins in biblical history; their names were Esau and Jacob. Deborah cared for these boys with energy and passion. She was well advanced in age and lived a healthy life. She was honoured to look after the children of the patriarch and was totally devoted to them. She was never married and never had children of her own.

*Deborah influenced and impacted the lives of these boys. When the boys were grown, she died of old age. The entire family lamented the passing of this irreplaceable woman. As a result, she was given a state funeral in full honour by the patriarch and his relatives. She was buried at Bethel, under the oak tree. This tree was then known as the **weeping oak** in Bethel. Not only did the family of Rebekah weep for her, but nature joined in the expression of sadness for a veteran godly woman. Deborah's memory lived on for generations.*

It must be noted that Deborah's legacy included service to three generations of elites in ancient times. She was buried in Bethel, a burial place for dignitaries not servants. Bethel was known as the house of God (Gen. 28:16–19) therefore she remained in the house of God. If she existed in the twenty-first century, she would be honoured in the *Guinness World Records* as the longest-serving nanny.

Modern-Day Reality: Displayed great commitment to the calling with dedication, service, and sacrifice

CHAPTER 18

Leah

(Genesis 29:16–18; 30:9–21; 31:1–55; 33:1–20;
34:1; 35:23–26; 46:8–15; 18; 49:2–4)

One of the major commitments of the daughters who attended the flock
and frequented the well was to attract a man to marry her...
Countless romantic experiences started as water was drawn...

The famous city well was more than a place where animals drank water; it created a window of opportunity for virgins to meet eligible bachelors. Countless romantic experiences started as water was drawn from the well.

Her family reminded her constantly, about the squint in her eye which made her appearance unattractive. Her younger sister was far more beautiful than she was. Constant negativity made Leah lack self-confidence, suffer from insecurity, and have a low self-esteem. If she lived in today's society, she would be diagnosed with depression.

Laban, her father, knew he had to act quickly to ensure Leah was married and 'off his hand'.

In biblical times, if a father had no son, the eldest daughter took care of the flock. Laban did not have any confidence in his eldest daughter Leah so she was not chosen to care for his flock. Laban confided in and completely relied on Rachel, his younger daughter, to care for the flock.

One of the major commitments of the daughters who attended the flock and frequented the well was to attract a man to marry her and possibly her sister. Leah was not selected even though she was the eldest; she could not look after the flock. She could not represent her sisters nor would she have been selected by any man as their bride. Leah was lonely and spent her days weeping, as she was constantly reminded by all the people around her, that Rachel is the **pretty one**.

Her father knew what the famous well represented. Laban did not send Leah to the well as he knew she would not attract a mate. Laban's action made Leah feel that external beauty is all that counts. He did not take a moment to discover her inner beauty. Leah felt she had nothing to offer. She was not sociable and could not hold a conversation with a stranger. Laban knew that if his younger daughter Rachel fell in love, he would make sure that Leah gets married first. Since in those times the culture placed emphasis on the elder sister getting married first.

Wedding ceremonies then differ greatly from those of present times. The father of the bride determined the intricacy of the wedding. In this case, the big celebration was held and the groom did not even know who his bride was.

As it happened Laban's nephew Jacob had tricked his older brother Esau and was on the run. Jacob was sent to his uncle Laban to live and hopefully get married to his own relative. Jacob came to the well and spoke with the men who were there with their flock. The men waited until Rachel came and introduced her to Jacob at the well. As Jacob's eyes caught a glimpse of Rachel, he knew fully well it was love at first sight. Rachel went home and told her father Laban about Jacob. Laban hurried to the well and brought Jacob to their home. Jacob told his uncle Laban how he felt about Rachel from the moment he saw her at the well, and that he would like to marry her. Laban and Jacob agreed that seven years of labour for Rachel would be enough.

At the end of seven years, Jacob went to Uncle Laban and asked him for Rachel's hand in marriage. Laban sponsored a big party, the wedding for his daughter. Jacob was very drunk. Laban tricked him and sent Leah, his eldest daughter, into bed with Jacob.

Jacob:

- *woke up the next morning and found that Leah was the woman he slept with the night before.*
- *was unhappy, but he had to take Leah as his wife.*

Jacob still had feelings for Rachel so he spoke with Laban, who asked him to work for another seven years for Rachel. His love for Rachel surpassed time, so he agreed.

There were lots of disagreements and sibling rivalry between Leah and Rachel. Although Rachel knew that she was the one whom Jacob loved, she had to allow the culture of the time to dictate. She must allow Leah to marry Jacob, and when the time was right, she would become his wife also. Leah was able to have children, unlike her sister Rachel. It took Leah many years and the birth of her sixth son Zebulum to feel as a woman whom her husband wanted. She spent most of her life feeling lonely and unloved. All of her children were given names that spoke about her feelings of doubt, insecurity, and lack of self-worth.

Jacob spent more time with Leah than his other wives. This showed he honoured her as his first wife. The result of the quality time was clear, as she had more children with Jacob than the other wives. In fact, Leah had three times more sons than any of the other wives and as many sons as the other three wives combined. Yet, Leah did not overcome her childhood rejection. The names of her sons were a reflection of her feelings of inferiority and low self-worth.

Leah had sons named: **Reuben** *(the Lord has seen my trouble and my husband will love me);* **Simeon** *(she was not loved, that is why God gave her this son);* **Levi** *(her husband will get close to her and love her);* **Judah** *(she will give thanks to God). Leah gave her slave girl Zilpah to Jacob and she had two sons with him. Their names were* **Gad** *(I am lucky) and* **Asher** *(I am happy and other women will see it). Leah had two other sons with Jacob,* **Issachar** *(God gave me what I paid for) and* **Zebulum** *(which is my husband will recognise me). She also had a daughter named Dinah.*

It must also be noted that the children of the slave women who dwell with their mistress were considered as the children of the mistress. With this in mind, Leah was the mother of eight of the twelve tribes of Israel. From her lineage came kings, including King David and the King of all Kings, Jesus Christ.

Leah probably never realised that she represented great wealth and carried generations of outstanding dignitaries. Her husband Jacob acquired much wealth and decided to make a fresh start after more than twenty years. He took his wives, children, and all the properties he had gained while he was living with his father-in-law and they all journeyed to Mesopotamia. Leah as a grown woman relocated from her birthplace and familiar surroundings to make a new start in life. She was adaptable. She signified greatness and historically, could be known as one of the greatest mothers who ever lived. She had unwrapped resources of undefined wealth and unimaginable prodigiousness.

Modern-Day Reality: Self-confidence is an important facet to success.

CHAPTER 19

RACHEL

(Genesis 25:27–28; 28:1–22; 29:1–35; 30:1–43;
31:1–55; 35:16–20; 25; 46:19–22; 1 Samuel 10:2;
Jeremiah 31: 15 – 17)

God answered her prayers. She became pregnant and
gave birth to Joseph.

In Israel the older brother's right was an endorsement of the blessing, headship, and a double portion of his father's wealth. Twin brothers who have been fighting from within the womb had become of age. They were sons of Isaac and grandsons of Abraham. Jacob the younger son tricked his older twin brother Esau into giving up the blessing and entitlement as head of the family. Esau, knowing what this meant for him, pursued Jacob with the intention to kill him. Jacob robbed him of the well-deserved family legacy of power, position, and prestige. Isaac, his father, was afraid for Jacob's safety and thought Jacob would be safe in another country. So Jacob was sent to his mother's relative in Mesopotamia. After a tedious journey, Jacob finally arrived in Mesopotamia. He went to 'hang out' at the most popular spot, the famous well. He then enquired where his uncle Laban lived. At that time Rachel, his first cousin, came to the well to get water for the sheep. The people of the city introduced Rachel to Jacob as her cousin. When Jacob saw Rachel, she wooed his heart. He was a gentleman so he offered to remove the stone from the well and help her water the flock. He kissed Rachel then turned his face away, sobbing.

In all excitement, Rachel ran home to tell her father Laban about Jacob. Laban hurried to the well to meet Jacob. He hugged and kissed Jacob inviting him to his home. Jacob took over the job of looking after the flock. His uncle Laban thought about all the hard work Jacob was doing and felt he should pay him. He asked Jacob what he would like as payment for looking after the sheep. Jacob's choice was Rachel's hand in marriage. Rachel was a beautiful young woman, the younger of two daughters. Laban knew that Jacob was in love with Rachel and felt that if Jacob worked for seven years, it would be enough work for Rachel.

When seven years of hard work came to an end Jacob asked his uncle Laban for Rachel.

Laban:

- *had no intention of giving Rachel to Jacob after seven years, since his older daughter Leah should marry first.*
- *had a big feast as Jacob celebrated; he had a few drinks and was not in control; however Jacob trusted his uncle's judgment, expecting him to be fair.*
- *sent his older daughter that night to sleep with Jacob.*

Jacob was totally unaware that Leah shared his marital bed that night and not Rachel as he expected. Jacob had sex with his new bride not knowing whether it was Rachel his first love or her sister Leah. When he awoke the next morning, to his surprise it was Leah in bed with him, not Rachel. Jacob had to work for another seven years. He loved Rachel and was willing to work hard for her, so he started another seven years of hard work. Jacob was committed to Rachel and worked for her since she was his first love. The second seven years ended and Jacob wed Rachel, the one he always loved.

Rachel:

- was a young beautiful shepherdess.
- took over the role of the elder sister when she went to the well to water the flock.
- shared a husband with her sister and slave girl.
- was barren while her sister Leah had children one after another.
- was envious of her sister and angry with her husband because she had no children.
- prayed and God answered her prayers. She became pregnant and gave birth to Joseph.

Jacob took his wives, children, all that he had acquired and secretly escaped in the dead of night from Laban's jurisdiction. Jacob did not know that his wife Rachel had stolen her father's idol and sat on it. Laban chased after then in search of his idol. He checked every where but could not find it. Rachel asked to be excused from been searched, her rational was, she was having her monthly cycle. Rachel was not truthful. As they

SECRET: FAME OR FAILURE

journeyed, Rachel who was pregnant went into labour and gave birth to her second son; sadly, she died in childbirth. Jacob called this son Benjamin. Rachel was buried on the road to Ephrath, Jacob her husband put a rock on her grave as a tombstone.

The Prophet Jeremiah noted in Ramah a painful sound was heard as Rachel who could not be comforted weeps for her children who were dead. Rachel asked for either children or death (Genesis 30:1). God blessed her womb; she had children but died in childbirth. A reference to Pharaoh's action in Moses' times and Herod's action in Jesus' times (Exodus 1:16; St. Matthew 1:16). Rachel is a type of all who experience impossibilities, even barrenness. God miraculously intervened and blessed her; however she died without enjoying her children. Rachel did not miscarry, nor had a still birth. She reproduced life, impacting legacy. A character of hopefulness, she is seen as one who accepted death for herself while refusing death for her offspring.

Rachel died at a very early age. She did not live to see her sons grow up and realise their dreams. However, her son Joseph was a hero. He was raised by his stepmother and became the most impressive young man of his time. He went from prison cell to becoming prime minister in another country. He was reputable, of outstanding character with unquestionable morality.

Rachel must receive a posthumous award; from her womb emerged greatness, integrity, bravery, and excellence.

Modern-Day Reality: Barrenness has no place.

CHAPTER 20

Bilhah

(Genesis 29:28–29; 30:1–8;
37:2; 46:22–25)

Bilhah must be greatly honoured for raising Joseph, a godly young man.

H er master Laban was a very wealthy man. His wealth included slaves who cared for his children. He had many acres of lands and many herds. Rachel, the younger daughter of Laban, was the young woman whom Jacob loved originally. Laban promised Jacob that he would be able to marry her after seven years of hard work. He changed his mind and gave another daughter to Jacob for his wife. Jacob had to work another seven years for Rachel. After the wedding, Laban gave Bilhah, one of the servants, to Rachel and Jacob to become their slave girl.

A few years after her marriage, Rachel's frustration was evident when she could not conceive; she was devastated since her sister had conceived and bore children. So Rachel gave Bilhah, who was her slave girl, to her husband Jacob to become his wife. Bilhah became pregnant and had a son called Dan. Rachel thought the name Dan meant God heard her prayer. Bilhah had another son with Jacob and she called him Naphtali. Rachel thought the name Naphtali gave vengeance to her feelings since she struggled with her sister.

Rachel later conceived and had two sons; unfortunately, she died in childbirth and Bilhah took care of these two boys. The two children were Joseph and Benjamin. Bilhah must be greatly honoured for raising Joseph, a godly young man. Joseph knew Bilhah as mother. He was treated cruelly by his brothers who sold him to the Egyptians to become their slave. Joseph was of high moral standing and integrity. As a result he was promoted to the position of prime minister in Egypt, a strange land.

God's mercies prevailed to Bilhah, as she was the subject of an extramarital affair with her stepson, Reuben, who was Jacob's firstborn. God detested a man having sexual relation with his father's wife, as Reuben had done. Bilhah was ashamed of her ungodly deed and repented of it.

From the twelve tribes of Israel, Bilhah was the mother of four of the heads. Two of whom were her biological sons and the other two she raised after the untimely death of their mother in childbirth. She must be credited for the godly upbringing of her sons. She recognised and encouraged greatness in Joseph even though he was not her biological son. It seemed as she was willing to invest in that which belongs to someone else, more than she invested in her own. She was outstanding.

Modern-Day Reality: God can entrust greatness in your hand, though it comes from another source.

CHAPTER 21

TAMAR 1

(Genesis 38:1–30; 46:12)

*Tamar knew full well that Judah was not faithful in
keeping his promises...*

Under Jewish law, the freedom to choose who they married was taken out of their hands. Whether they agreed or not, their parents chose the man or the woman their children married. Judah, one of Jacob's twelve sons, was the father of three boys. He went out 'wife hunting' for his eldest son. He thought Tamar was the perfect choice as she was beautiful. Although she was not an Israelite, she was selected. She was honoured to marry someone from another race, a Jew. Judah gave his eldest son Er to Tamar. In the Jewish culture when a woman gets married, she leaves her parents' home to live with her husband among her in-laws.

Tamar loved Er and found him very attractive. However, he was wicked, as he did not want to know the God of his father Judah. He worshipped false gods and was involved in heathen practices. His father counselled him and showed him the ways of God. He was defiant and stubbornly continued in his evil path. God was displeased with him. He went to bed one night and never woke up. Tamar was greatly distressed when her marriage ended abruptly. Tamar felt aggrieved as she became a young widow. She mourned the loss of her husband for months, wearing mourning clothes; she did not go to her hairdresser, or wear makeup and jewelry. Her father-in-law comforted her. Tamar stopped grieving when her father-in-law propositioned her to marry again.

Tamar knew that under Jewish culture she was entitled to marry again to the brother of her deceased husband. After the official period of mourning, a second wedding was arranged. She was given Onan, Judah's second son, to marry. The Jewish culture also dictated that when a man dies without children, his brother should have children for the deceased. Onan did not want to have children for his dead brother, so he interrupted the sexual act to prevent Tamar becoming pregnant. Onan's action displeased God, so he collapsed and died in bed. God took his life since he failed to have children for his dead brother. Tamar was inconsolable, she felt guilty and thought God was punishing her. Her burden of grief was incomprehensible becoming a widow all over again (twice in a few years). Her emotional instability caused her to be mentally unsound. She expected a comforting word from her father-in-law, as she felt she could not go on living.

She was shocked when Judah, her father-in-law, asked her to return home to her father's house, as the last son was too young to get married at that time. Judah reassured her that when his last son Shelah was eligible for marriage, he would bring her back so she could marry him. Tamar was obedient; she trusted Judah. Tamar could not stop her tears from flowing as she packed her bags and headed home to her father's house. She had to readjust to life at her father's home. Time had passed as she

*checked the mail, expecting an invite from her ex-father-in-law Judah.
Many years had passed and Judah's wife was now deceased. Judah, fearing his last son would also die suddenly, was determined that Tamar
would not marry his third son. Tamar finally concluded that Judah had
lied to her. His betrayal and deception stung her heart.*

*Tamar had an informant in Judah's house. News reached her that
Judah was planning to visit Timnah.*

Tamar:

- *painted her face and shaved her head, disguising herself.*
- *arrived close to Timnah and waited for Judah.*

Judah:

- *saw her and thought she was a prostitute.*
- *had no idea that the woman was his ex-daughter-in-law.*
- *took her to a motel and had sex with her.*

*Judah did not recognize Tamar's voice when she asked him for pay-
ment for sexual pleasures. He did not have the payment for his act of
prostitution, so he promised Tamar a goat from his flock. Tamar knew
that Judah was not faithful in keeping his promises and asked him for a
guarantee or a deposit until she received the goat. Judah willingly handed
over his seal and his walking stick.*

*A few days later, the servants went to Timnah in search of the 'pros-
titute' to give her the goat; she was nowhere to be found. They asked the
people who knew the area very well, but they did not know who the servant was speaking about.*

Three months later Judah heard that Tamar had become a prostitute and she was pregnant. Judah was angry and wanted Tamar to be killed. He sent his servant to get her so that she would be put to death. Tamar sent a message back to Judah, telling him that the **owner of the seal and the walking stick** was the father of her baby.

A few months later she gave birth to twins. The delivery record was unique; one baby's hand was delivered first, and the midwife put a red label on that baby's hand. Seemingly, as if that baby had a change of mind, not wishing to be first, he retracted, allowing his brother to be born first. These boys were called Perez and Zerah, both were mentioned in the genealogy of Jesus Christ in the New Testament (Matthew 1:1–3).

Judah realised how unrighteous he was and repented. He thought Tamar's retaliation was a direct result of his deception for failing to give his third son, Shelah, to her in marriage. Judah was ashamed and admitted that Tamar was much more God-fearing than him.

Tamar did not allow the fact that she was taken advantage of, lied to, and shamefully dispelled from the house of her in-laws to dominate her thinking. She refocused and God gave the wisdom that allowed her to discredit the deceiver, securing a blessing. She did not have grandchildren for Judah while she was married to his sons, but she had children for him through trickery and deception. She became the predecessor of Jesus. Her cunning craftiness worked for her and it guaranteed her a title in Christ's genealogy.

Modern-Day Reality: God gives the grace to overcome unjust treatment.

CHAPTER 22

DINAH

(Genesis 30:21; 34:1–31; 46:15)

Dinah knew God through her father,
since they worshipped Him as a family.

H er father's life was equal to that of a slave who had run away from his master. Jacob arrived in Mesopotamia and lived with his mother's relatives for almost three decades. He stayed with his uncle Laban who later became his father-in-law. This was a safe haven; he was a fugitive, running away from his brother Esau whom he tricked. Jacob had many wives including Leah who had six sons, and she also gave birth to their first daughter Dinah. Jacob craved for his independence and felt it was time to have his own home. He decided to move away from his father-in-law and start life as a free man.

He took his wives, children, and all that he owned and journeyed to Shechem in Canaan. On his arrival he decided to settle, so he bought lands from Hamor, one of the most influential rulers in that country. Jacob was conscious of the God who protected him and brought him back to his homeland. He felt his priority was to erect a place of worship, an altar where he could make sacrifices to God.

Dinah knew God through her father, since they worshipped Him as a family. She was beaming with excitement as they moved into a new neighbourhood.

Dinah:

- *felt isolated and wanted to meet the women of Shechem and make friends.*
- *loved to explore and went to the city the next day.*
- *was always protected by her six brothers and had no reason to distrust men, since her brothers loved her dearly.*
- *met the son of Hamor the king, a Hivite called Shechem. He was young and friendly and offered to orientate her to the city.*
- *did not realise that her actions of befriending the young prince would set off a series of tragic events in her life.*

Shechem was lustful and deceptive. He led Dinah to his house then seduced and raped her. After this, he tried to cover up his abominable act by admitting that he was madly in love with her. Dinah was severely embarrassed and demeaned.

Shechem:

- *thought that as the king's son he had the authority to go into bed with any of the young women.*
- *sought reparation for his seduction of Dinah and went to his*

father with an offer of marriage. Dinah told her father Jacob what Shechem had done. He was outraged.

- *knew that Jacob's anger was not appeased by his offer and he could kill him for what he had done to Dinah.*

Shechem went to his father Hamor and told him some aspects of the story. He told his father he was in love with Dinah and she was the one he wanted to marry.

Dinah's brothers heard what Shechem did to their sister and wanted revenge. Hamor tried to negotiate with Jacob and his sons. Hamor told them that they can come together and intermarry. Jacob responded to Hamor that under religious rites, his daughter cannot marry a man who was uncircumcised.

Hamor was the chief leader in the city, so he arranged an urgent meeting with all the men in Shechem. He felt he had good news and told the men of the city if they were to be circumcised, they would be able to marry any of the Israelite women. They would live together in the same city and share their wealth. All the men in that city welcomed the news and wanted to be circumcised so that they could marry the Israelite women. They were all circumcised and three days later, when the pains in their private parts were at its highest, two of Dinah's brothers, Simeon and Levi, knowing how vulnerable they were, took a sword and savagely attacked all the men in the city, including King Hamor and his son Shechem. They were all killed by Dinah's brothers, who felt justified for Shechem's violation of their sister.

Jacob feared that the actions of his sons Levi and Simeon could provoke a riot. All the neighbouring cities could come together and attack them. Levi and Simeon were daring and felt justice was served since they could not allow anyone to treat their sister Dinah, as a prostitute. They *were very protective of her and willing to wipe out an entire nation in revenge for their sister's violation.*

Dinah thought she was mature enough to handle life without the defense of her protective brothers; she was sadly mistaken. She encountered a man who was evil, sexually abusing her as a result. She later felt justice was served, since her brothers destroyed an entire nation in revenge. She learnt wisdom as she realised that there are good and evil people around her. She could only decipher and discern good or evil with God's help.

Modern-Day Reality: Justice will be served.

CHAPTER 23

KETURAH

(Genesis 25:1–10; 1 Chronicles 1:32)

*Keturah was not prejudiced by the fact that Abraham was
more than twice her age.*

H er lover was in search of a bride at age 137. It sounds ridiculous,
but it was her reality. At age 137, her husband began a national
search for a wife. He was a celebrity in his time. Women in all the
nations knew Abraham as the greatest man who lived in their era, and
many of them did not think about his age. It was an honour in Israel
to be the wife of this great patriarch. Hundreds of women were eligible. However, he chose Keturah to be the wife of his old age. She was
highly selected among many other women to be his second wife after
the death of Sarah.

Abraham:

- was the father and founder of faith and did many great things for God.
- obeyed God by relocating his family without a known address of where he was going.
- made an agreement or a covenant with God. The covenant meant Abraham was going to give up his people, property, and power to become what God wanted of him.
- saw many miracles in his life as he obeyed God, and was willing to give up his son after he waited twenty-five years for him.

Keturah:

- accepted Abraham's proposal to become his wife.
- had qualities that attracted this great hero of faith.
- gave Abraham more children: Zimran, Jokshan, Medan, Midiam, Ishbak, and Shuah.
- spent thirty-seven blissful years of marriage with her husband before he died.

Abraham:

- was exceedingly wealthy and gave most of that wealth to Isaac.
- also gave his other children some of his wealth.
- was very experienced and chose a godly woman as his wife.

She was a woman of child-bearing age. Keturah would most likely have been much younger than Abraham, possibly eighty to ninety years younger. By virtue of her age, she could have been considered as Abraham's daughter or granddaughter.

Keturah was not prejudiced by the fact that Abraham was more than twice her age. She was delighted and honoured to be the wife of the greatest father of faith and man of God in her time. She knew her reality was many women's dream. Keturah knew about Abraham's miraculous encounters even though she was not his wife at that time. She knew that Abraham became a dad at one hundred years of age. She read about Sarah conceiving a son in her old age. She felt honoured to have children for Abraham since God had promised that Abraham's children would be many and great in the earth. Not only Isaac was Abraham's son of his old age, Keturah's children were also conceived and born many years after the birth of Isaac.

While the birth of Isaac as the child of Abraham's old age is a dominant theme, it must also be understood that Keturah also mothered many children for Abraham decades later. Isaac was not a one-off miracle but the beginning of a series of miracles. Keturah's womb was the carrier of the subsequent miracles. She also produced nations, though sadly some became ungodly. She was also integrated into the greatness ascribed to her husband since great men rise with the help of great women.

Modern-Day Reality: It's never too late for a miracle.

CHAPTER 24

ASENATH

(Genesis 41:44–57; 46:19–20; 48:1–22)

He selectively chose a bride, a woman of God, a virgin and
the daughter of a priest.

Her husband was among the seven most handsome men in Bible times. All the virgins in the land thought of him as prime husband material. He selectively chose a bride, a woman of God, a virgin and the daughter of a priest. Asenath was the daughter of Potiphera, a priest from the nation of On. She was not from the Jewish nation. However, God allowed her union with Joseph, a mighty man of God. Their marriage produced two sons, Manasseh and Ephraim.

The name Manasseh was chosen as Joseph thought God brought him through so much trouble by making him forget those experiences.

The name Ephraim was chosen in appreciation of God, who allowed both Joseph and his wife Asenath to have children or blessing; in the same place they had many troubles in the past.

Her husband struggled with ill treatment from his eleven jealous brothers, since his father thought highly of him. They sold him and he became the pharaoh's servant in Egypt. The pharaoh's wife lusted after the teenager; making advances, she grabbed his shirt, but Joseph ran away topless. He jumped through the window to escape from her. Joseph subscribed to a life of purity and having sex with his master's wife was beneath his integrity.

His master returned home and found his wife very distressed and distraught. She told him her version of the story; Joseph was thrown into prison immediately to serve a sentence for a crime he had not committed. He was a disciplined teenager with godly principles. God used him in prison to interpret dreams. He interpreted a dream for the king when all the wise men and magicians could not interpret the king's dream. This merited him instant promotion. He became the only person in Egypt who was almost as powerful as the king.

Asenath was beautiful and attracted to Joseph, Egypt's most powerful man. She felt this was one of the highest honours in life. She was equally a woman of principle and integrity. God had prepared her for the role of the wife of a great man of God, even though she was not an Israelite. She was a daughter of a priest and she was taught the ways of God by her parents. God's revelation of His knowledge was declared not only to His people the Israelites. The scripture highlighted that God's mercy and His power was demonstrated to people who were not from the tribes of Israel, but also to those who had a consciousness of God's power in the earth.

Asenath:

- knew from her family background what the office of the priesthood meant.

- was taught about caring for people and sacrificial giving of her life for the cause she believed in.
- could not identify with Joseph's life of turbulence, but she did identify with his life of purity and integrity.
- knew she was chosen by God to be the wife of a powerful man of God, an Israelite.

Joseph and Asenath were in charge of Egypt in a period of plenty and seven years of fruitfulness. The crops produced seven times more harvest than years past. The animals also produced abundantly. The increase was astronomical. Joseph and his wife were involved in preserving crops and livestock in preparation for a prolonged period of famine. The other countries had a severe shortage of food and the people in those countries were dying of hunger. Messages and official letters were received on a daily basis from the government of all the countries outside Egypt. They all requested for help, since all the foods they had stored up for the famine were finished. Joseph's office was managed by Asenath, his wife. He knew she would ensure that those working under her were accountable and responsible while he managed the province. The crops and animals they had stored away were used to feed people from many of the other countries for seven years until the famine was over. There was great organisation, excellent management and efficiency in ensuring that the sustenance was preserved and distributed appropriately.

She was not only credited for her roles and responsibilities in the famine, her children received extraordinary blessings from Israel, Joseph's father. This blessing granted them equivocal status as their uncles, who were leaders of the twelve tribes. They became the only grandchildren of Israel who inherited portions of land (Cities) in Canaan, which was the highest recognition in that time. Israel blessed Ephraim, the second *born, with the blessing that was rightfully given to the firstborn, as he was about to die. The blessing of Ephraim (Joshua 16:1–10; 17:15–18) outstripped that of Manasseh's (Joshua 17:1–18). Samuel was one of the descendants, he was a remarkable judge from the tribe of Ephraim, since his father was an Ephramite (1 Samuel 1:1).*

Asenath's children received the highest recognition in the land even though she was not a Jew. Their blessings were in proportion to the sons of Israel, who were a generation above them. She raised stalwart, men of renown. She was righteous, and knew the God of the chosen people. God's mercies and favour are demonstrated through her, as God is no respecter of persons. He honours all who will fear him, and indeed she was greatly honoured.

Modern-Day Reality: God's blessings are given to non- Jews also, to make them govern and rule.

CHAPTER 25

Rahab the Harlot

(Joshua 2:1–24; 6:17, 25; St Matthew 1:5
Hebrews 11:31; James 2:25)

She was the only person mentioned in this hall of faith from the
heathen nation as a biblical heroine.

One summer day as Rahab sat on her porch, her eyes roamed the street for *business as usual*. It was not unusual for strange men to visit her home, as she was Jericho's well-known **prostitute**. Jericho's city was built high above sea level, surrounded by massive walls. The unique location together with its architectural design created a robust security system. No one could go in and out of the city unnoticed. It was impossible to believe that men of God, doing His business would walk into the home of a notable prostitute late at night. It seemed ridiculous that these men were crawling into a **red light district**, but this was exactly what happened in Jericho.

God is sovereign. He uses any open door, even the door opened by a prostitute. These two Jewish men were led by God into Jericho, without a hotel reservation or an address where they were going to stay. Rahab recognised the wandering men by their appearance—**Jews!** She invited them into her home. Rahab was well informed about the Jewish history and heard about all the miraculous occurrences the Jewish people did. Rahab was not Jewish, but she knew the principle of hospitality to even those who were supposed to be enemies of the people of Jericho.

News spread about God working wonders through His chosen people, the Jews. They were warriors who fought and conquered many of their enemies, known to be strong and undefeated. Rahab told them all that she had heard and the men confirmed the accuracy. The men explained the purpose of their mission. Rahab knew the men could not escape security as they entered the city.

Rahab:

- *knew that her house would be targeted as one place in the city that the men would visit, so she expected a knock on her door.*
- *hid the two men in a room close to the roof where she dried wheat.*
- *was expecting security to do a full search, so she covered the men over with straws and dried leaves.*
- *knew she was risking her life and the lives of her family to accommodate these spies, since these Israelites were their enemies.*

The king of Jericho heard that the two men had breached security and were hiding within the walls of Jericho; he sent out a search party to find the men and kill them. The search party came to Rahab's house and asked her for the men from Israel. Rahab lied, telling them that the men came by but left hours ago. She pointed in the direction she wanted the search party to pursue.

When the king's search party left, she went up to the roof to tell the men what had happened. She also told them, God had sent them and God would cause Israel to defeat her own people of Jericho. The people of Jericho feared the Israelites and their God. Rahab reiterated the story of the Israelite conquest as they led the pharaoh and his chariots through the Red Sea. Pharaoh and his army drowned as they pursued the Israelites who escaped Egypt.

A woman of faith, a 'prophetess', Rahab was fully aware of the future of Jericho before it happened. She saw the impending destruction of Jericho and asked the two men to make a covenant with her to save her life and the lives of her family. Being family-oriented, it was important to Rahab that her family was saved also. She was the only person God trusted with a secret. It was not only the secret of hiding the spies, but she was also the only person in Jericho with knowledge about its impeding destruction.

The Israelite men made a covenant with Rahab. She was expected to invite all her family into her house, leaving a rope dangling outside the window. The men would be able to identify her house and save all those who were staying inside.

God accepted Rahab; she was defined by God, not by her lifestyle. It was her act of faith and her obedience that stood out.

As a prostitute, Rahab had acquired lots of skills that made her highly secretive. She was 'streetwise', and told the men to escape in the hills and hide for three days before they returned home. In Israel, a search is unsuccessful and abandoned after three days by the search party, if they failed to find the person(s) they went out to seek. Rahab was physically strong, so she was able to help the men down through the window by a rope. She left the rope dangling from her window so that the Israelites could identify her house when they returned to destroy Jericho. The Israelites returned with a seven-day plan to destroy the people and the city. Jericho was completely demolished and the only survivors were Rahab and her family.

She was the only person mentioned in this hall of faith from the heathen nation as a biblical heroine. Rahab was recorded with patriarchs and prophets like Abraham, Moses, Isaac, and Jacob. This woman of Jericho can be seen as the female equivalent of Abraham. Her faith was great as Abraham's even though she was not one of God's chosen people, the Jews.

Rahab encountered God on her journey of life, putting her faith to work since faith without corresponding works is dead. Faith always works for those who believe in God's word, as God honours faith. Rahab's act of faith meant she disobeyed the laws of men, sacrificing her life and the lives of her entire household to save the spies. Historical records in biblical times placed Rahab and her family as living among the Israelites. Rahab became part of the ancestry of Jesus Christ and was mentioned in His genealogy. Her faith evoked God's favour, propelling her into divine destiny.

Modern-Day Reality: Fear always precedes defeat and destruction, but faith creates life.

CHAPTER 26

The Daughters of Zelophehad

(Numbers 27:1–11; 1 Chronicles 7:14–16)

Women can stand for change in the law, even when they were originally
excluded from the drafting of the constitution.

FIVE WOMEN CHANGED THE INHERITANCE LAW IN ISRAEL!

The headline news the next day was groundbreaking. This was the most memorable day in their lives; they were tired of lousy excuses from men who told them what they could not do. They took their case to their leader and the result they received was greater than winning the jackpot.

Five sisters were constantly being told they could not get the land deed and title because they were women. Zelophehad, their father, had left Egypt to go to the Promised Land to settle there. He died *en route* with thousands of other people. Moses distributed the lands to all the leaders of Israel before they entered the Promised Land. Zelophehad was a descendant of Manasseh, who was the son of Joseph. He was given lands in Canaan with all the other leaders of the tribes of Israel. The tradition dictated that only the male descendants could inherit the lands and legacy to preserve the family name.

Zelophehad had no sons to inherit these lands; it meant that the other male relatives would be entitled to claim the land title by default. A greater understanding of the work of the ten spies who went to spy out the land, they were supposed to inform the leader of the precise acreage of the lands they proposed to inherit. These lands were distributed to the tribes before they entered and possessed the Promised Land. This was a complete act of confidence, faith, and trust in God. Moses read out the names of all the leaders and the portion, as well as the location of the lands they were expected to inherit, when they arrived in Canaan. These five sisters were attentive as their father's name was mentioned and the portion of land that belonged to him.

Zelophehad's five daughters—Mahlah, Noah, Hoglah, Milcah, and Tirzah—approached Moses and the priest requesting their father's portion of land since their father died and had no sons. The law concerning inheriting property was silent and never mentioned what to do in such exceptional circumstances, or in the case where there was no son. These girls thought it was fully time for an amendment to the law concerning inheritance. What was very important in handing down property was that the name of the previous owner be kept 'alive' so that the deceased person was not forgotten. This was of great significance in Jewish times. Therefore when a woman married, she took on the name of her husband and all his wealth. Wealth was transferred only through the male lineage.

These five girls stood up for the passing on of wealth to the female lineage in Israel for the first time. Moses was confused and did not know what to do. He consulted with God and a new legislation took effect regarding the inheritance of property. This legislation was known as the **Daughters of Zelophehad Law.** The new law stated that when a man died leaving no sons, his wealth did not go to any of his male relations if that man had daughters.

In a male-orientated society these five sisters fought for what they believed was rightfully theirs. They were fearless and went to the main leader of their time for justice. Standing firmly on their belief, they refused to have their father's name erased and inheritance handed over to another relative or the state. The sisters did not view the law regarding inheritance as binding and unchangeable. Women in Israel seldom stood up against men in those times when their belief contradicted common practice.

Women can stand for change in the law, even when they were originally excluded from the drafting of the constitution; this was what happened in the case of these five sisters.

Modern-Day Reality: Women petition for change by doing what was never done before.

CHAPTER 27

ACSAH

(Genesis 15:18–19; Numbers 26:65;
Joshua 14:6–14; 15:13–20;
Judges 1:12–15)

Acsah was the daughter of Israel's greatest optimist and warrior.
Her Father taught her to always dream big and aim high.

Her dad was the greatest optimist of his time. He came face-to-face with giants and he never thought he was too small in stature to challenge his opponents and defeat them.

Caleb was the son of Jephunneh, a Kenizzite; his origin was not from the twelve tribes of Israel. Bible scholars believe that the Kenizzites were from the descendants of Esau and were also known as Edomites. With such background, it is only likely that Caleb's father, Jephunneh, followed Abraham and became as one of the Israelites. Caleb associated himself with the tribe of Judah and was referred to as Caleb son of Jephunneh from the tribe of Judah. The identification of Caleb son of

Jephunneh (who was associated with the tribe of Judah) must be made as there was another Caleb from the tribe of Judah.

Caleb descended from an ungodly nation. However, he believed God was with Abraham. When all the leaders of the Edomites were mentioned in (Genesis 36:1–43), Jephunneh was not mentioned since he was not known as a leader. Caleb followed Abraham, aligning himself with the tribe of Judah. Caleb went into the land of Canaan as one of the twelve spies. His association with Abraham could have changed his perception and made him a leader as he returned from Canaan with only positive news. Caleb was ready to conquer the enemies and take his portion of the lands in Canaan. It took the Israelites forty years to arrive in the land of Canaan with only two survivors from the older generation. Caleb was one of those two survivors.

After five years of settling in Canaan, Caleb went to his leader Joshua and requested his mountain/territory. At age eighty-five he was not suffering from joint pains or arthritis but was prepared to climb mountains, and defeat and destroy the enemies who had made their home there.

Acsah was the daughter of Israel's greatest optimist and warrior. She saw her dad Caleb compiling a list of strategies for war. Her father was preoccupied with fighting and defeating his enemies. He visited and explored the lands the enemies dwelt in and he brought back a positive report about the land. Acsah saw her father return home with a winner's attitude, after challenges, opposition, and negativity. Her dad taught her the secret of conquest, to always think positively and take decisive actions.

Acsah was no doubt a daddy's girl. Her mother's name was not mentioned in the scripture. Caleb was a loving and caring dad, so he had heart-to-heart talks with his daughter. She listened attentively as her father discussed with her about the man she would marry one day.

Acsah's husband:

- *must be a **winner and a warrior**.*
- *must be a man of integrity, a man as brave as her dad, and one who is a champion warrior.*

Acsah knew all that her father told her was mere information; she did not have any choice in the matter. Her father would choose a husband for her whether she loved him or not.

Her father put out an advert, which read:

Warrior Compulsory!

Task: Fight and conquer our greatest enemies.
Reward: My beautiful daughter's hands in marriage.

*Othniel, his nephew, saw the advert and became excited. He had never been out fighting on his own before, but he decided that he would take the challenge. Othniel worked out a strategy for war, fought, and won the battle. Caleb kept his promise, Acsah was married to Othniel, her cousin. Caleb inherited an extra-large portion of lands, handed over to him as a result of his incredible strength and bravery. It was **not** normal in that cultural setting for fathers to give lands to their daughters, since inheritance was given to sons. It was phenomenal as Caleb favoured his daughter, giving her a portion of land. Despite the knowledge that it was abnormal for daughters to be given land, she went to her father shortly after, requesting the entire countryside.*

Acsah:

- *felt that the land she had received was very dry and not fertile.*
- *was not prepared to remain in a land that was barren.*
- *went to her father to ask him for a well-watered, fruitful land.*
- *asked for high places with springs. Her father gave her lands with great springs in the upper and lower parts.*
- *knew the principle of asking and receiving.*
- *had a productive mind, making her aim for the best of the lands.*
- *was not hindered by the fact that lands were given to sons. In her heart, lands belong to all children.*
- *was moved by faith, as she knew without faith it was impossible to please God or to get anything from God.*

She applied spiritual principles, **seeing the thing that did not exist as if it did** and was not prepared to remain in dryness and futility. One prerequisite to receiving the blessings of God is a refusal of the current situation and a craving for greater blessings. Acsah was taught by her father to seek after that which was good and settle for nothing less than the best.

Modern-Day Reality: All children are equally entitled.

CHAPTER 28

DEBORAH 2

(Judges 4:1–14; 5:1–31)

There was no warrior in Israel until I Deborah arose,
I arose to be a mother in Israel.
Wake up, wake up Deborah,

Her courtroom was in a very strange location, it conveys her sentiment, a love for nature and the outside world. She spent the majority of her day between Ramah and Bethel in the mountains of Ephraim. As a prophetess and a judge in Israel, she utilised the open space under the palm trees as her courtroom. A place of tranquility, where she felt so relaxed. From sunrise to sunset the children of Israel visited her to settle their disputes and disagreements under the open skies. She was not only a judge but also happily married to Lappidoth.

Deborah judged fairly as she dealt with matters of dishonesty, fraud, unscrupulous landlords, unjust slave masters and many other social ills. She had *zero tolerance* for unrighteousness and wanted to stamp out injustice in Israel. Deborah knew that the Israelites had many enemies whom they must fight and conquer. It would be counterproductive for the Israelites to have so many internal struggles and disparity, if they were to succeed in accomplishing the task of prevailing against their enemies.

The enemies of God's people were at war with the Israelites. The war was fierce. Their opposition had one intention: to wipe out the name of the Israelites from history. Deborah awoke one morning with a vision from God. She saw the war and God's people singing and dancing after the fight. She knew that Israel would defeat their enemies from Sisera. In Israel the mark of conquest was realized when the king had been captured, then the kingdom would transfer hands. This is exactly what happened when David defeated Goliath.

Deborah asked Barak, the chief commander of war, to prepare the armies to fight Sisera. Barak was very timid for a captain. He turned to Deborah and told her that he would go, **only if she went with him, but if she didn't he would not go**. *Deborah, being a woman of war, told Barak,* **'I am ready for war'.**

Deborah, the head warrior was accompanied by Barak and her army. They attacked the enemies and God sent confusion in the camp of the enemy. At the height of the confusion, the king of Sisera thought he could run faster than his horse, so he jumped off his horse and started on foot. The Israelites chased and killed the men of Sisera and not one of the men was left alive, but they had not conquered the king. There was no victory for Israel until the king was conquered. God took care of Sisera, since the king ran into the wrong place for safety and was killed. **Israel won the victory**.

That day Deborah and Barak wrote the words of the songs, and led the people of Israel into praise and worship about the greatness of God.

Sisera's mother looked out through the window,
She looked through the curtains, and she asked
Why is Sisera's chariot late?
Why are the sounds of his chariot horses delayed?
They must be having a good time as they conquer.

How great and awesome is our God,
Before whom the mountain shakes in terror.
The skies rained and the cloud dropped water,
The stars fought from heaven,
From their path they fought Sisera,
And the Kishon swept Sisera's men away.

There was no warrior in Israel until I Deborah arose,
I arose to be a mother in Israel.
Wake up, wake up Deborah,
Wake up, wake up and sing a song,
Get up Barak, go Barak, go and capture your enemies.
Let all Israel's enemies die this way, Lord
But let all the people who love you be powerful like the rising sun.
There was peace in the land of Israel for forty years.

Modern-Day Reality: We all need to possess a warrior spirit ready to fight and defeat the enemy.

CHAPTER 29

JAEL

(Judges 4:17–22; 5:24–31)

Sisera asked for water but she gave him milk,
In a glass fit for a king.

Who trained her to be a warrior?
She gave him drink to quench his thirst.
She spread a blanket over his feet, making him warm.
He felt secure within her tent,
And off to sleep he went.

She knew the rules of war. Never rescue a wanted man or all your house/tent would be completely destroyed. Her husband was Heber, a Kenite. Sisera ran into her tent nervous, breathless and shaken. She met him by the door. She knew without a doubt this was not an honourable occasion. It was her worst nightmare, a king trying to seek safety from war in her home.

Jael was aware of all that was happening in the land, and as a wise woman she had a plan. She smiled and welcomed the king into her home/tent. She reassured him that all would be well. He was perplexed and exhausted as though he had been running for his life.

Jael knew the war was on. Her humble tent became a place where the noble king hid himself from his enemies. She showed him hospitality by covering his feet with her new thick blanket. Sisera was relaxed enough to ask for a drink. In her pantry, Jael found a goat skin bag with milk to give the king. She was commanded by him to guard the tent door and not let anyone in, as he lay to rest for the night.

*A moment of panic came over Jael: She knew if caught hiding the enemy of the Jews, this meant **death** for herself and her family. Jael decided to conclude the war Deborah and Israel had started. She took a peg that fastened her tent, hammering it into Sisera's head straight into the ground. The Israelite army came running to her tent to witness the victory.*

Jael, wife of Heber, is blessed more than all the women
who lived in tents.
Sisera asked for water but she gave him milk.
In a glass fit for a king she served him milk, which was rich
with cream.
Jael reached out and took the tent peg and her right hand reached
for the hammer.
She struck him
Smashing his head.
At Jael's feet he sank and fell
And there he lay dead.

What a *warrior*, a woman of war. Who taught her to fight? She knew how to finish a war; the head of a king was all that was needed to prove that the war had ended. Jael held the trophy as proof of Israel's victory that day; she concluded the war without stepping outside her home.

She was never recruited as a general in the army, although she was a strategist and qualified to be a warrior. Her humble tent was cosy and comfortable, just the right place for a King who had escaped his enemies. Jael did not reveal her secrets to the king. His status did not intimidate her. She devised a plan and pursued it. Jael saved her people that day, and she was heralded as a champion in Israel.

Modern-Day Reality: Courage and conquest; one brave act secures victory for a nation.

CHAPTER 30

A WOMAN ENDED THE LIFE OF A WICKED KING

(Judges 9:24; 50–56)

Ready to use what she had: a stone to defeat a militia that was very experienced with swords and armoury.

A Woman Ended the Life of a Wicked King!

That was headline news in Israel. Gideon the king was a mighty warrior, a conqueror in battle. Gideon fought the enemies of God, securing victory every time. He lived a polygamous life, having many wives, and from these relationships he had more than seventy sons. Abimelech was one of his sons. Abimelech's mother was one of Gideon's servants from Shechem. After Gideon's death there was a major family dispute about who would reign as king. Although Ablimelech was not the firstborn, he sought power and wanted the throne. He carried out a bloody massacre, killing seventy of his brothers. Only one of his brothers escaped.

Abimelech:

- became king by default. The people became rebellious and revolted against his leadership; they were devastated by his wicked act of killing his brothers.
- fought many wars and won.
- waited in ambush and set fire to cities.
- created great fear in the hearts of the people. In one city a group of people found a safe place in a tower, as Abimelech set fire to that tower and killed one thousand (1,000) men and women.

Abimelech was proud of his major achievements, beating his chest, thinking he was invincible. He came to the city of Thebez. This city had a tower also. The inhabitants of Thebez climbed into the tower to hide, fearing for their lives. King Abimelech laughed as he knew the people were hiding in the tower, and he felt this made his task of destroying them effortless. Using a previous war tactic, he came near the door of the tower and attempted to set the tower on fire.

Unknown to the king, a woman had climbed into the tower with a purpose. The woman did not have any modern weapons, but she chose her grinding stone, knowing its power was parallel to that of a sword or spear. *Stones had domestic uses; they were used to grind wheat into flour (Deuteronomy 24:6).* She prepared herself to fight, opting not to leave the task to any other person hiding in the tower.

This fearless woman:

- *was hundreds of feet above ground and wanted a **fight**.*
- *navigated well; dropping the stone, it hit Abimelech, causing a large laceration to his head.*

King Abimelech fell to the ground. With the little strength he had left, he called his soldier to kill him with the sword. His pride would not allow him to have it rumoured that a woman killed him with a stone.

Of all the people who sought refuge in the tower, this brave woman had a plan not only to escape from the wicked king but to save the city.

She:

- *had a strategy and the right weapon for war.*
- *had enough of wickedness and wicked men.*
- *wanted to put an end to terror and terrorists.*
- *was not frightened by all that Abimelech had done.*
- *was ready to use what she had: a stone to defeat a militia that was very experienced with swords and armoury.*
- *was a mighty warrior, ready for her success story.*

A nation could not claim victory against its enemy if the king was still alive. This woman's strategy was to destroy the king. Knowing if she relied on the strength of the Almighty God, she would succeed, and her rock (stone) is a type of Christ.

The woman's name was never mentioned in scripture but she is known by her victory. Her actions were greater than an army. She was not just trying to escape. She spent time thinking about God's people and their safety. This woman was not deterred by the fact that female warriors were not officially enlisted for war in her times. She was a selfless woman who took action. Her thoughts reflected collectivism, patriotism and a love for God.

Modern-Day Reality: Fearlessness and faith work hand in hand.

CHAPTER 31

MRS. MANOAH

(Judges 13:1–25)

She knew that if a woman cannot have a baby,
it was a stigma within the Jewish culture.

Not known by her name. Could it be she was not an important figure in her society? She lived in the times of the judges; approximately three hundred years after the Israelites entered the Promised Land and partially inherited it. The nation of Israel faced many challenges with the enemies who lived around them. God expected the Israelites to drive out their enemies, as they were never meant to coexist. When the Israelites obeyed God and served Him, they won the battles over their enemies. However, when they took on the lifestyle of their enemies they displeased God and were defeated by their enemies. The Philistines were one group of enemies who reigned over the children of Israel for a long time. God is sovereign and compassionate, He planned to deliver the Israelites who lived in Zorah from the wicked Philistines.

God had a unique plan how He would bring about deliverance in Israel.

Mrs. Manoah was a childless woman. She knew being childless was a curse in Israel. Her status depressed her as she tried continuously with her husband to conceive. From time to time she prayed for a baby. One day while her husband had gone into the town, a strange man appeared.

This man told her about preparing for preconception and postnatal care, as she would become pregnant and have a baby in nine months. She was not expected to eat certain foods or drink certain drinks since her baby was going to be an extra-special child. Mrs. Manoah was gobsmacked. She did not know who this stranger was, but she believed all that he told her.

To her amazement, her husband arrived a few minutes after the stranger left, and she related to him all that the man had said. He was bewildered and wondered for a moment if his wife was hallucinating. After giving it some thought, her husband prayed that the stranger would return.

The same man returned a few days later, much to her surprise and secret expectation. She asked the stranger to wait a moment as she run to the farm to get her husband. The Manoahs hurried back and found the stranger waiting outside their home. The stranger gave instructions for her pregnancy and postnatal care. Manoah was suspicious and questioned the stranger, trying to find out who this stranger was. The stranger gave no clue who he was. However, the couple was convinced that the stranger was trustworthy even though they did not know him. Their eyes lit up in amazement as they hugged each other. They decided to be hospitable by cooking a celebratory meal for their guest. He refused to indulge and made a request instead. The Manoahs were asked to offer a sacrifice to God, a burnt offering (Leviticus 1:1–17).

*At first they pondered the request, knowing that only the priest was expected to offer sacrifice on an altar to God. They were God-fearing and wanted to please God always. In complete obedience, they fetched a goat as a burnt offering to God. (Offering could be a bull, a goat or birds. The couple belonged to the middle class in society and could not afford a bull like the upper class.) The goat must meet certain specifications: it must be a male, of a certain age, and be perfect or without any health defects. A **burnt offering** was God's method of purging his people of their sins in that time. God wanted this couple to be holy and separated for Him, as He desired to use them to accomplish His plan. God was about to bless them with a son who would be a mighty warrior, bringing victory against the enemies of the children of Israel. They prepared the goat for sacrifice, lit the fire and put the goat on the altar.*

*There arose a large fireball. As the flame ascended, the stranger disappeared with the burning flames. They stood in awe and only then did they realised, it was the angel of the Lord who visited them. In utter dismay, Manoah fell to the ground and his wife fell subsequently. They worshipped God for hours while lying on the ground. After that lengthy episode of being prostrate, they stood up trembling and frightened, the sound of every heartbeat still audible. Manoah told his wife that **death was imminent** as they had seen God. Mrs. Manoah reassured her husband that God would not reveal Himself to them and bless her womb with a son, then kill them. She told him that God was pleased with them and their sacrifice; it was a seal of God's approval of their lives. They continued to be God-fearing and devoted. Mrs. Manoah became pregnant; she spent the next nine months praying over the child in her womb. She went into labour and gave birth to a son, whom she called **Samson**. They were careful to obey all the instructions that the angel gave them for this baby, whose manual arrived long before he was born.*

Samson:

- *was taught the word of God and knew what was expected of him.*
- *strayed from the path that he was instructed in, but he later returned to the path God had destined for him.*
- *married a Philistine woman, and even though God instructed the children of Israel not to marry anyone who was not from the tribe of Israel, the scripture stated that God allowed Samson to marry a Philistine so that His purpose would be accomplished.*
- *became one of Israel's judges and was a powerful warrior. He was the only leader who killed more people while he was dying than when he was alive. He was also the only judge who secured victory against the Philistines after his death.*

Mrs. Manoah:

- was not known by an official name, but she was the person God chose to visit and reveal His will and purpose.
- believed God and was in close fellowship with Him.
- knew God's thoughts about her and the family were good. His plans were to prosper and do her good not evil.
- went from infertility to becoming a mighty warrior's mother in a few months.

Mrs Manoah might not be the topic or title of many sermons, but she was indeed a woman of character and renown. She was the one chosen by God, through whom He revealed Himself. She and her husband offered a sacrifice to God, a task carried out by the priest in those times. Her worship to God was a sign of God's acceptance. She knew how to reassure her husband about the difference between God's judgment and God's acceptance. She knew God in a personal way and never relied on the faith of her husband.

Modern-Day Reality: Insignificance in the eyes of men does not equate to insignificance with God.

CHAPTER 32

Delilah

(Judges 16:4–31)

To achieve much for God, we must be persistent, goal-orientated,
and not deterred by anything.

H er husband worked in the fields; he looked macho as though
he was always working out at the gym. He was strong, mus-
cular with a well-built physique, also referred to as the powerhouse.
His uncommon strength made him achieve what hundreds of men
put together could not do. He was the subject of lust and envy by
many women for his unique masculinity. He chose to fall in love
with a woman from Sorek named Delilah. Over time Samson and his
wife had attracted many enemies who were intrigued by his amazing
strength. Their enemies, the Philistines (descendants of Ham), were
unsuccessful in discovering Samson's strength. They believed Delilah
could help them. They agreed to partner with her, offering her a very
big bribe. After many years of marriage she never knew the secret of

her husband's 'storehouse' of energy, neither was she bothered about it. However, with the prospect of a big reward she became curious.

Her job was to find out the source of her husband's extraordinary strength. She believed she knew his vulnerable points. One night after a sumptuous meal, she stroked her husband's head, telling him all the great things he had done since they became a couple. Delilah spoke directly to his ego and complimented him for his powerful body. She reassured him how proud she was to be his wife. Samson thought Delilah's generosity could only mean, she wanted something from him. Delilah asked him what made him powerful. Samson, however, was not impressed since he never told anyone his secrets before. Samson did not know why his wife wanted this information, but he lied to her about the origin of his strength. Delilah, acting in deception, went secretly to the enemies, telling them what Samson told her. The enemies tried to weaken Samson, but they could not. Delilah was devastated. Her husband had lied to her.

She was determined to find out the origin of her husband's strength, so she came up with a better plan. Dressed in her finest lingerie, she doused him with hugs and kisses. Samson again did not reveal to Delilah the true secret; it was now the third time. Still not discouraged, she felt the need to work harder, believing this will cause her husband to reveal his secret. **'How can you say you love me, yet you lied to me three times?'** *Eventually, Samson gave in and told her his secret.*

When Delilah told the enemies, they attacked Samson and conquered him. Samson was so weakened that the weakest man could tie him up and beat him. Finally, it was a euphoric moment for Delilah as she received her reward from the Philistines.

Delilah:

- displayed virtues of consistency and persistence.
- never gave up even when her husband continuously lied to her.
- didn't lose her calm but developed new strategies, and sought to get to know her husband more than she ever had.
- deceitfully worked with her enemies to achieve their purpose.
- was not in unity with the man she 'loved' and married. Money was more valuable to her than true love.

Delilah utilised remarkable characteristics. However, they were used for a negative cause. She employed the rule of consistency and stayed with the task until she achieved her goal. She had a plan; she took action and revised her plan. She never gave up until she got the answer. This fundamental principle works whether for good or evil. Her lesson for us is: to achieve much for God, we must be persistent, goal-oriented, and not deterred by anything.

Modern-Day Reality: Purpose and persistence bring rewards.

CHAPTER 33

Jephthah's Daughter

(Judges 11:1–40; Hebrews 11:32–34)

She inspired her dad to stay committed to his promise to God,
knowing the cost.

Her father became the head of his father's house though he was the son of a prostitute.

Animosity among his siblings and power struggle caused him to run away from home. He fled empty handed. Jephthah was a man who feared God and demonstrated that he was a good leader. The enemies swarmed in on the Israelites who were defenceless. These enemies were the Amonites, descendants of Lot through his younger daughter (Genesis 19:36–38). His brother felt that only Jephthah was qualified to subdue the enemies, so they sent for him. Jephthah knew the God of wonders and wanted to demonstrate this to his enemies.

Jephthah took on the challenge to fight the enemies, envisaging his moment of victory. He had a flash of spiritual ecstasy, making a vow to

*God, which lacked specifics and was overly generous. **'I will sacrifice the first thing that comes to greet me after my victory'**. God who is all-knowing knew who would be sacrificed, so He held Jephthah accountable to his promise. Men often go out to war for weeks or months and their wives, or a senior female figure would eagerly await their return.*

Examples:

- *David's conquest; his wife was looking out for his return from battle (2 Samuel 6:14–16). The women met David the warrior (1 Samuel 18:6–7).*
- *Another account is in Judges 5:28; Sisera's mother kept looking out for him.*

Jephthah thought the women in his house, one of his wives or servants, was not indispensable so he was willing to offer one of these women as a sacrifice.

After the war, to his greatest surprise it was a young girl who first opened the door with singing and dancing, as her dad returned from conquest; she was an only child. Jephthah, forgetting the exuberance of the moment, was heartbroken as he could not recant his vow. Jephthah told his daughter his vows and she inspired her dad to stay committed to his promise to God, knowing the cost. The text referred to Jephthah's daughter going away with her friends for two months to bewail her virginity. Some scholars have concluded that she was not put to death, but she was committed to a celibate life.

Jephthah's only daughter:

- *knew about faith in God from her father. His name was mentioned in the famous hall of faith in the account of all the heroes (Hebrews 11:32–34).*
- *knew about the God of covenant; she knew it was better not to make a vow than to make one and don't pay.*
- *made one request of her father: she wanted to go on a spree with all her friends for two months before she was sacrificed.*
- *went away to the mountain. Her friends wept bitterly week by week; it was a sad time for them.*

This remarkable young lassie returned home at the scheduled date, the day she would be placed on an altar as a sacrifice to fulfil the vow made by her father. She was sacrificed.

Scripture has a reference to a male equivalent (Genesis 22:1–13). Abraham was asked by God to sacrifice his son Isaac, his only son after waiting twenty-five years for his birth. However, God provided a lamb, sparing Isaac's life.

The question: why didn't God spare this young girl?

In Abraham's case, God asked Abraham to sacrifice his son, whereas in the case of this young girl, her father volunteered the first thing that came out of his house as a sacrifice, which happened to be his only daughter. He was gobsmacked since the idea of his daughter coming out to meet him was remote, something he thought would never happen.

Both cases were tests of obedience. However, in Jephthah's case, a vow or a promise was made to God. Vows are binding; they create covenant and contract.

Abraham did not tell his son what he was about to do but Jephthah told his daughter, who submitted to her father's covenant with God. She was willing to die for God.

God interrupted Abraham's act of sacrificing his son, providing a lamb. However, this virgin girl was sacrificed to God.

*Judging from face value, it seemed partial and unfair. Crucial to the understanding of this account is the significance of vows that are made to God. This father was not specific, and if he was specific he would not have promised God to sacrifice his young daughter, his only child. God takes vows/covenants as serious as when He Himself makes them. Her father was tested for truthfulness to his words. What God asks us to do (**command**) and what we promise God we will do (**vow**) seemed to be judged differently. The scriptures admonish that one should be quick to listen but slow to speak (James 1:19). Abraham was quick to listen, whereas Jephthah was quick to speak.*

God's sovereign rule allowed Isaac to be spared and this young girl to be sacrificed since He knows the heart of the one who made the promise. Jephthah's daughter was a teenager of integrity on par with Joseph who was sold into slavery and thrown into prison for his faith. She lived for two months knowing she would die. She never hated God or her father who made the vow. God is a life giver and can make a demand on us for the life He has given us at any time. Jephthah's daughter knew she owned nothing not even her life. Isaac in the Old Testament is known as a type of Christ; however, he was replaced by a lamb. He escaped death, but she was sacrificed.

Jephthah's daughter was close to her God and knew the demands of a vow made to God. She safeguarded the lives of her father's household, knowing that if she was not sacrificed as promised, the entire household would die. She knew about celebrating God after victory. Being bold and brave, she was the first in her father's house to grab her instrument of music with singing and dancing as an act of worship and thanksgiving. Her purpose was to honour God in what she did. She was trustworthy; her father sent her off to 'enjoy' life for two months, knowing she would return as promised. As a virgin she knew that she would never get married. Jephthah daughter's life was not in vain. Israel honoured every anniversary of her death, allowing all the women to get away from home for four days. This event was a memorial in celebration of her life.

Modern-Day Reality: Selflessness and sacrifice are required on the journey.

CHAPTER 34

NAOMI

(Ruth 1:1–22; 2:1–23; 3:1–18; 4:1–22)

The series of unfortunate circumstances were too much
for any woman to bear.

L ife for them had gone from being among the wealthiest families in Bethlehem-Judah to finding it impossible to survive. No rain meant no vegetation; no vegetation meant no livestock and no livelihood. They owned lands and houses before the prolonged drought, which forced them to sell all they had. The family became migrants automatically as they sought a better life in a foreign land. Naomi, her husband Elimelech, and their two sons moved to the country of Moab. The government of Moab heard their story and was sympathetic to them, leasing lands to this family for a new start. They settled in and commenced farming. An agreement was made to honour the monarchy before they could settle in Moab.

Transitioning from a Jewish lifestyle to the life of a Moabite was a cinch for the family. They worked happily together as a family, becoming increasingly prosperous.

Tragedy strikes! *Elimelech died. Initially the family's reaction was one of numbness since he was healthy, with no health challenges prior to his death. The family mourned his death for months. Naomi held the family together, supporting her sons in trying moments. Mahlon and Kilion along with their mother Naomi continued farming, as they were determined to get on with their lives in Moab.*

One year after her husband's death, Naomi was elated with the great news that both sons had fallen in love with Moabite women. Mahlon and Kilion introduced Ruth and Orpah to Naomi. She was pleased with their choices. The sounds of wedding bells brought joy to Naomi's heart. Naomi was able to put the loss of her husband behind and looked forward to getting to know these girls better. Naomi was pleased with both Ruth and Orpah, as they helped her to understand the Moabite customs.

*Mahlon and Kilion went out in the field that day. Naomi had her worst nightmare, as tragedy struck the family again. This time it was a freak accident. Sorrow spiralled out of control for Naomi as she lost both sons in quick succession. The series of unfortunate circumstances were too much for any woman to bear. She lost all her property and in an effort to secure a better life, she moved out of Bethlehem. Losing all she originally left home with, firstly her husband and then her two sons, this was heart-rending. Naomi was devastated. She questioned God, '***Why me? Does God really care about me***'? Surprisingly, Naomi did not allow her grief to control her thinking. She did not lose her ability to rationalise and to look for the opportunity to improve her situation. Naomi and her daughters-in-law consoled each other as they grieved for months.*

Naomi followed the news from her homeland closely and heard that the famine was over and that the people in Bethlehem-Judah had plenty of food. So Naomi decided to return to Bethlehem-Judah. In the Jewish culture of the times, the surviving widows were expected to live with their mother-in-law until they were remarried to any other sons the mother-in-law had, or a close male family member of their deceased husband. Naomi knew this but she begged her two daughters-in-law to return to their parents' homes. She hoped and prayed that they would get married again.

Though she was a Moabite, Ruth knew the Jewish culture. She also remembered her vows: 'Your people shall be my people and your God shall be my God'. As the moments drew closer for Naomi to return to her homeland, both Ruth and Orpah wept. Orpah said her goodbyes to Naomi, but Ruth had a binding contract and refused to leave.

Naomi's life was certainly one of challenges and adventure.

She:

- moved out of famine and into a strange land, living among strangers.
- did not realise that her entire life would change as she stepped out. She became a widow.

Then a moment of exuberance followed when her sons got married. To her surprise, this moment was only to be short-lived as both sons died. Naomi did not allow famine, hunger, the death of her husband and two sons to separate her from God's love. She had great faith in her God, since she had proven Him as the One who is more than enough. She was not going to allow her heart's sorrow, bitterness, pain and her negative emotions to dictate how she served God or what happens to the rest of her life.

Naomi:

- knew that not only good things happen to good people, but unpleasant things also happen to good people.
- trusted God to take her through difficult times and to do the impossible in and through her.

The villagers of Bethlehem-Judah were happy to have her back. She told them about all the troubles she had been through and her determination to make a fresh start even in her old age. Naomi experienced restoration by the king's order, all the lands she owned previously and any profit made during the time she was away would be restored.

She then sold the land to her husband's nearest relation, Boaz, who was expected to marry her deceased son's wife. Boaz married Ruth and they had a son called Obed. Within their culture, when a woman's husband dies, if she remarries and have children with her second husband, the children carried the first husband's name. Therefore Obed carried Mahlon's name and was known as Naomi's grandson. Naomi's heart was filled with joy as she held Obed and nursed him as her own son.

Modern-Day Reality: Living a life of hope in the midst of hopelessness, knowing God is faithful.

CHAPTER 35

RUTH

(Ruth 1:1-22; 2:1-23; 3:1-18; 4:1-22)

Ruth felt only death could separate her from her mother-in-law...
A story of true love.

Has it ever occurred to you how two women from different cultural and ethnic backgrounds could be so close and develop a bond so powerful that they become almost inseparable? Their commonalities included being widows at an early age. Ruth made a vow to Naomi that was so strong it could only be separated by death. Ruth's ancestors were from Moab. They were descendants of Lot. After Lot left Sodom, his two daughters tricked him. They had sex with him and both girls became pregnant. Lot's son with his elder daughter was called Moab, he became the father of the Moabites (Genesis 19:31–38). At an early age Ruth married an Israelite. This cross-cultural union was not the norm for either Ruth or her husband.

Ruth's ancestors for ten generations were exempted from the

meeting place to worship God because they were not hospitable towards the Israelites. They refused to allow the Israelites to pass through their lands or to give them bread and water. They also hired Balaam to curse the children of God (Numbers 22:1–41). Therefore, God cursed them for ten generations (Deuteronomy 23:2–3). Ruth was privileged to escape the generational curse and was able to worship and serve God without hindrances.

Ruth was happily married. She enjoyed spending time with her husband as they looked forward to many years of marital bliss. All of her hopes and dreams vanished when her husband Mahlon died unexpectedly. Her heart was torn apart; she felt the pain of grief and death. Ruth had a great mentor and looked to her mother-in-law for lessons on how to deal with loss. She wanted to emulate all the godly qualities she saw in Naomi. Ruth knew she was committed to Naomi for the rest of her life.

Naomi adopted Ruth as her own daughter and nurtured her. She showered her with love and blessings, which created a magnetic bond, making it impossible for Ruth to leave. Naomi knew that nothing in life was worth holding on to so tightly. Naomi asked her daughters-in-law to return to their parents' homes after the death of her two boys. Ruth chose to stay with Naomi instead of returning home. This was a story of true love.

She travelled to Bethlehem-Judah with Naomi and settled there; this was a new experience. The law in Israel stated that farmers must be concerned about the poor and needy. The farmers could not harvest all their crops and sell them. They must leave some of their produce for the orphan, the widow and the poor of the land (Deuteronomy 24:19–21).

Ruth:

- *went to the field to gather crop that was left for the poor, where she met a close relative of her deceased husband.*

Naomi noticed that Ruth came home quicker and she had a larger quantity of fruits and vegetables. Ruth told Naomi that she met a young man called Boaz. Naomi was Ruth's confidant and advisor. She coached Ruth on how to make herself a woman that a man would find attractive.

Naomi told Ruth that personal appearance matters. Ruth was expected to get the best perfume, wear her finest outfit, then go to the threshing floor ensuring that Boaz noticed her. Naomi told her to keep a keen eye on Boaz.

Ruth:

- *was given practical advice on how to fall and stay in love.*
- *was supposed to watch where Boaz went to rest for the night and go lie at his feet. This statement of interest symbolized her humility to serve him.*
- *obeyed Naomi and Boaz found her lying at his feet in the middle of the night.*

Ruth and Boaz spoke to each other, then Boaz could not sleep as he was determined to find out if he was in line to marry this beautiful woman. Boaz did his research and found out that he was not the nearest relative of Ruth's deceased husband, but second in line. He spoke with the nearest male relative, who was not interested in marrying Ruth.

In Israel the nearest relative was expected to redeem the property, marry the wife of the deceased, and raise children for the deceased (Deuteronomy 25:5–6).

Culturally, Boaz, who became the nearest male relative, was expected to marry Ruth and have children bearing her deceased husband's name. The terms of the covenant: he must take off his shoes and give it to a third party who witnessed the agreement. Boaz fell in love with Ruth and he was willing to redeem the property, marry her, and have children for her previous husband Mahlon. Ruth married Boaz and had a son called Obed. Ruth became the great-grandmother of King David. She was the ancestor of kings, even King Jesus Christ. Ruth was willing to leave her people and follow Naomi. She gave up all that was familiar to gain all that she needed.

Modern-Day Reality: Mentorship is key. Be willing to explore new territories; all that you need might not be in the place where you are.

CHAPTER 36

ORPAH

(Ruth 1:1–15)

She came to the moment of making one of the most
powerful decisions in her life.

O rpah was no doubt an attractive young woman. She fell in love with the son of the Israelite, Kilion, who had just arrived in Moab. His family fled from famine and were refugees in the country of Moab. Marrying a Jew was not customary in her times, but she did not view it as unacceptable. Ruth was another Moabite woman who had married Orpah's brother-in-law. She also knew of the account of Rahab the prostitute who was not a Jew, but sacrificed her life to protect the Jews. This was a sign that other nations could be at peace with the Jewish nation. The story of Rahab created an awareness that non-Jews could be grafted into the Jewish race by Divine providence and be saved from destruction.

Whilst Orpah's story was only captured in a few verses within the book of Ruth, it does not mean her story is insignificant. She was married at a young age; her blissful years of marriage came to an abrupt end when her husband died suddenly. The pain was amplified by the untimely death of her only brother-in-law, her husband's brother, Mahlon. With the help of her mother-in-law (Naomi) and sister-in-law (Ruth) she was able to navigate the difficult times. The trio consoled themselves and often cried and prayed together.

Time passed, healing from the pain of loss occurred, and they were ready to embrace the next phase in life. Naomi decided she would return to her homeland in Bethlehem. It was culturally accepted for the daughters-in-law to go with their mother-in-law. This tradition made provision for passing on the family legacy. If Naomi, the mother-in-law should get married again and have sons, then they were expected to marry Orpah and Ruth, widows of her sons Kilion and Mahlon. Naomi knew she was too old to get married and have children. And even if she did get married, by the time her sons became of age, Orpah would have to wait her whole life.

Orpah:

- had two options: either to return home to her parents or to go with Naomi.
- chose the former.

Her life's account concluded after she left Naomi. She came to the moment of making one of the most powerful decisions in her life.

We never knew what happened to Orpah, whether she remained a widow or remarried.

Orpah walked back to Moab, the place of the familiar. She relinquished care of her elderly mother-in-law in a strange land. This meant no account of her life and no book of Orpah as there is a book of Ruth. Orpah walked away from her inheritance, an abundant blessing that Ruth received. She could have met Mr. Right again. Orpah did not realize she carried a connection to great men and kings as the daughter-in-law of Naomi. She would have been a part of the family's ancestral wealth, which culminated in Christ.

Modern-Day Reality: Fulfilment in life calls for selflessness and sacrifice, knowing when to walk away and when to stay committed.

CHAPTER 37

HANNAH

(1 Samuel 1:1–28; 2:1–21)

In today's society, people who are misunderstood or wronged would hand out harsh treatment, including social exclusion.

Since she was not the only woman in his life she knew about rivalry, competition, rejection, being mocked and laughed at. Her life was a constant fret through her rival's effort to humiliate her. She suffered such humiliation because her husband had more than one wife. Elkanah, her husband expressed his love in different ways, however she felt it was inadequate since she had no children. He was a proud dad, fathering children from his other wives. Although he daily verbalized his love for her, it was not enough to deal with her infertility. Hannah knew in the Jewish culture a son meant one who preserved an inheritance. From the account with Leah in Genesis, a son meant *my husband will love me more*. She struggled with the curse of barrenness or childlessness, which had no place within a marriage.

Hannah's annual family trip to Shiloh was her most painful

experience. Peninnah, her rival, humiliated, and taunted her by showing off her children. These inhumane gestures made Hannah's heart groan with pain. She felt sad, isolated, hurt, and embarrassed, making her yearly trip to Shiloh synonymous with pain and distress.

As the time drew closer to the journey to Shiloh, Hannah would weep ceaselessly, almost inconsolably. Elkanah could not understand why she was so distressed. In an effort to reassure and console her, he said to her, *'You know that I will always love you and I love you much more than Peninnah. You are the best thing that ever happened to me, and I love you with my whole heart'.*

Her husband tried very hard to reassure her of his love, he told her she meant more to him than ten sons hoping this would captivate her heart. Elkanah said this, knowing that childlessness was a curse in Israel. So was he really honest with her?

Hannah thought her husband's insensitivity, to some degree, was understandable. However, she believed the pastor/priest would understand her and be much more sympathetic. She went to the temple in Shiloh thinking it would offer her peace and tranquillity, and a place away from her rival.

Hannah's Façade

She:

- pretended to have had such a peaceful demeanour, as though there was emotional and mental stability in her life.
- acted as though the hurtful words of her rival had no adverse effects on her.

- was prayerful and felt the altar was the place to pour out all her sorrows.
- knelt down, praying inaudibly as she spoke to God, asking for a son and promising to give him back to God as long as he lived.

The priest was in the temple, standing on the altar when his eyes caught on to this unusual sight. The woman kneeling at the altar, her lips moved but no sound was heard. In Old Testament times, prayer and petition to God for the people were made by the priest. Hannah took on a priestly role. This was prophetic, as Hannah represented the church, the body of Christ, who will pray directly to God. Eli, the priest/pastor, became judgmental and accused her of being drunk. He completely misunderstood Hannah's actions.

Hannah, filled with the love of God in her heart, replied, *'No, Pastor/Priest Eli, I am not drunk. I have not had a drink. I am overburdened and sad because I have a need'*. She was a woman of godly qualities; she chose to respond in love when she was grossly misunderstood. She did not say or think, **What kind of a pastor/priest is he?** Nor did she think, **Is he really a priest, when he does not know the difference between someone who is drunk and someone who has a need and is pouring out their heart to God?**

Negative thoughts did not enter Hannah's mind. She could have said, 'I am a praying woman of God and have to pray for this Priest'. Hannah did not focus on what Pastor/Priest Eli had done. She never thought she must leave this temple to go to another to worship because she was misunderstood, embarrassed and humiliated by the priest.

Hannah:

- understood her role and the priest's role in God's mandate. She understood the difference between the person of the priest and the office of the priesthood. It was not for her to take care of that which belongs to God and the priest. With a pure heart seeking after God, she modelled godliness. She focused on her God and her needs.
- knew Pastor/Priest Eli even when he completely misunderstood her, held the answer to her emptiness. Pastor/Priest Eli pronounced the blessings and said, 'Go in peace and may the God of Israel give you the desires of your heart.'
- meditated on those words; whether the priest understood or was able to diagnose rightfully, she knew she got a word from God.
- was told something quite negative and hurtful, yet she humbled herself and accepted human error. She exercised patience and self-control. She never took offence, when misunderstood or she would have missed out on the answer to her prayers and the prophetic utterance over her life.

Hannah stopped praying and fasting immediately; she got off her knees, washed herself, threw off her mourning clothes, and was ready to celebrate motherhood. She was ready for her baby. Hannah walked away empowered to face her enemies and any other challenges.

Months later Hannah was pregnant; she was overcome with excitement as she shared the good news with friends and family. Her rival heard about it and was furious; she spoke unkind words about Hannah and sent threatening messages, which Hannah completely ignored.

*The day finally came when Hannah gave birth to a handsome baby boy; she named him Samuel. His name meant **asked of God**. When Hannah prayed for a son, she made a promise to give her son back to God. She could either honour her promise and be true to her words or think it was just empty words. Hannah looked at Samuel. He was handsome, innocent, and precious; the child she had always wanted. Her friends could not understand why Hannah would wait for a child and then give him away for adoption. Hannah loved God so dearly that she had no choice but to honour her promise. She told Elkanah that Samuel, their son, was going to be given to Pastor/Priest Eli for adoption. Elkanah was astounded; he thought she had lost her mind.*

The tenacity of this mighty woman of God to take her firstborn, her only child (at that point in her life Samuel was her only child), and give him up for adoption to God via Pastor/Priest Eli was shocking. Eli was the same priest who misunderstood and judged her wrongfully in the temple, but Hannah understood some principles about God, His sovereignty and faithfulness. She knew that without faith it was impossible to please God. This woman of God knew about man's limitation and she looked beyond man's imperfection and kept her eyes fixed on God. *The people who know the mind of God shall be strong and shall do that which seems impossible* (paraphrased Daniel 11:32). Hannah released her seed and planted him in the house of God, and allowed God to water him as he grew. She knew it was vain to put confidence in man, but she relied completely on God. Even when Pastor/Priest Eli and his sons' hearts were turned away from God, the child Samuel grew and became a powerful man of God, a priest. He flourished in the midst of godlessness and knew God for himself.

Hannah was a tremendous woman of God; her love for God and her maturity in God is worth aspiring for. She received a plate of injustice, yet she returned a platter of love. In today's society, people who are misunderstood or wronged tend to retaliate with such harsh treatment, including social exclusion. There is a tendency to talk about the wrong done and to justify oneself. Hannah covered Pastor/Priest Eli with her prayer, love, reverence, and gratitude. She knew God can use Pastor/Priest Eli despite his weakness, both the person and the office of the pastor/priest demanded respect. Even when she did not agree, she submitted and obeyed. Her focus was not on an earthly priest but on a Heavenly One.

Hannah was totally given over to God, as she gave up her treasured possession, her only son *Samuel*, to Priest Eli. She demonstrated a life of humility. Hannah emptied herself of her own will, desires, and selfish ambitions. Hannah's life demonstrated Christian maturity and a level of strong faith; this should be emulated by all Christians.

Only a woman with the heart of God would take her child to live with a priest who once called her drunk (when she was on the altar praying and pouring out her grief-stricken heart to God).

Only a woman with a heart of God would take her son to live with a priest whose sons were going astray from God. She did not question what example or what influence they were going to have on her son.

Hannah's heart reflected love, forgiveness, and faith, she understood some deep, godly principles for living. In our Christian walk, when people do us wrong, the average believer tends to be vengeful and retaliates. It is often like adding wrong to wrong to try to make it right. Hannah chose not to gossip or live in unforgiveness and bitterness. She chose not to be judgemental; she remained in that **same** temple and worshipped. God expects us to have a heart like Hannah's, too small to hold a grudge, but big enough to love unconditionally.

Hannah's Thanksgiving (Ch. 2)

God has made me strong.
He filled my heart with joy.
My wicked enemies
Have been thrown into darkness,
And completely destroyed.

I will sing for joy
Knowing they will never rise again,
Nothing will save them, not even their wealth,
And people who know them cannot redeem them.

God cares so much for me,
The foundation of the world belongs to Him,
He hangs the world upon it.
By His great power and might.

God is all-knowing,
He has met my needs.
God also changes my time and season,
By turning my sorrows into joy.

He is the only King with great power and strength.
I sing my song to Him,
There is none holy like my God,
And no God like my God,
There is no rock to lean on like Him.

Modern-Day Reality: Forgive and keep forgiving. Let nothing stop you.

CHAPTER 38

Mrs. Phinehas

(1 Samuel 2:11–17; 22–26;
4:10–22; 14:2–3, 18)

Refused to live in a land void of God's presence.

The family role in society demands sacrifice, a life of high moral standing and uprightness of heart. Her husband was the son of a priest and was groomed to take over the monastery when his father died. His life did not exemplify the qualities of a priest's son. He was vile and reckless; he committed sexual sins in the temple with the women who came to meet with God. Her husband and his brother Hophni were both sinful in their actions; they were extreme in their sinful desires. The victims of their unrighteous sexual acts constantly made reports to Eli about his son's evil behavior, but Eli trivialised the despicable sexual acts of his two boys.

Mrs. Phinehas:

- knew that her husband was unfaithful even though he was supposed to be living a godly life and serving in the temple.
- remained faithful and committed to her marriage to a husband who was very unfaithful.
- did not deny him his marital privileges or sexual pleasure since she was now pregnant with his second child.
- was a godly woman and was deeply hurt by her husband's ungodly lifestyle.
- prayed about her husband's lack of conviction and his insensitivity to God daily. However, she felt that his attitude and actions did not improve.
- longed for her husband to spend quality time with her and to assume his leadership role in their home.

She was pregnant with her husband's second child, thinking this would improve her fragmented relationship. Her husband became more vile and promiscuous. Her pillow was wet with tears every night as she felt the burden of the evil that was occurring within the house of God. She had many sleepless nights, which she spent praying.

It was a few weeks before her baby was due and her labour was pre-empted by bad news.

Mrs. Phinehas:

- *heard that the Ark of the Lord was captured by their enemies.*
- *understood the spiritual significance of the Ark of the Lord, a representation of God's power, His presence and His favour.*

- *heard that three of her family members—her father-in-law Eli, her husband Phinehas, and her brother-in-law Hophni—were murdered.*
- *had just enough strength, with the encouragement of those around her, to give birth.*
- *was in a stupor, anesthetised by a state of shock.*
- *named her son Ichabod, a name that served as a reminder to the nation of Israel. It was a day that the nation would never forget, as God's presence fled from His people. His name meant **God's glory has departed**.*

Mrs. Phinehas refused to live in a land void of God's presence. She died in childbirth and her two sons became orphans. When they were older, her eldest son Ahitub, had a son. This grandson continued the priestly lineage. She knew that her husband, his brother, and their father would not escape God's wrath because they failed to show a godly example in the house of God. God's judgment started in the house of God. Her worst nightmare was not the death of three family members, but the Ark of God (His Presence) taken away from God's people.

She loved God and was the type of woman who sought after God's righteousness and His holiness. Although giving birth to new life is often a joyous event, this mother felt her life was meaningless without the presence and power of God. Mrs. Phinehas was convinced that life had little or no value without the presence of the Most Holy God.

Modern-Day Reality: Only God's presence can preserve life.

CHAPTER 39

MERAB

(1 Samuel 14:49; 18:17–19;
2 Samuel 21:8–14)

She was jilted since she was promised to be David's wife.

Merab inherited special privileges and rights, being the eldest daughter. In Israel the eldest daughter was given in marriage before her younger sisters.

Merab was:

- jilted since she was promised to be David's wife. However, her father Saul sought revenge against David and changed his mind, and gave her to Adriel of Mehalah.
- bitterly hurt and secretly outraged by her father's actions, though she could not display these emotions.

- crushed by feelings of inadequacy inflicted by her father. She could not rebel against his insidious decision.
- rendered powerless.

King Saul had gone away from God and did not serve Him according to His requirements. Merab knew her father did an unprecedented amount of **evil**, *including numerous attempts to destroy David's life.*

Saul formally destroyed a nation who had a covenant with Israel. The terms of the covenant meant the nation should live among the Israelites and become one with them. The Gibeonites who remained, came to David seeking revenge for what Saul had done. The Gibeonites felt justice would be done if King David handed over seven of Saul's son or descendants. They did not want to destroy the entire nation of Israel. King David thought it was a reasonable request. King David handed over two of Saul's sons and five of his grandsons to the Gibeonites.

Merab's life depicted the life of someone who was always taken advantage of. She knew that all her sons would be sacrificed. The sins of the father visited the second generation. Merab was never a part of the decision-making process. She had no voice, was not recognised, never honoured or appreciated. She was not a favoured child of King Saul.

It seemed justifiable that Merab's siblings, Jonathan and Michal's actions of defending David from the wrath of Saul (saving David's life on numerous occasions), would have influenced the king's decision. David owed his life to them, therefore in showing his gratitude he would have spared their sons. Since Michal was barren (2 Samuel 6:20–23) David turned to Merab, Saul's other daughter and Rizpah, Saul's concubine for their sons to be the ultimate sacrifice for Saul's diabolical crime.

Merab:

- *felt life was very unfair.*
- *was not assertive and had no one who would mediate for her, or who felt the deep pains of her loss.*
- *washed her face in the day and saturated her pillow with tears at nights.*
- *was numbed by grief and felt at times that her life was in vain; she could not face such a seemingly hopeless future.*

Yet in the process of time, this remarkable woman was able to survive such a horrific ordeal — ill treatment. It caused anguish in her soul, torment of her mind, and the incurable wounds of her emotions. She was able to live, laugh, and find peace again. An extraordinary woman of faith, she believed in her dreams and knew that once there is life within her there is hope.

Modern-Day Reality: Though it is not obvious at that moment, grief, sorrow and pain have a limit.

CHAPTER 40

RIZPAH

(2 Samuel 21:7–14)

...Patient for the change that she anticipated...

S he was greatly honoured, the 'wife' of a king, the first king of Israel. However, their relationship was not monogamous. Rizpah was Saul's concubine, a slave daughter of Aiah. However, she had rights and privileges as a royal. Her relationship with Saul was characterised by a series of dreadful moments. The Israelites made numerous treaties with the surrounding nations when they left Egypt. This agreement was binding and irrevocable, giving the affiliated nations the same rights and privileges as the Israelite nation. The Gibeonites had made a treaty with Israel during the reign of King Saul. Saul was an evil king since he did many horrid deeds. One such evil deed was violating the terms of an agreement, killing some of the people of Gibeon. The remaining Gibeonites were utterly displeased; therefore, they made a covenant among themselves to kill all of Saul's surviving relatives.

There was a period of severe famine during King David's reign; he asked the Lord why there was such a famine in Israel. The Lord confirmed that the famine was secondary to Saul's diabolical act by breeching a treaty and killing the Gibeonites. David met with the Gibeonites expeditiously and negotiated with them. The Gibeonites were happy to take seven of Saul's male relatives and destroy them for this violation. The news reached Rizpah, who was widowed, that David had made an agreement with the Gibeonites to take her sons. She was inconsolable as she wept bitterly at the thought of her boys being 'sacrificed' for the wicked deeds of their father. Two of Rizpah's sons, whom she had with Saul, and five of Saul's grandsons were chosen to be slain as a repercussion for what Saul did to the Gibeonites. The sins of the father visited the first and second generations (Exodus 34:7).

Rizpah:

- *took sack cloth, dressing as a woman bereaved.*
- *came to the rock and waited from the beginning of the harvest until the rain came. (This was a type of her coming to Christ who is the rock and waiting for the abundance in her life, which was signified by the harvest).*
- *waited for months, sitting by the bodies of these dead men, making sure that the birds and the wild animals did not touch them.*
- *was certainly no coward; she sacrificed her life in the forest, with no thought that she was at risk of being killed by the wild animals.*

Guarding dead bodies in an open field would be described in contemporary terminology as psychotic, or having severe mental problems. She had a strong conviction since her loved ones died without dignity. Rizpah was determined that their bodies would be disposed of properly.

The news finally reached the palace; King David heard what Rizpah had done. He ordered that the bones of these men, including that of King Saul's and his son Jonathan's, be removed from the open field and that they should be given a decent burial or cremation.

There is a grave spiritual significance in placing herself at the rock; she put herself in God's hand since **the rock** is a type of Christ. She made a powerful commitment to rely only on God as her source of strength.

Rizpah:

- was patient for the change that she anticipated so she waited through seasons.
- enjoyed the harvest but had a future in mind; she wanted the rains.
- was fed up of the dryness she had experienced and yearned for much more.
- knew that the present harvest meant the here and now, but the rains meant future harvest.
- did not only live for the present moment; she believed God for harvest upon harvest.
- was a powerful character as her faith worked, producing miracles for justice.

Rizpah was not afraid of the dead as she took care of the corpses of her loved ones. She was extremely courageous; her actions were consistent and repetitive, pressuring the king to take action. Her determination brought about the desired result since she was not prepared to take no for an answer.

Modern-Day Reality: Be patient through the seasons; change will come.

CHAPTER 41

MICHAL

(1 Samuel 14:49; 18:20–21; 19:11–17; 25:43–44;
2 Samuel 21:1–8; 3:13–16; 6:13–23)

She saw God at work in David and knew he was
destined for the throne.

Michal could be described as a 'spoilt brat' since she demanded from her father the handsome young man she wished to marry. This was unheard of in Israel. She was the daughter of Israel's first king, Saul. She was no doubt born into wealth and prestige. King Saul knew that his daughter's demand did not fulfil cultural norms; she was the second daughter and could not get married before her elder sister. He was also expected to choose the man she would marry.

Saul:

- had a close relationship with Michal so he underestimated the love his daughter Michal had for David. David was well

known to the family and spent time in Saul's home with his best friend Jonathan, Saul's son.
- was overly jealous of David's success and was preoccupied in trying to kill him.
- made numerous attempts at David's life, but was unsuccessful every time.

Saul's first daughter was also in love with David. In an effort to hurt David's ego, Saul promised David his first daughter as his wife, but gave her to another man. Saul interpreted Michal's request to marry David as the right opportunity to carry out his long-awaited plan.

The people favoured David, making him a threat to Saul. When Michal admitted her desire to marry David, Saul was extremely happy. Saul saw David as dead from that moment. The king instructed his servants to talk to David and find out how he felt about becoming the son-in-law of the king. Thinking that David would be elated with pride to be honoured by the king; David's humble response, essentially a decline, shocked him.

Saul:

- *thought he would trap David and have him killed, so he welcomed the idea of his daughter Michal getting married to David.*
- *asked for a gift in exchange for his daughter; he was very confident that David would not survive the Philistine camp. He asked for one hundred foreskins of the Philistines.*
- *thought that the Philistines would kill David. David and his men went out, killed two hundred Philistines, and brought their foreskins to Saul.*

- *was angry with himself as David became unstoppable and his daughter Michal became David's wife.*

Despite Saul's prolonged jealousy over David's success, Michal loved David. She defended and protected David from her father's onslaught. Life in general was strenuous and extremely stressful as David was constantly running from Saul to save his life. David would tell her all about his narrow encounters and near misses. This was frustrating for Michal as her father's deep hatred for David made her life and their marriage **hell on earth**.

Michal was in secret contact with her father's house. News leaked from Saul's house that he would send men to David's home to kill him. When Michal and David were made aware of Saul's evil plan, they also sat down and devised a plan. Their home was built on the wall and Michal knew she must be strong to help David escape. Later that night she took a rope, letting her husband down through a window, allowing him to escape for his life. Michal created a manikin to place on David's bed. She dressed it in David's clothes, put goat's hair on it's head and covered it over with a blanket.

David had already escaped when Saul's messengers came knocking. Michal told them that her husband was sick. The men saw what they thought was David lying on his bed. They returned to Saul, relating to him what had happened. Saul was furious, telling the men to bring David back to him on his sickbed immediately. The men returned to Michal's home shortly, to find that David was not there. Michal knew her father would go ballistic. His imminent rage would mean severe punishment, but she was prepared for the consequences.

Just as she anticipated, there was a vehement knock on her door. She opened the door and found Saul standing outside, infuriated that Michal let his enemy escape.

Saul ordered her to sign a divorce bill against David. Then gave her to another man to marry, she then became the wife of Phaltiel from Gallim, someone she hated. Saul wanted to teach Michal and David a lesson. Michal was mortified, feeling she would have to live her entire life very unhappy because of her father's jealousy and inferiority complex over David.

Michal had dark moments in her life, she felt David's behaviour was not dignifying as he celebrated his victory over the enemy by dancing foolishly before God. Michal spoke negatively about David and his worship to God, which resulted in barrenness until her death.

She was married to David prior to him becoming king, then later given to another man to become his wife. Yet, she lived in King David's house as his wife when he led the people in an exuberant episode of dancing and revelling before God, as the ark of God returned to Israel. This could only be possible since King David reclaimed her as his wife from Phaltiel, after Saul's death. David asked her elder brother, Ishbosheth, to bring Michal back to him. Paltiel knew his respect and reverence for David meant he must allow Ishbosheth to return Michal to David.

After she was reunited with King David, she looked through the window and saw the king dancing in an uncouth manner. David celebrated the return of God's glory as the ark of God returned to Israel after a very long time: more than twenty years (1 Samuel 7:1–2). Michal thought David was not acting or behaving in a dignified manner, as kings should.

Michal showered David with love by saving his life. She saw God at work in David and knew he was destined for the throne. Despite her emotional roller coaster, she was caring and became an amazing wife to her father's opponent. Her marriage to David exemplified strong love, devotion, and commitment. She was a model wife. Her love and loyalty to David was greater than her allegiance to Saul, her father. She knew God's plan for David and played her unique part in that plan. Michal's upbringing in an ungodly home shaped her life, so she had limited knowledge about the God who deserved her all. She was not punished for her limited knowledge, but for her pride.

Modern-Day Reality: One's life can have a lasting impact even though one's upbringing is from a negative environment.

CHAPTER 42

THE WITCH OF ENDOR

(1 Samuel 28:1–25)

The witch fed the king his very last meal.

Wealth was synonymous with success in Israel. Kings who obeyed God won battles, causing them to become successful and exceedingly wealthy. To the contrary, Saul, the first king of Israel, was disobedient, abusing his authority while he was on the throne. God's punishment for Saul's disobedience was to remove him from the throne and to prevent his descendants from reigning. It was common knowledge in Israel that God spoke to prophets, priests, and kings. King Saul did not hear from God while his enemies were threatening to wipe out all of God's people. A king hearing from God meant, His authority and power was with the people and no one could harm them.

Saul was afraid of his enemies, the Philistines. He prayed to God for help, but there was no answer. Panic arose; he was completely helpless, with no strategy on how to fight his enemies. Before Saul became so defiant, he stopped all witches and wizards from operating in the land. Saul was in a predicament since the enemies were about to destroy the people of God and he could not hear from the Supernatural.

News got around and he heard about the witch in Endor practising illegally. He put his mask on, to disguise himself, then visited her by night with his men.

Saul:

- *asked the witch to bring up the spirit of someone. The witch was afraid since she was practising illegally.*
- *reassured the woman that she would be spared and that no evil would come to her.*
- *asked her to bring up Samuel the prophet from the grave. The woman did not know it was Saul who wanted Samuel brought up from the grave.*

The woman then realised that it was Saul who was behind this request. She stood dumbfounded, shocked, and petrified.

Saul assured her that there was no need to panic. The woman gave a detailed description of who she saw, a spirit in the form of an old man wearing a coat. Saul knew exactly who she saw and who she was describing, it was Samuel.

Saul:

- *had a conversation with Samuel and told him that the Philistines were fighting against him and they were winning.*
- *admitted that God had left him. Samuel told Saul this was because of his disobedience to God. Samuel confirmed that the*

kingdom would be given to David, and in twenty-four hours Saul and his sons would die.

- *collapsed and fell to the ground in shock.*
- *was weak as he had not eaten for one day.*

The witch:

- *begged Saul to get up and eat but he refused. The two servants also begged Saul to get up and eat.*
- *prepared a feast. She killed her fatted calf, baked bread, and fed the three men. The men ate, and later that night they left.*
- *fed the king his last meal before he died.*
- *sacrificed her fatted calf and was hospitable even though she was involved in witchcraft.*
- *disobeyed the king's command; paradoxically the king himself sought her help when God had departed from him.*

Practising witchcraft illegally, in defiance of the king's command, she risked her life and the lives of all around her. Her witchcraft practice seemingly was on par with the king hearing from God. Someone recommended her to the king, it was important for the king to hear from God for directions. In biblical times, people tried to substitute hearing from God, by seeking out many other sources, but only God could give right directions for living.

Saul visiting a witch **'to hear from God'** seems inconsistent. How do we explain God associating himself with such evil? God's nature is against evil. God can fulfil His purposes through those who do not even know Him. She could only exhume the prophet Samuel by the power of God.

Since God's gifting and calling are without repentance (Romans 11:29), it could be that she was gifted without fully realising her gifting; it is possible she had a gift of miracles. Since God cannot associate Himself with evil and disobedience, she operated on a supernatural level. Witchcraft is always against the nature of God. God had commanded that wizards should be put to death (Leviticus 20:27). There is a tendency to do more than required to prove one's power. If greater demands were placed on her to produce miracles all the time, she could have dabbled in the occult, seeking something that will produce miracles all the time. Did she bring Samuel the prophet back to life by the spirit of God?

Another thought was God is sovereign and He can do whatever He wishes; He made a harlot protect his servants from the wrath of a wicked king (Joshua 2:1–7) and made an animal talk when Balaam rode high on his mission to curse the people of God (Numbers 22:22–29). God used a witch to bring the prophet Samuel back to life. He told King Saul, God's plans and purposes. God is incomprehensible; therefore human beings will never be able to fully understand the diversity of His ways and thoughts (Isaiah 55:8–9). If God is fathomable He would cease to be God.

The witch:

- was bold and fearless.
- was in the king's presence in his final moments of life, without him realising it.
- knew how to celebrate and be hospitable, she did so by killing her fat calf that was reserved for an impromptu occasion.
- survived in the presence of Samuel even though she was

practicing witchcraft, yet Saul did not survive. (1 Samuel 15:23) Rebellion is as the sin of witchcraft.

She had little knowledge of God, but she was compassionate and was drawn to God by His mercy. Her life was transformed from that moment onwards. An ungodly woman encountered God's mercy and understood God's power.

Modern-Day Reality: Bold and compassionate, transformed by the grace and mercies of God.

CHAPTER 43

ABIGAIL

(1 Samuel 25:1–43; 27:3; 30:1–5; 18;
2 Samuel 2:2; 3:3; 1 Chronicles 3:1–2)

Abigail accepted the proposal to become the king's wife.

There was a vast contrast on the same strip of desert lands, which was seemingly divided by an invisible wall. Unknown to them, the shepherds of Nabal were grazing their flock on the treacherous mountain plain at night. The servants of David were also out with their flock. They knew the desert very well and ensured that their flock was safe. David's servants realised that the entire flock of Nabal was in danger. They knew that if Nabal's flock was left there overnight, none would be alive by the morning. His servants kindly assisted Nabal's shepherds with their flock, taking them to a place of safety. They created a human shield around the flock to keep them safe from predators overnight.

Nabal, originally from Maon, was a millionaire; his assets included thousands of sheep, goats, and acres of land in Carmel. However, he was mean, harsh, uncaring, and unkind. His wife was quite opposite. Nabal's wife was wise and beautiful woman, named Abigail.

David's servant related to him all that happened while they were out tending the flock. David sent his servant to Nabal requesting payment for the work done by his servants who protected Nabal's endangered flock. Nabal was at home cutting wool from the sheep when the servant arrived. David's servant told Nabal that they were kind to the shepherds, protecting the flocks day and night. Anger stirred inside Nabal when he heard David's request. He insulted David's servant, making derogatory remarks about the king. He then chased them away empty-handed.

The servant told David what Nabal said, which made David extremely furious. David felt Nabal was looking for war. So he decided to go with his army and fight Nabal.

One of Nabal's servants who witnessed the episode with David's servant related to Abigail all that happened.

- *David's servants were kind to them.*
- *David had sent his messengers to Nabal, who insulted them and sent them away empty-handed.*

Abigail was too embarrassed; she had no discussion with her husband. She took immediate actions by preparing bread, wine, cooked meat, cooked grains, raisins and figs, and sent them with one of her servants on a donkey. Abigail, wishing to appease David's anger, sent her servants ahead with gifts for David. She followed closely after them, knowing that if David accepted the gifts then she and her family would live.

Abigail:

- *knew urgency as she went to meet David and his army, who were on their way to destroy Nabal and his entire family.*
- *was good at saddling; she rode her donkey with speed to meet David.*
- *carried a two-course meal with complimentary drinks to give David and his army of two hundred men.*
- *fell prostrate at David's feet and apologised for the behaviour of her husband. David accepted her gift and decided that he would not destroy Nabal and his family.*

Abigail returned home and could not discuss with Nabal what she had done since he was too intoxicated. The following morning Nabal awoke; he was sober then. Abigail relayed to him what she did. Nabal had a heart attack and never recovered; he was dead within two weeks.

David never forgot Abigail's wisdom, nor her cool, calm, and collective manner, used to defused the situation. After the grieving period, he sent his messengers to ask Abigail to become his wife. Abigail accepted the proposal and her second marriage was to the valiant king. The following year, Abigail had a son for David.

Abigail experienced great and breath-taking moments in her life. She moved to the 'Davidic Village' Ziklag among the Philistine and lived there with David for more than a year. Their enemy, the Amalekites attacked their homes, setting it ablaze. Abigail was kidnapped and held hostage. David found her a few days later, rescuing her.

While she was married to Nabal, Abigail knew all of her husband's business ventures and his weakness; she refused to sit back and lose all her assets and her life.

Abigail's action was extraordinary. In her society, decision-making process was made and totally controlled by men. Women could not oppose their husbands' decisions. However, women like Jezebel and Sapphaira changed the decision of their husbands. Abigail realized that all she owned including her life and her husband's were at stake. She was highly involved in her husband's business venture and knew when bankruptcy was looming. She was wise in her plans, knowing favour, acknowledgement, and credit, must be given when due. She knew when to consult her husband and when she should work secretly to bring about a change. Abigail was generous in her gifts and aware that life was about giving and receiving.

Modern-Day Reality: A strategy for winning includes the antidote for inflicted wounds.

CHAPTER 44

AHINOAM

(1 Samuel 25:43; 27:3;
30:1–5; 18; 1 Chronicles 3:1;
2 Samuel 2:2; 3:2; 13:1–33)

Beauty and poise attracting her to royalty,
but she did not secure an heir to the throne.

Overall a young woman's role in that society falls into one of these three categories: slaves living with their masters and mistresses, married and living with their husbands, or single and living at home. One of the greatest honours in Israel was to be selected by the king, or would-be king, to become his wife. These young women groomed themselves daily in an effort to become eligible; it was every single woman's ambition to be the wife of the king. Unofficial pageants were held. Young unmarried women in Israel, keenly followed David's itinerary. However, David's choice of women, were from those with a beautiful physique, small waistline, and the curves in all the right places. He demonstrated this as he was willing to kill any 'competitors' to take away their wife.

Ahinoam was young, beautiful, single, and very attractive. She emerged as number one in the king's choice of women. Although she was not an Israelite, she successfully wooed the heart of the handsome Israelite above thousands of women. It must be noted that David was married before to King Saul's daughter Michal. Saul made numerous attempts to hurt David even by ordering a divorce bill for his daughter Michal. Saul then ensured she was remarried to Phaltiel from Gallim. Ahinoam's relationship with David resulted in the birth of their first son, called Amnon. She knew that David's popularity would take him to the palace and she never expected a monogamous relationship. It was not long after David had the next woman in his life.

Ahinoam's reality was another woman's dream as she was attracted to one of the most handsome young men in Israel. King David selected her as one of his eight wives and she was the mother of his first son Amnon.

She:

- *was born in the town of Jezreelites.*
- *felt honoured to become the mother of the king's first son. In Israel, the first son was usually the heir to the throne.*
- *tried to prepare her son Amnon to take up his role, since she thought he would be the future king of Israel.*

She was highly honoured as the 'first wife' above the other wives, and the woman who gave birth to the king's first son. Her son was the one who was undoubtedly earmarked to succeed his father on the throne of Israel.

Amnon:

- *was a troubled young man. His emotional disparity went unnoticed into adulthood.*
- *was wicked and lost respect for women, including his sister.*
- *was a trickster, pretending to be very sick.*

Tamar, his half-sister, visited him; the cake she made for him was in her hands. Amnon, who was supposed to be at the point of death, grabbed his sister into bed and raped her. When Ahinoam heard the news she wept bitterly. She could not believe that instead of raising a worthy heir to the throne, a son of the king, her son had become an abuser and a rapist.

Ahinoam had beauty and poise, attracting her to royalty, but she did not secure an heir to the throne. Her son was disqualified from kingship and he never reigned on the throne of Israel. He lost his life as his own brother arranged for his friends to murder him.

Ahinoam secured the most honorable opportunity all mothers in Israel envied, an opportunity to have their son reign on Israel's throne. However, her parenting skills were subjected to scrutiny when she raised a son whose actions were dishonourable and disrespectful to women, including his own sister. Could it be the actions of both parents contributed to their son's life of crime? It appeared that her husband, King David was busy winning wars to the detriment of losing the battles of raising decent, law-abiding children. It is quite possible that he did not ensure, his children were disciplined and honourable. However, God viewed him as a man after His own heart.

Ahinoam was in love with David before he became king and was aware of all of David's near misses, when his life was greatly endangered. She supported David, knowing he was great at poetry. She lived a nomadic life along with David; they were constantly on the run to escape Saul's death threat. They moved to live among their most deadly enemies, the Philistines, for more than a year. While David and the army were away from home, fighting their enemies (this could be a period of many weeks), the Amalekites invaded their home. She and her son were captured and taken hostage; David returned home and everything was reduced to ash. He was frantic, searching for his family, but he found out that they were not burnt to death. Ahinoam and her son were found alive after a few days; this was a grand family reunion. She experienced all the difficulties and challenges of a woman whose husband was a valiant warrior with many enemies. Her husband was absent from home for lengthy periods. Ahinoam experienced anxiety, stress, and worry about whether her husband would return home alive. Her greatest fear was that the battle and war will never end.

Ahinoam lived a life of regret and never forgave herself for raising a defeatist. Could it be that she did not fully uterlise her maternal influence to instil discipline, morality, and respect for God and for others? She had some regrets, since her son led a life of disrepute and shame. She died broken–hearted and never impact legacy.

Modern-Day Reality: Excellent start; what happens in between determines the outcome.

CHAPTER 45

MAACAH 1

(1 Chronicles 3:1–2; 2 Samuel 13:13–32; 14:21–28; 15:1–20; 18:9)

Her beauty got her to the throne of Israel.

She was the daughter of a king. Her father was Talmai, the king of Geshur. She was not an Israelite but competed with the Israelite women, for the noble position, the wife of the king. Kings were never known to have one wife. However, all the women in Israel and the surrounding nations would never miss the opportunity to become one of the king's many wives. This was a worthy status and none of the women worried about their rank. She was young, attractive, and fit into the Davidic profile of femininity, so she was selected as one of David's wives. Maacah became pregnant and gave birth to King David's third son Absalom. David was busy devising strategies for battle and being involved in war; he spent less time fathering his son.

Her son Absalom was an angry young man and did not learn forgiveness.

Absalom:

- had hatred in his heart even when the incident occurred two years previously.
- never forgave or forgot his brother's violation of their sister.
- waited for the opportunity when he felt everyone forgot.
- arranged a boys' night out with all of his brothers.
- went to his father, King David, and asked if Amnon and his brothers could hang out with him. Amnon was the firstborn and was entitled to the throne. He could not go out without his father's permission.
- reassured his father that he would look after his brothers and that they would be safe.

Absalom was dishonest and had arranged with his servants to kill his brother Amnon, when he was intoxicated. Amnon was murdered, David was inconsolable as he wept bitterly for his son. Absalom commenced a life on the run which lasted for two years; he knew his brothers wanted to kill him also. During Absalom's two years as a fugitive, his father David never tried to contact him. He felt it was time to let go of the past: he asked Absalom to return home.

Absalom:

- had an appetite for power and arranged a coup to overthrow his father from the throne.

- *fought against the servants of his father with his troops.*
- *was trying to escape the battle, rode his horse and came through some oak trees.*
- *was riding at such speed that his head got caught in the branches of the tree while his horse continued to go; he was left hanging above the ground until he died.*

Maacah grew up in a palace as a princess, the daughter of a king. She was not one of God's chosen people, but she was exposed to the ways of true worship to the Living God through His servant David. She was held in the arms of the psalmist, the writer of the scriptures. Her upbringing conflicted with that of her husband's as she grew up in a culture that was polytheistic, worshipping many gods. Absalom's childhood was characterised by a state of confusion as his mother often worshipped the gods of her parents, whereas his father, King David, worshipped the true and Living God. David's household was troubled and dysfunctional. There was sibling rivalry, sexual abuse, and power struggle. David's action was disobedient to the ways and Commandment of God, even in his choice of women. The Israelites were instructed by God not to marry women from ungodly nations. God told the Israelites that these nations would turn their hearts away from Him, yet David was seen as one who loved and sought after God with all his heart.

Her honorary position as one of the wives of the king of Israel was the highlight of her life. She was proud, as she felt her background as a princess would maintain her royal status, but it did not. Her time was spent trying to outstrip her rivals as she sought to make herself the most attractive wife of the king. Although she knew royal protocol, her life was no different from many of the other wives who were never raised in a palace. She had a son for King David. Their son, like most of his siblings, lived extremely troubled and disruptive lives. Although they were heir to the throne, their ungodly upbringing failed to make them realise their full potentials. Maacah's pride caused her to concentrate more on herself than raising her son in a manner that befitted a prince.

Modern-Day Reality: Inner beauty and godliness is what counts.

CHAPTER 46

HAGGITH

(2 Samuel 3:2-4; 1 Kings 1:5-27;
2:13-25; 1 Chronicles 3:2)

Eyed the throne for her son and was willing to have him reign
as king at any cost.

A handsome young man ascended to the throne and became Israel's second king. When the king was in search of a wife, she was chosen because of her beauty. King David was attracted to her, adding her to his 'collection of wives'. Young women in Israel and surrounding nations lived in expectation, desiring to become one of the king's wives. The prestigious role was envied by all the young women. The woman selected as the king's first wife received the highest honour. However, any woman who was selected as a wife of the king, regardless of the position, it was an honour.

Haggith was very attractive and she lived with high expectations that she would be selected as one of the king's wives. That day finally came. King David propositioned her and invited her to the palace to be one of his wives. She was respected as a 'queen' of Israel. Haggith became pregnant and gave birth to King David's fourth son, who was called Adonijah.

Haggith:

- *cared for her son and groomed him to become king of Israel in place of his father.*
- *completely ignored basic royal protocol since the first son was entitled to the role of kingship in succession of his father.*
- *eyed the throne for her son and was willing to have him reign as king at any cost.*

Haggith was the main disciplinarian for her son, since his father was busy with wars and royal duties. She was responsible for instilling discipline and loyalty in her son. However, it was possible that she spent the time thinking about her son's ascension to the throne as the next king of Israel in place of his father David. Haggith prepared herself to become the head of the monarchy, but David promised Bathsheba, who was also one of his many wives, that their son Solomon would become the next king. Adonijah was jealous and even when his father did not approve of him as king, he planned a coup to make himself king instead of his father David. His mother Haggith was complicit and did not reveal Adonijah's evil plans to his father.

Adonijah had a coronation, this was no secret to his mother. He invited all of his close friends to join him in the big moment. His stepmother Bathsheba knew she had to protect the interest of her son

Solomon; when she heard of what Adonijah did, she immediately broke the news to her husband, King David, that his son Adonijah had made himself king.

King David asked Nathan the prophet, Zadok the priest, and Benaiah son of Jehoiada to take his youngest son Solomon and put him on the king's horse. They were expected to take him to the spring called Gihon and pour oil on him, blow the trumpet, and announce that Solomon was the king of Israel and Judah.

As Adonijah was finishing his celebration meal, he heard that Solomon was officially made the new king of Israel. Adonijah and his friends knew they were a threat to the new monarchy. Their lives were endangered because they attempted to overthrow the king. The celebration party ended abruptly as they fled for their lives.

Adonijah ran nonstop to the temple and held on to the altar for safety. Culturally, when someone flees to the altar because their lives were endangered, no one could kill them. The altar was a safe haven. King Solomon sent his servant to get Adonijah; he forgave him and allowed him to go home in peace. Adonijah bowed down to the ground and acknowledged that his brother was king. Adonijah later went to his stepmother and asked her, if she could ask King Solomon to give him the slave girl Abishag to become his wife. King Solomon was furious; he knew Adonijah's deception. King Solomon knew that he wanted access to the palace. King Solomon ordered that Adonijah should die. Adonijah was put to death by King Solomon's servant.

Haggith:

- carried many negative traits.
- was self-absorbed, envious, and angry.

- did not educate her son of his unique position in the palace and his entitlement as the king's son.
- raised her son to be deceptive, to take power by force even when she knew the king's decision was paramount on the successor to the throne.
- failed to use her motherly influence and her entitlement in the palace in a positive manner.

Adonijah's status as the king's son entitled him to royalty, apart from the throne. However, he eyed the throne and his mother colluded and conceded with him about being the successor.

Haggith did not help him achieve his greatest potentials or goals in life as the son of the king. As a result he spent his entire life chasing that which could not be his. Adonijah grew up producing the kind of fruits that reflected his upbringing: greed, deception and negativity. There could be a human tendency to chase after position, fame, and recognition not intended to be our own. Such driving force can often become so strong eroding the true purpose in life. Haggith did not realise she had only one chance to parent her son, and her parenting ability is a major contributing factor to make him rise or fall.

Modern-Day Reality: Parental role impacts lives positively or negatively.

CHAPTER 47

BATHSHEBA

(2 Samuel 11:1–27; 1 Kings 2:13–25;
1 Chronicles 3:5–8)

She trained her son Solomon to kingship even though he was not
the firstborn son of the king.

Young women in Israel did not have a choice about who they married. It was a serious matter when the king of Israel murdered her husband, then took her to become his wife. King David observed her external beauty from his balcony, while she was having a bath.

The nation of Israel was at war with the Ammonites and kings were expected to be out fighting for their nation. King David excused himself from war and sat on his balcony overlooking the river. The river was a place most women frequented as they performed purification rights. Bathsheba, the daughter of Ammiel and Eliam, was performing her post-menstrual ceremony of purification in the river when her life changed drastically.

King David:

- *was expected to be out fighting the war with his soldiers who depended on him. He was a man of conquest and strategy after he won the victory against Goliath.*
- *was accountable to no one, so he decided to relax and leave the rigours and risks of battle to his officers.*
- *frequented his balcony, which overlooked the river. He had a detailed view of all the woman taking a bath in the river. His eyes zeroed in on Bathsheba; he loved her shapely physique, with curves in the right places.*
- *felt she was the most eye-catching among all the women in the river. He sent his servant to fetch her.*

Bathsheba could not understand why the king interrupted her cleansing ceremony, inviting her to his palace. She went to the palace, since disobeying the king was not an option.

King David:

- *took her to his private luxurious suite and empathised with her about her husband being away and how lonely she must have been without him.*
- *pretended to be sympathetic to her.*
- *had a few alcoholic drinks, offering Bathsheba the same.*
- *had sex with Bathsheba even though he knew that she was married.*
- *then sent her home to get on with her life.*

Bathsheba was most probably in her mid teens and was married for at least one year. Since warriors were allowed to stay at home with their new bride for one year before they go to battle (Deut. 24:5) Bathsheba's husband Uriah was out at war, fighting for the survival of his people. Uriah was totally committed to the war and wanted his nation to win the war and be at peace. One month later Bathsheba had morning sickness then found out she was pregnant. Her husband had been at war for a few months so she knew she was pregnant with King David's child. She sent a message to King David to inform him that she was pregnant.

King David:

- knew that he would be found out, so he tried to cover his sin.
- hurriedly sent his servant to the officer in charge of the men at war.
- requested that Uriah should be summoned to see him immediately.

Uriah was a devoted soldier and wanted to stay and fight, but he knew he could not disobey the king or he would die. The same day Uriah arrived at the palace, most confused. He could not understand why the king singled him out to return from war. King David entertained Uriah then enquired about the war. Uriah gave the king an account of what was happening on the battlefield. The king wanted to allay suspicion, so he asked Uriah to go home and spend time with Bathsheba since he was away from home for many months. Uriah, being a man of high principles, refused to go home to see his wife. He slept outside the palace.

One of the servants told King David what Uriah had done. The king called Uriah again, begging him to go home and spend time with his wife.

Uriah told the king that he could not go home and enjoy life with his wife when the ark of God and his colleagues were in tents. He did not think it was right for him to eat, drink, and spend time with his wife when all the other men were risking their lives to save the nation. Uriah refused to go home. David, realising that his plan had failed, thought of another plan. He had two reasons to take action; Bathsheba was pregnant with his child and Uriah refused to take orders from him.

King David:

- *wrote a letter and asked Uriah to deliver the letter to the officer in charge of the war.*
- *asked the officer to send Uriah into the hottest part of the battle ensuring that he was killed.*

The officer obeyed the king and Uriah was killed. Years later, King David was known as the man who did right in God's sight, with this malicious, heinous act against Uriah as the only exception on his character.

Bathsheba mourned for her husband, and when the period of mourning was over, King David sent his servant to get her and she became his wife. A few months later Bathsheba gave birth to a baby boy. The prophet had already visited King David when Bathsheba was pregnant. He told him what he did was wrong, and as a result the baby would die. The baby was quite normal at birth; however, within seven days he died. Bathsheba wept for her baby and was inconsolable. She mourned the loss of her baby for many months, while still dealing with the death of Uriah, her husband.

By the next year she had another son called Solomon. She became mother to the wisest man who ever lived. She trained her son Solomon to kingship even though he was not the firstborn son of the king. Solomon was selected by God to build His house, a magnificent edifice and a place where God dwells. This temple was the first church building erected for God's glory in Israel's history.

Bathsheba's son, Solomon recorded in Proverbs 22:6: "Train up a child in the way that is right and the child will never depart from it." This statement reflected Solomon's childhood, as he was trained in the ways of God. A reflection on David's other children and their childhood makes Solomon the star child, the child with kingly qualities fit to reign on the throne of his father. Solomon was his father's successor on the throne of Israel.

Bathsheba saw greatness in her son and was determined to secure his place in leadership. She was David's favourite wife since David discussed with her his intention to have Solomon reign after his death. David spent his final days with her and not his other wives. She also ensured that Solomon succeeded David as king when his brother tried to overthrow David and take the kingdom. She was a wise and faithful wife. She knew that training and discipline were essential assets in the life of her son if he was to qualify for the throne, and she instilled these qualities. She could be recorded as the mother-in-law with the most daughters-in-law in history, since her son Solomon had one thousand wives and concubines.

Solomon's demise came as a result of his disobedience to God. He allowed heathen women to seduce him to the extent of diluting his belief and worship in the True and Living God. Solomon's lifestyle as an adult was in complete contrast to the training he received as a youth. (1 Kings 11:1-13).

Bathsheba was the mother of the third king who reigned over Israel. It must be noted that very little had been recorded about the mothers of the two previous kings, King Saul and King David. Bathsheba's life is recorded from teenage years to late adulthood. She was indeed remarkable.

Modern-Day Reality: Godly qualities are crucial in the life of a child.

CHAPTER 48

TAMAR 2

(2 Samuel 13:1–39; 1 Chronicles 3:1)

*She was physically violated, emotionally devastated, and
mentally traumatized.*

Her identity was wrapped in her traditional wear, as it signified her mark of purity and her status as the king's daughter. King David was her father, yet she was one of the most innocent women in Israel. She was also known for her profound beauty and notable godly influence. Tamar was a humanitarian, welcoming every opportunity to help the needy in her community. She displayed Godlike characteristics without malice or hatred.

Her brother Amnon was the complete opposite. Amnon premeditated evil all the time. He stayed awake at night feeding those evil desires and ungodly motives, which became so strong they overpowered him.

A deceptive Amnon crawled into his bed as though he was dying.

He was never known to refuse food, especially his favourite dishes, but now he had lost all appetite.

Amnon's condition as he lay in his bed:

- Fixed eyes, filled with water.
- Shallow breath with froth in his mouth.
- Heavy tongue, slurred and inaudible speech.
- Extreme restlessness and appeared to be groaning in pain.
- Indecisive as to whether he was too warm or cold and wanted the bed cover on and off constantly.
- Nothing seemed to ease his discomfort.

Many of his relatives came to visit him and were emotional. They stood speechless, in disbelief as they saw Amnon's condition. Amnon's mother, Ahinoam wept ceaselessly. She was crushed, as she found it difficult to come to terms with the events of the past twenty four hours. The sudden onset of her son's illness coupled with his quick deterioration before her eyes, intensified her pain. Amnon's relative kept a constant vigil at his bedside as death seemed imminent. Ahinoam regained her composure and asked her son if there was anything she could do for him. He muttered a few words; he could hardly be heard or understood.

Everyone visiting was surprised when he perked up, but it was momentarily. He spoke again, barely audible; however, his mother recognised two words from his utterance: *Tamar's cake*. His mother felt he was recovering, as he had not eaten or drank anything for twenty-four hours. She felt as though there was a glimpse of hope, so she sent someone to fetch Tamar. Amnon's heart was evil and secretly loaded with lust towards his sister Tamar. He was self-absorbed; as he lay in his bed at night, his mind regurgitated on the wicked plans he had for his sister.

Tamar was ambitious and domesticated; she loved baking cakes. A 'dying' Amnon filled with deception convinced the family that his sister's cake would make him better. Tamar being caring, innocent, and sincere was ready to do anything to aid her brother's recovery. She was overjoyed at the thought that her cakes were the 'only remedy' to make him recover.

As she visited her *'dying' brother*, it appeared that Amnon had only moments to live. Amnon's distorted and distressed relatives, could not cope with the thought of his inevitable death. They did not hold back their feelings of sorrow and grief as their faces were stained with tears.

Tamar was a professional baker and was able to bake a cake for Amnon very quickly. She placed the cake on a silver platter and garnished it. Then Tamar handed the scrumptious cake to the servant who waited on her brother. Amnon was filled with ulterior motives: he refused the cake that was baked for him. He pretended he was about to take his last breath, then he made a gesture with his hands to be left alone. His mother was about to leave the room when she heard him mutter, **'Tamar'.**

The family was in a state of shock and confusion when they convinced Tamar to serve the cake as this might be his last request. Tamar allowed herself to be vulnerable. She went into the room, her eyes filled with tears, it was distressing to witness her brother gasping for breath. Amnon, who was supposed to be dying, beckoned to his sister to close the door. He made another sign, inviting her to sit on his bed; at this point she was completely emotional as she moved closer to her brother.

Tamar's Horrible Ordeal

*Amnon, who was much bigger and stronger than Tamar, grabbed her wrist with both hands and threw her into his bed. Tamar, frozen in shock and disbelief, was speechless as her 'dying brother' was completely revived. She could not process her thoughts, thinking she had a terrible dream. Amnon held a pillow over her mouth, threatening her. She screamed but no one could hear her. Tamar tried to bargain with him, '**Don't do such wickedness. This is shameful, and it is not worth it**'. However, a determined Amnon ignored his sister's rationale and her cry for help. He carried out his premeditated thoughts, raping her, then he realised that he absolutely hated her. He shouted at her to get out of his room; he no longer wanted to see his sister. Tamar told him that his evil actions would be found out. She reminded him that according to the custom of Israel, he was expected to marry her for taking away her virginity. She left the room distraught and embarrassed. He was also expected to pay her father two-thirds of a kilogram of silver (Exodus 22:16; Deuteronomy 22:28–29). Tamar wanted her brother to do the right thing even after he had done something horribly wrong. A heartless Amnon ignored her pleas and wanted her out of his sight.*

King's daughters who were virgins wore special clothing according to the tradition and custom. In Israel, being a virgin was no secret, nor was losing one's virginity outside of marriage. Tamar put ashes on her head and tore off the special clothes. Placing both hands on her head, she screamed loudly as she wept. She was hysterical. As part of the custom, when someone suddenly suffered grief or lost something valuable, they would tear their clothes and scream as an expression of their sorrows. Tamar went away completely devastated.

After such a traumatic episode, Tamar relocated and went to live with her brother Absalom. She was depressed, sad, and isolated because of the evil deed that Amnon had done. Absalom counted Amnon as dead and waited for the opportunity to kill him.

Tamar often reflected on the fact that she was abused, violated, taken advantage of, and raped even when she was doing what was right. She was physically violated, emotionally devastated, and mentally traumatized. Despite, being spiritually challenged, she maintained her integrity.

The Bible mentioned that **man's heart is evil and wicked, only God knows and detect it** (Jeremiah 17:9). Tamar never bore bitterness, carried an unforgiving spirit, nor was she vengeful even when she had a reason to be. She never joined with Absalom for vengeance. Amnon's evil deed revisited and he was murdered. Tamar displayed qualities of love and forgiveness, as a woman with a heart seeking God.

Tamar seemingly had the right to be hateful and angry because of what she suffered. Her brother's wicked actions had damaging consequences on her physically and emotionally. However, she did not feel justified to hate him. Tamar had so much love in her heart even though she hated her brother's sin.

What a godly woman; she knew what the scripture meant by *vengeance belongs to God (Deut 32:35).*

Modern-Day Reality: Love conquers all.

CHAPTER 49

Two Wise Women
with Strategies

(2 Samuel 14:1–20; 20:1–22)

*The woman made a request to see King David
and her request was granted.*

T hough they were raised in the palace as children of the king, their lives failed to depict children raised by the monarchy. One son was so jealous of his brother that he wanted to kill him as he eyed the throne. The king's son Amnon raped his sister Tamar. His other son Absalom killed Amnon in revenge. Absalom fled for his life and was in hiding for three years.

Joab, who was servant of King David, knew the king missed Absalom and was grieving for him. Joab called the wise woman from the city of Tekoa, begging her to pretend she was someone else. She was expected to disguise herself as a depressed woman in mourning. He told her exactly what she must say to King David. *The woman made a request to see King David and her request was granted. Her appearance wasn't appeasing to the eye, nor was it in keeping with royal protocol, but she went to meet the king. Invited into the king's palace, the servant showed her to the king's mini conference hall. She was served an appetizer, but she refused to eat, showing her misery.*

She related her fictitious sad story.

She:

- *told the king she was a widow with two sons.*
- *related to the king an incident involving her two boys. They were fighting out in the field and the younger son killed the elder. As she spoke, tears filled her eyes.*
- *was heartbroken by the ordeal as she not only lost one of her sons, but the family planned to kill her other son for his transgressions.*

King David was so moved by the story and promised the widow that this would never happen under his reign as king. The woman was trying to get a message to the king, so that he would deal with his own family matters. She then told King David that this was the situation with his son Absalom. The king realised that this woman was wise; by creating a fictitious account of love and forgiveness, she exposed the inconsistencies of the king. Her tale was effective, as it made the king realise that he needed to forgive his son Absalom for murdering his brother Amnon.

Her wisdom was profound and she was sought after by many of the villagers to settle difficult family disputes. She had an unbeaten track record in resolving disputes and was known as **Lady Wisdom**.

Modern-Day Reality: The king is accessible. This also refers to King Jesus.

The woman assured Joab that Sheba's head would be thrown over the wall.

Another coup in Israel, as some young men revolted against David's judiciary, vowing to have nothing to do with the king and his kingdom. Amasa was part of the conspiracy, along with Sheba and his men. King David and his army knew all about the planned revolt. Deception and falsehood was everywhere, absolutely no one could be trusted. Joab, King David's servant, pretended to have a friendly conversation with Amasa, sneaked up on him, drew the sword from his waist, and killed him.

There was jubilation after that victory as Joab and his servants were invigorated. They then chased after Sheba and his men by surrounding the city. Joab and his men seized the city. They dug under the wall, hoping that the city would collapse.

The wise woman knew what was going on both inside and outside her city and shouted to Joab's men from within the city walls, **'Listen to me and go tell Joab I want to talk to him'**. *She knew exactly how to distract and delay a destructive course of action. Joab felt it was a good idea, as it would give him the opportunity to get closer to his enemies. Joab welcomed her discourse.*

The woman told him:

- *that many people came to her seeking advice, and their problems were solved.*
- *she was one of the peacemakers in the land and was a loyal citizen of Israel.*

- *he was trying to destroy the city of God. He could not fight against God and win.*

Joab told the wise woman:

- *it was not his intention to fight against God or to destroy the city of God.*
- *that Sheba, the son of Bicri from Ephraim, revolted against King David's authority and was hiding in the city.*
- *that he wanted to ensure that Sheba did not continue with this wickedness.*

The woman:

- *assured Joab that Sheba's head would be thrown over the wall.*
- *was not the main leader of her city since women were seldom leaders in those times.*
- *assumed a leadership role by calling an emergency meeting for all the citizens.*
- *chaired the meeting with one item on the agenda.*

*The citizens decided that they would cooperate with the woman, ensuring that the entire city was not destroyed. Sheba was hiding in the city, ill-prepared for battle. They chased after him, decapitating his head, which they threw over the city wall. Joab took the head of Sheba and blew the trumpet. In Israel's culture, a king won the battle over his opponent and celebrated victory when he had in his possession the head of the enemy, even as David did with Goliath. The sound of the trumpet was a sound of **victory**.*

Her diplomacy and bravery are commendable. It was unusual in her times for women to be enlisted as warriors; in fact none of the armies recruited them. She was not insecure being a woman or unskilled in war.

This woman was on par with David who was victorious against the Philistines. She secured victory for Israel over the enemy.

Modern-Day Reality: Strategies for winning: knowledge and negotiation.

CHAPTER 50

TAMAR 3

(2 Samuel 13:1–2; 2 Samuel 14:27)

She ensured that her offspring did not ascend to the throne
through revolt and rivalry.

Though born and raised in the palace as royals, their behaviour did not reflect their status since King David's family was dysfunctional. Serious questions were raised about the King's parenting skills. The family dynamics was one of disloyalty and disrespect. His children sought to overthrow him and seize the kingdom. There was constant fighting and even murder among them. His firstborn son Amnon viciously violated his own sister and lived without remorse. Absalom, the king's other son, was full of vengeance towards his elder brother Amnon for raping their sister Tamar and bringing shame on the family. He walked around for two years with vengeance in his heart, waiting for the opportunity to kill Amnon. When the moment presented itself, Absalom murdered his elder brother for violating Tamar.

Absalom:

- loved his sister Tamar very much and was willing to protect and defend her.
- highly regarded his sister for all the excellent and exceptional qualities she possessed.
- wanted a lasting memorial in his sister's honour so he named his daughter after her.

Tamar was:

- *the daughter of Absalom and granddaughter of David.*
- *tall, attractive, godly, and upright.*
- *gracious as her aunt Tamar (2).*
- *versed in royal protocol and the day-to-day activity in the king's palace.*
- *very knowledgeable of the family rift. She witnessed her uncles and Absalom struggle for power, rivalling one another to ascend to the throne.*
- *traumatised by the countless bloodshed and unrealistic expectations, as her father lived his life wishing he would be king one day. She knew when her father tried to overthrow the king and seize the throne.*

Yet, all this negativity had no adverse effect on the way she lived. She was not disloyal or seductive. She ensured that her offspring did not ascend to the throne through revolt and rivalry.

Tamar reversed the generational curse on her family and her descendants. Her family reigned on the throne for many generations. Her *great-grandson King Asa's reign was peaceful. Many of the previous kings did evil in the sight of God and their reigns were characterised by war and destruction. Asa's peaceful reign could be attributed to the fulfilment of scripture, as he was four generations after Absalom. **The sin of the father visits up to the third and fourth generation** (Exodus 20:5). Absalom's sin visited three generations but stopped at King Asa, the fourth generation.*

Tamar knew that her descendants would be chosen to be an agent of peace in Israel. Though such peace was not realised through her daughter, it came through her great-grandson. God's blessings and prosperity on the nation was manifested, a state of tranquillity never realised in Israel for centuries. She never allowed the doom and gloom around her to define her destiny and that of her generation.

Modern-Day Reality: Faith for great thing. Success will come even if it's through your descendants.

CHAPTER 51

ABISHAG

(1 Kings 1:1–4; 15; 2:17–22)

Served the king with great respect and dignity.
*Their relationship was **not** an intimate one.*

It was summer, the temperatures were soaring; most people found the warm days and nights unbearable. Even with such unendurable heat, King David was suffering from hypothermia, and just could not get himself warm in bed. He had lost a large proportion of his body fat due to the aging process. His wife and servants tried tirelessly to keep him warm with all the blankets, socks, and hats, but he shivered and complained of feeling cold.

The king's servant, caring for him, thought of this brilliant idea: if he found a young woman to lie in bed close to him, then he would become warm. The idea seemed weird at first, but they decided to search for a young woman to keep the king warm. The advert went out and many women thought this was a great opportunity to live in the palace full time. It was seen as a prestigious job with attractive pay. Many young women applied for the job to keep the king warm in bed. Abishag, the Shunammite, was successfully chosen.

Abishag:

- *was very young, beautiful, and caring.*
- *served the king with great respect and dignity. Their relationship was **not** an intimate one.*
- *was highly trusted and trustworthy.*

Abishag was a much younger woman, therefore this was the highest degree of trust one woman could expect from another. Bathsheba was no longer the young and beautiful woman who was at the river bathing, when the king looked out from his balcony and thought she was a must-have. She had aged gracefully. Bathsheba had no doubt that, Abishag was honest, trustworthy, and disciplined. Bathsheba trusted Abishag to get in bed with her husband, primarily to keep him warm.

Abishag got into bed with King David. His body temperature went from hypothermic to becoming completely normal within a short period of time. She produced enough warmth in King David's bed, making him lively and happy. David had already handed over the throne to his son Solomon. Abishag worked faithfully in the house of David and gained favour and promotion. Adonijah, who was also the son of King David, found Abishag very attractive. He approached his brother Solomon, asking him for Abishag's hand in marriage. Adonijah's intentions were not honourable since he tried to become king instead of Solomon, by revolt. King Solomon knew that he would not allow Adonijah to walk into the palace and take this godly woman to be his wife. He felt Abishag was a woman of class and prestige, and his brother was not deserving of her.

Abishag was known as the young woman with the most unusual vocation; she was respected by all men and trusted by all women. She was extraordinary and exceptional, and known as the most trustworthy subject in the kingdom. After King David's death, she was promoted in the palace to an honorary position. Abishag lived in an era when many women were famous because of their close relationship with the king. Her story is rare; a wife allowing another woman to sleep in bed with her husband, only to keep him warm. She was an excellent example of morality since she did not have a hidden agenda or an ulterior motive.

Modern-Day Reality: Trustworthiness can take you to a king's palace and sustain you.

CHAPTER 52

Naamah

(2 Chronicles 12:13–14; 1 Kings 11:1–13)

*... her name was the only one mentioned in scripture among
Solomon's one thousand (1,000) women.*

S pending one day with each woman would take him almost three
years to see them all. Obviously he had irregular contacts with
many of these women in his life. She was one of a thousand, since 999
other women dated and slept with her husband, the wisest man ever.
His wisdom was attributed to the fact that he asked God for wisdom
instead of wealth. King Solomon's 1,000 queens originated from various nations, including Moab, Edom, Ammon, and Sidon.

Solomon, the son of King David, was chosen to build the first
temple for God. He built the most magnificent building in history.
Naamah supported her husband, King Solomon, as he built the
temple unto God. Solomon's fame was well known: he was the most
popular king who ever lived. However, it was to his detriment when

Solomon allowed his wives to influence him, causing him to turn away from God to serve idols. God was very angry with Solomon and promised him that his kingdom would be taken away from his successors after him.

Naamah, an Ammonite was most likely Solomon's first love, or the woman who bore his first son. In her era it was an honour to be the wife of a king even though it was highly competitive. She was exceptional as the king's wife with the greatest honour. Naamah exercised tremendous patience, coping with her husband's extraordinary love for women. She waited for Solomon to return from visiting his many wives. The disparity was evident as women were expected to be a faithful wife even when the king had hundreds of wives. None of these women could have an extra marital affair. Naamah loved Solomon dearly. She had a son called Rehoboam, who ascended to the throne after the death of King Solomon. Naamah taught her son about the downfalls of Solomon his father, who allowed too many women to capture and turn his heart away from God. She told Rehoboam that Solomon's compromise cost the kingdom. Rehoboam obeyed the advice of Naamah: he had seventy-eight wives. Although it was a large number, it was still fewer than ten percent of the women of his father.

Naamah is credited as one of exceptional repute, her name being the only one mentioned in scripture among Solomon's one thousand (1,000) women. She was the 'wife' of the wisest man who ever lived and the most outstanding of all his 'queens'. She experienced the building of the temple and the glory of God visiting His people in the temple. She was involved in all the finesse and professionalism surrounding the palace. Naamah fully assumed her parental role since Solomon was constantly away from home. She raised a son who succeeded his father on the throne. She survived intense competitiveness, jealousy, hatred and malice from hundreds of rivals. In spite of all the challenges, she maintained her honorable position as the king's number one wife.

Modern-Day Reality: Honourable and outstanding.

CHAPTER 53

THE QUEEN OF SHEBA

(1 Kings 4:20-34; 1 Kings 10:1-29; 2 Chronicles 9:1-12)

Wanting to associate with and celebrate greatness,
...she planned a trip to Solomon's palace.

G ood news about the fame of the king arrived in her palace at
Sheba. King Solomon's fame had travelled far and wide through
the province of Asia. Stories about the magnificent edifice, King
Solomon had erected to worship God, spread throughout the lands
like wildfire. The report described the temple's interior and exterior
as beautiful beyond imagination and second to none. The queen of
Sheba also heard about Solomon's wisdom. He ruled with fairness
and justice. Solomon was the son of King David and Bathsheba. As
the third king on the throne of Israel, he was so renowned that his
fame spread globally. Solomon's success was greatly ascribed to the
fact that he sought God for wisdom to rule the nation of Israel, unlike
his predecessors.

The queen of Sheba sat in her palace giving much thought to what she had heard. She decided to visit the king and get to know him personally. She was eager to be associated with and to celebrate greatness. Weeks before her visit she did some brainstorming, writing down all the hard questions that she wanted to ask the king. She gathered the best spices, gold, and jewels as her gift of appreciation for this remarkable king. Her servants ensured that the camels were laden with every valuable gift. A royal chariot was mounted and the convoy set off on the long dusty road to King Solomon's palace. The journey took a few days, stopping at various motels. As she got closer to King Solomon's palace, the queen of Sheba was exuberant and beaming with excitement. Although she was no stranger to royal protocol, she became apprehensive envisaging what her first encounter with the king would be like.

When she finally arrived at Solomon's palace, the king was delighted to meet her. They greeted each other then she presented her gifts to him. Entertainment at the palace comprised of a parade and a special meal with a few dignitaries. The king then had a private conference with the queen. The queen commended him for the extraordinary work that he had done. This was her chance; time to ask the questions she had brainstormed before she embarked on her journey. However, to her greatest surprise, Solomon answered all her questions before she could ask them. She was overly impressed and thought, **what a wise King.**

She admitted, despite her status, her own palace could not be compared to King Solomon's. She observed the order and high standards with which the king managed his palace, making her secretly envious of him.

The queen of Sheba confessed that Solomon's wisdom, wealth, and fame exceeded all she had ever known. So she poured out her treasures of gold, silver, and precious stones into the temple, ensuring that Solomon had shiploads of the finest wood. When the wood arrived, Solomon used them to make musical instruments like harps, organs, and to maintain the temple.

The queen of Sheba:

- *spent more than a week in Solomon's palace; during her visit and when she returned home, she honoured King Solomon with gifts.*
- *found it difficult to contain her emotions as she reflected on the overwhelming sovereignty of God through His servant, King Solomon.*
- *sat and wept as she reflected; she found the experience mind-boggling.*
- *seized a life-changing opportunity to associate with and to celebrate greatness.*
- *did not feel sufficient in her own role as a queen.*
- *submitted herself to what was greater in magnitude and splendour.*
- *was overly impressed with what she had experienced that she placed Solomon and the temple on her list, to receive gifts of gold and other precious stones annually.*

The queen of Sheba was not self-absorbed or proud. She strived for excellence, knowing it could be found elsewhere. She was willing to be vulnerable and submit herself to a young king with less experience, but more wisdom. She was completely astonished by Solomon's effortless manner in managing his kingdom and the professionalism with which all aspect of life happened in the palace.

Modern-Day Reality: Submission to and celebration of that which is greater.

CHAPTER 54

THE PROSTITUTE IN SOLOMON'S JUDGEMENT HALL

(1 Kings 3:16–28)

The king sympathetically listened to their arguments then asked his servant to bring him a sword.

They lived together for many years as if they were sisters, sharing one large bedroom; however, each woman had her own bed and own space. They understood each other well as they were engaged in the same 'profession': prostitution. They thought it was unusual, but neither of them was surprised when both of them became pregnant around the same time. Their babies were expected to be born a few days apart. Both women had an uneventful pregnancy and looked forward to motherhood. As time drew closer for the birth of their babies, the women were regularly seen out shopping, buying all the essentials for the babies.

Both women gave birth to sons, days apart. They took turns to babysit each other's baby; this shared responsibility made them grow even closer.

The women were advised against co-sleeping with their babies, especially if they had a drink or were tired. All the reports from the health professional noted that both babies were gaining weight and developing well. One night one of the women was so tired she fell asleep, with her baby in bed. Unaware of her actions, the woman rolled over on her baby. She awoke frantically in the middle of the night and was mortified at the sight of her lifeless baby. Not wishing to cause a panic or to be heard by her flatmate, she tiptoed and swapped the babies.

A few hours later the other woman awoke to feed her baby, she found a lifeless child in the Moses basket. In shock, she screamed and wept inconsolably. Then in the midst of her distressed, in a moment of clarity, she soberly recalled that her flatmate had gone to sleep with her baby in bed. She remembered the clothing her baby wore when she put him to sleep and concluded that the deceased baby was not hers.

In the early hours of the morning a bitter argument ensued over the ownership of the living baby. Argument was heard in their living space, which was unusual for these women since they were always able to resolve minor squabbles. The quarrel was quite heated and none of them got any sleep. They agreed that there would be no justice without the intervention of a judge, so they sought the king to handle the matter.

Early the next day both women took the babies to King Solomon. They told the king their versions of the story and each claimed that the living baby was hers. King Solomon had no access to a laboratory and a deoxyribonucleic acid (DNA) test couldn't be done. The king sympathetically listened to their arguments then asked his servant to bring him a sword. His decision was to divide the living baby with his sword and give each woman a half. The biological mother of the living baby was greatly moved with compassion; she then asked the king to give her child to the other woman, sparing the boy's life. The other woman was overcome by excitement, completely agreeing with the king to have the baby divided.

She was uncaring and unsympathetic, not being concerned about the loss of a life if the king should kill the innocent baby. She was coldhearted, selfish, and callous. The wise king knew, no mother with a heart of love would want her baby to be divided into two. He realised that the other woman was the mother of this little boy.

The rightful mother had a heart of compassion, willing to go home with a dead baby and bury him as if he was her baby.

This is an illustration of two groups of people; one group would rather give away their own than have it destroyed. Another group would destroy their own and campaign for the destruction of someone else's belonging, calling it equality.

Her love and compassion influenced King Solomon's decision, as a man filled with wisdom; his judgment ruled in her favour since no loving mother wanted her baby to be divided in two. She was a wise mother who displayed the love of God, with mercy and compassion.

Modern-Day Reality: The cliché 'half a loaf is better than none', does not apply. Never settle for less.

CHAPTER 55

MAACAH 2

(2 Chronicles 11:20-23; 2 Samuel 3:2-3;
2 Samuel 18:9-18)

She stood out among her contenders as her husband's favourite wife.

Image the competition, being one of seventy eight wives. What made her unique? She stood out among her contenders as her husband's favourite wife. Maacah was her husband's first love; it was a special privilege to see him on a regular basis. Her husband, King Rehoboam divided his time among so many other wives, that he saw some of them less frequently. She came from a kingly lineage; her grandfather was King David and her father was Absalom.

Negativity and woes characterised her childhood. Maacah was raised by a father who murdered his own brother. Her father was obsessed by the desire to become King. He sought to overthrow his father, which led to his untimely death since he was caught by the branch of an oak tree while riding his horse. Her father Absalom did not have a good relationship with his relations, however it would appear that he absolute adored his mother and honoured her by called his daughter Maacah. The same name as his mother.

Maacah was married to her first cousin, the son of her uncle. Rehoboam, her husband, was the son of King Solomon. Maacah and Rehoboam had a good marriage despite all the competition with other rivals, which was quite acceptable. The king had great respect for her. She was the 'distinguished' wife of King Rehoboam. Abijah, Attai, Ziza, and Shelomith were the four children produced from their union. Undoubtedly, Rehoboam inherited great wealth from Solomon, since his entitlement as firstborn was a double portion. Rehoboam had twenty-eight (28) sons altogether. He distributed this wealth to all his children and also gave his first son Abijah a double portion of his riches. Maacah and Rehoboam spent time with their family regularly as they groomed Abijah for the throne.

King Rehoboam put Abijah in charge of all his brothers, making him heir to the throne. Maacah supported her son as she was aware of the dangers he faced. The road to the throne was plagued with sibling rivalry. Abijah experienced challenges such as hatred, malice, jealousy, and murder.

She was a granddaughter of King David and the niece of King Solomon, Maacah knew the challenges of kings and their kingdoms. She knew the full history of all the assassinations and evil within the family in pursuit of kingship. She was an outstanding model in her son's life as she taught him many principles of success. She supported her husband, knowing that his other wives would attempt to have their sons reign as king. During the reign of King Rehoboam there was war in Judah, causing a rift in the kingdom. King Rehoboam died and Abijah succeeded him as king. Maacah felt that her grandmother was unsuccessful in raising her father in the fear of the Lord. Her determination to turn away from the ungodly influence was evident when her son ascended to the throne, becoming king of Israel. Her descendant commenced generations of exceptional kings.

Modern-Day Reality: Determination to succeed is a positive driving force.

CHAPTER 56

ZERUAH

(1 Kings 11:26–43; 12:1–25;
2 Chronicles 13:6–7)

An amazing mother, a single parent teaching her son loyalty,
discipline, trust, and honesty.

She was a descendant of Ephraim, the son of Joseph, one of the patriarchs. Her husband Nebat was an officer in King Solomon's army. They lived in the town of Zeredah. Zeruah and her husband had a son called Jeroboam. Jeroboam was born around the same time as King Solomon's son Rehoboam. Jeroboam and Rehoboam were often mistaken as bothers. In some instances, they were referred to as twins. Zeruah's husband was hardworking and trustworthy. He worked hard to maintain his reputation and the king's trust. It was under strange circumstances that Nebat died suddenly at a young age. Zeruah became a very young widow overcome by grief and sorrow, she spent months weeping for her deceased husband. As time passed, her grief and pain became numb. Zeruah made a decision to forget the past and move on. Her motivation was to raise her son in a godly way, she remained unmarried and a single parent. Zeruah invested time and energy in her son as she prepared him for the challenges in his life. King Solomon expressed his gratitude to Zeruah and her son Jeroboam after the death of Nebat.

As a gesture of goodwill and an expression of his empathy over the loss of his father, the king put Jeroboam in charge of the city of Ephraim and Manasseh.

King Solomon was surprised and overly impressed with Jeroboam's upbringing. The young man was disciplined, hardworking, and trustworthy like his father.

*Jeroboam performed his duty responsibly. His journey home daily, was through the street of Ephraim. One day on his way home Ahijah, the prophet, met him halfway. They sat by the side of the road and spoke about strategies to manage the two cities and future plans. Jeroboam became perplexed when Ahijah took off his new coat and tore it into twelve pieces. Initially, Jeroboam was lost for words, he then asked Abijah, **'Why you are tearing your expensive new coat?'** Ahijah replied, **'It will become clearer soon. Just take ten pieces of this coat. The Lord has taken the kingdom away from King Solomon and you will be the king over ten of these tribes. This will happen when Solomon dies'.** Jeroboam went home and could not escape reality as he tried to process his thoughts. He was still shaken as he related to his mother the happenings of the day.*

The news got to King Solomon that Jeroboam would be king. Solomon felt threatened and was no longer caring and empathetic. He was furious and sent his soldiers to kill Jeroboam. While Solomon was planning to murder Jeroboam, his mother Zeruah told him that King Solomon would not be happy with the news, so she made arrangements for him to escape. Jeroboam fled to Egypt to preserve his life. He sent a message to King Solomon, informing him that he no longer wanted to be in charge of the two cities. Many years later, when King Solomon died, the people sent for him.

The people asked Rehoboam, who succeeded his father as king, to make their work lighter. He said he would reply to them in three days. King Rehoboam asked the senior men what he should do about the people's request. They told him to listen to the people and honour their request. Then he asked the younger men, who told him that the people were idle and needed more work to do. So he listened to the young men and made their work much harder. The people revolted and refused to have anything to do with David's kingdom. They then made Jeroboam king over the ten tribes.

Zeruah was a single mother who supported her son and raised him as a disciplined, trustworthy young man. Her son was chosen to be the king of the divided kingdom. In Israel it was the son of the King who would normally succeed his father on the throne. However, Zeruah's son became king even though he was not entitled to the throne; none of his ancestors reigned.

Zeruah was an amazing mother, a single parent teaching her son loyalty, discipline, trust, and honesty. She 'unknowingly' groomed her son to reign on the throne of Israel.

She was a wise woman making sacrifices for her son, ensuring that his life was saved from the wrath and envious plans of the king. Her success could be attributed to the fact that she raised a 'godly' son, preparing him to sit on the throne.

Modern-Day Reality: Success can be derived from what you already have.

CHAPTER 57

Azubab

(1 Chronicles 3:10; 2 Chronicles 20:31;
14:1–15; 15:1–19; 16:1–13)

Azubab was an integral part of her son's success;
she cradled and nurtured a champion.

A polytheistic nation would aptly describe the nation of Judah. They had constructed sacred altars everywhere to worship false gods. The nation was noncompliant with God's divine requirements; serving both the true and Living God and idols made by their own hands. Their apostasy evoked God's wrath as the people drifted further and further away from Him. The kingdom of Israel was divided into two. Azubab, daughter of Shilhi, lived with her husband, King Asa, they governed Judah. This royal couple had a son whom they knew would ascend to the throne to become Judah's next king.

She and her husband gave much thought about how they could make a difference.

Azubab and Asa:

- *were dwelling in the middle of a nation that served many gods.*
- *started a major construction enterprise, building high walls to protect the cities.*
- *repaired the broken altars and replaced the furnishings of the temple.*
- *created unity among the many Israelites living in Judah. Asa was a respected king; the people saw that he pleased God.*

King Asa had a big celebration for God. He had trumpets and singing, as they promised God, they would always ask Him for instructions first. They made a covenant with God not to follow the ungodly nations. God honoured His agreement and there was no war in Judah for many years under their reign.

Asa, wishing to honour God and keep his covenant, dethroned his mother Maacah because she made an idol called Asherah. The king completely destroyed the idols, burning them. He was determined to serve God and to rid the kingdom of idolatry. Asa and Azubab had a son called Jehoshaphat. They raised their son in a godly manner, he ascended the throne, after the death of his father. Jehoshaphat prayed to God and asked for help against his enemies, he fought against them, prevailing every time. God gave him unusual strategies to fight his enemies by asking them to form a choir and practice a song. They had an excellent practise session: their voices harmonised, the enemies were confused and they started to fight among themselves. There were numerous fatalities and casualties; they were perplexed by their own actions. There was no explanation why they resorted to self destruction.

Azubab was an integral part of her son's success; she cradled and nurtured a champion. She knew that her son would not ascend to the throne based on his rights as first born son, since the monarchy was a much sought-after position. However, integrity and loyalty were necessary qualifications to ascend to the throne. Jehoshaphat's success was attributed to his parents who taught him the ways of God in an ungodly era. Azubab served God in truthfulness and was a godly example to her son.

Modern-Day Reality: Success, a great legacy for future generations.

CHAPTER 58

AN INDEBTED WIDOW

(2 Kings 4:1–7)

Her situation changed from a negative balance and indebtedness to
owning assets and great wealth.

H er story made headline news, however she could only be
described by her circumstances. No one knew her real name
or the name of her husband. An attempt to identify her statistically,
would fall into the category of widows firstly, then widows with two
sons. She had been through many crises, including the death of her
husband. She knew about struggle. In biblical times health and social
service were a national agenda; looking after the widow and the fatherless. She inherited a huge debt after losing her husband; this debt was
her personal responsibility as the state took care of her needs and those
of her sons.

The widow:

- was expected to find monies to liquidate this debt.
- pleaded with her creditors for another week to acquire the money to pay her debts.
- had no idea where that money was coming from. The creditors were no longer swayed by her tactics and sent the debt collectors to her doorstep. They were coming to take her sons and sell them as slaves to pay her debts.
- was at her breaking point and needed serious answers and instant solutions.

This woman owed a tidy sum, which would be equivalent to the price of two slaves or the value of her two sons. In Jewish culture the price of a slave was thirty pieces of silver (or 120 days' pay for each slave). She owed sixty pieces of silver (or 240 day's work) to her creditors, equivalent to one year's wage. She felt isolated as none of her friends were willing to help her at this crucial time in her life.

The only person interested in her story was the man of God. She told the prophet that her husband was a God-fearing man, but he was dead. He accumulated huge debts while he was alive. The people whom he owed came to repossess all that remained; the heartbroken woman pleaded with the prophet for a **miracle***.*

Elisha the prophet asked her what she had left. She knew exactly what the prophet was asking her: did she have anything to use for financial gain/profit, or what could be used for a miracle? She knew that faith alone was not sufficient to produce her miracle. Faith needed a vessel or a vehicle to travel in, so that it could cover distance. Her cupboard was scant except for a bottle of oil, which she probably used sparingly to anoint herself and her sons daily as they prayed. This was insufficient to pay this debt or she would not have been in this embarrassing situation. However, she knew that a bottle of oil with faith and obedience to God was the key to her debt crisis. It was the key to the lack and poverty in her family. The widow obeyed the prophet and went to all her neighbours to borrow bottles. The neighbours became suspicious of her and these empty bottles that she was acquiring. Her house was filled with empty bottles of various sizes and description.

The widow, ensuring it was a family occasion, had her sons join her. As the door closed behind her, she poured oil from the bottle she had in her cupboard. She poured into one bottle that she borrowed, and then the next, until the last bottle that she had borrowed was filled. As the oil got to the rim of the last bottle she had borrowed, it stopped completely. God's miraculous working power excited her. She never assumed she knew what to do with the oil, but she sought the advice of the prophet for the next instruction. Elisha's instruction: go and sell the oil, pay your debts. and put the rest of the money in the bank for future usage. This family experienced one of the greatest miracles in their time of lack. The widow understood God's economy: **God could use little, even a little oil, with a little faith to produce gallons.**

Her situation changed from a negative balance and indebtedness to owning assets and great wealth. She went from severe poverty and embarrassment to becoming rich and wealthy overnight. The widow exercised great faith in crucial moments. She did not sit down to tell people how difficult her situation was. There was no blaming her circumstances on a dead husband. Widowhood, single parenthood and indebtedness did not affect her mental stability. Her bills were not paid, yet she believed that at the lowest moments in her life, she could make a difference.

It sometimes seems easier to be negative and to accept defeat when life appears to deal an unfair blow—or in her case, multiple blows. She sought help and carefully selected the source of her help by going to a real man of God who was interested in her and the circumstances in which she found herself. She became a success story because she believed, obeyed the prophet, and exercised great faith in God.

Modern-Day Reality: Nothing ventured, nothing gained.

CHAPTER 59

THE CAPTIVE GIRL FROM ISRAEL/NAAMAN WIFE'S MAID

(2 Kings 5:1–27)

She chose to be a part of the solution.

S lave trafficking was the norm in Israel. The Arameans went to steal from the nation of Israel; in the process they captured a teenager and sold her as a slave. Her name was not mentioned. As a foreigner and a slave she had no status in a foreign land; she was classified as an **immigrant** or a **refugee**. She lived with the enemies of her ancestors and had no choice in the matter. Her master was Naaman the king. She realised that amidst the fame, wealth, power, and position, he had a serious health challenge. Naaman's entire body oozed; it was putrid and he experienced excruciating pain. He had very little comfort in life and sometimes wished he would die.

This slave girl was sympathetic to her master's painful cries. She heard him repeatedly wish he was dead. His sickness and outlook on life made her job tedious.

She:

- saw the unhappiness and distress in her master's household even though they were wealthy.
- was a wise woman and knew exactly where Naaman could find help.
- knew in Israel people like Naaman visited the prophet and they were healed from any disease.
- thought about it for some weeks, but did not think she was authorised to give advice to her master. The moment finally came and she could not hold back anymore.

One day, as her mistress, Naaman's wife, was giving her the instructions of the day, the slave girl found courage to speak to her. She was shy and felt that her mistress might not accept what she had to say. The opinion of slaves was never given credence. The girl told her mistress she knew how Naaman could recover from his disease. This was news to Naaman's wife, so the mistress showed interest in what the slave girl had to say.

If Naaman could meet the prophet in Samaria, he would be healed of his disease. Naaman's wife found this simple and was happy with what the slave girl said. Going to her husband's bedside she repeated the words of the slave girl. A proud Naaman looked at his wife and wondered if she was losing her mind. He told her arrogantly, it was beneath his dignity to lower himself by visiting a religious fanatic in Samaria. Naaman's pride dominated, so he concluded, if the people heard about him going to see a religious figure, they would laugh at him. The king preferred to remain in his leprous state than to see the prophet. He didn't believe that the idea would work. The thought of humbling himself and visiting the prophet angered Naaman. Naaman's condition deteriorated as weeks passed by. He then decided to do something about the information. Naaman humbled himself and visited the prophet. The advised because the essential factor for his healing.

This captive girl was resourceful. She heard of the prophet's miracles; the dead being raised to life and great abundance in the time of famine. She did not concentrate on herself and her needs, but she shared vital information that was necessary to bring about miracles.

She was trafficked, living away from her family, friends and her familiar environment, as foreigner in a strange land. She decided against wallowing in self pity by blaming Naaman and his wife for her situation; instead she chose to be a channel of blessings. She chose to be a part of the solution instead of the problem.

Naaman was healed when he obeyed God. He made the greatest confession, there was no God in all the earth except in Israel. The slave girl became a missionary by introducing Naaman to the prophet Elisha. Her greatest moment came when Elisha then introduced her master to God. The entire family trusted in God. Peace and tranquility reigned in Naaman's house. The slave girl was promoted by her mistress and lived among them, since she was well liked and respected.

Modern-Day Reality: Shared information can bring life and healing to all.

CHAPTER 60

THE SHUNAMITE WOMAN

(2 Kings 4:8–37; 8:1–6)

She held on to Elisha until he stopped his meeting...

S he attracted such popularity among the villagers since she was the most hospitable woman in Shunem. It was of little significance to her whether or not the guests came from nearby villages or farther away. Her house was purpose built with extra rooms to accommodate guests. Elisha, a man of God, had just returned from seeing Elijah the prophet, taken up into heaven. He had received twice the anointing of Elijah; and was ready to do the work of God.

While visiting Shunem, Elisha looked for a room to spend the night and all the villagers recommended one house, that of the Shunamite woman. He felt welcomed at her house. She prepared him a sumptuous meal and allowed him to stay in the guest quarters. Elisha found her caring, friendly, and helpful. Despite the biblical account of the many great things that she did, her name nor that of her husband was not recorded.

Elisha, being overwhelmed by her hospitality, decided to stop by her home every time he came to Shunem. He became her regular house guest.

The woman:

- thought about how she could create a unique atmosphere befitting a prophet.
- wanted to make the man of God **comfortable**.
- discussed it with her husband and built a self-contained room in the loft of their house. Equipping the room with all the furnishing that the prophet needed, Elisha was touched by this woman's innovation.

Elisha visited the family in Shunem as usual. On this occasion he found a room prepared for him with a unique personal touch. He stayed overnight and slept comfortably. Elisha was greatly appreciative of the couple's kindness. Thinking how he could express his gratitude to them for their selfless deeds, Elisha asked the woman if she would like him to put her name forward to the king's honour list. She was humble and did not want to leave her home to live next to the palace. She wanted to live among her own people; she declined the promotion to sit in the king's palace. She never focused on her own needs. Elisha was not aware of her social or family history, and he did not know that the woman was childless as she never focussed on her childlessness. Her kindness towards Elisha was genuine, with no ulterior motives or thoughts of a reward. She was convinced that her kind deed was the right thing to do. *She knew it was more rewarding to be a giver than a receiver.*

Elisha's servant told him that the woman had no children. In the next conversation, Elisha informed the couple that they would become proud parents in one year's time. One year later the couple had a son, just as Elisha promised. The boy had a normal childhood. He spent lots of his time with his father as they enjoyed farming together.

The boy and his father went out and he complained to his father about having a severe headache. The boy started to vomit, and then he became weak and malaise. His father's first thought, it could be **meningitis**. *A servant was called to take the boy home quickly so that his mother could look after him. His mother gave him all the medicine she had and kept vigil at his bedside. Eventually, the boy's condition deteriorated and he died. Refusing to accept death or to give up on her son, his mother made a great statement of faith. She climbed up to Elisha's loft and placed her child on his bed. This woman heard words from Satan, which she completely ignored; they were words of discouragement and deception. She sent her servant ahead of her to fetch Elisha. Even in her distress, she was determined to speak to Elisha, so she ran to meet him although he was miles away.*

She met him on Mount Carmel and held on to his feet firmly. Elisha saw the woman's distress as she poured out her grief to him. He was in the middle of a spiritual meeting, so the most logical action was, to ask his servant to take his walking stick and lay it on the dead boy. Elisha believed the boy would come **back to life again**. *This woman was not interested in Elisha's servant and the walking stick. She was resolute, refusing to take no for an answer. She held on to Elisha until he stopped his meeting and returned with her to raise her son from the dead.*

The Shunamite woman:

- *was overwhelmed by grief and loss as any mother would, yet she saw it as a great opportunity for a miracle.*
- *refused to be short-changed.*
- *knew how to stay with the man of God until her situation changed.*
- *felt that Elisha's servant with the walking stick was not adequate for the kind of miracle that she anticipated from God.*

Elisha brought the revival meeting to a halt and went back to this woman's house where he found the dead boy. He restored the boy to life. She was a mother who would not settle for her son, the miracle child God gave her, to die prematurely. **This woman knew that God is a miracle worker.**

Elisha continued to visit her home. He told her, 'take your family and go to Philistine, there would be a famine in Shunem'. She obeyed and lived among the Philistines for seven years. On her return, she visited the king to reclaim her property. Much to her surprise, her name was first on the king's list for honour, although she had refused this honour many years previously.

One day the king called his servant to an important meeting, as he wanted to find out what the prophet Elisha had done in the land of Shunem. It was by sheer coincidence that while the servant was relating the story about the boy who was raised to life, the woman and her son were knocking at the king's door, rather desperate and needy. In the Jewish culture, after been away for seven years, one could have their properties restored. A command was given by the king for the woman to have her property restored, and she was expected to receive all the profit made from her land since the day she left.

Life is not without its challenges. This woman experienced child-lessness, then the loss of her son. However, God raised him from the dead. Her property, house and lands were taken; because of a famine she was relocated to the land of the Philistines. God took care of her for seven years while living among her enemies.

Modern-Day Reality: The magnitude of the trials faced is indicative of the magnitude of the anticipated miracles.

CHAPTER 61

Jezebel

(1 Kings 16:29–33; 18:17–19; 19:1–5;
21:1–28; 2 Kings 9:8–10; 22; 30–37;
Revelation 2:20–23)

Jezebel set herself up as a final authority in the land.
She displayed characteristics that God required of His people…

King Ahab lived a life of splendour in an exquisite palace with his wife Jezebel. She was a princess, the daughter of Ethbaal the King of Sidon. The palace had a beautiful exterior, marvellous garden, and immaculate interior. Naboth's home was located next to the palace. Being an ordinary man, he was not qualified to own properties or live next to the king. His garden bordered the palace on the north. He inherited the property as a family legacy. It has been within the family for many decades, and was sentimental. His meticulous nature meant that the garden was always neat and well-kept, he was the sole gardener. When he was not working arduously in his garden, he would spend his leisure time relaxing in his hammock, as it swayed leisurely in the wind. The king, along with many of the villagers was envious of Naboth. His garden boasted of picturesque views and grandeur. King Ahab looked out of his palace windows regularly, being overcome by jealousy; he thought, *such a garden should belong to the king and no one else.*

The king had ulterior motives when he invited Naboth for afternoon tea. Naboth felt honoured and accepted the king's invitation; he attired himself with his best outfit. The king was quite welcoming, as they spoke about life in Jezreel and how Naboth felt about living next to the palace. Then King Ahab propositioned Naboth to give up his garden so that it could become the estate of the palace. He was offered a large sum of money or another garden. Refusing to dispose of his family's legacy, Naboth declined.

King Ahab could not process the thought of being rejected, since he always secured the cooperation of his subjects. The king failed to recognise his authority over the land, since the lands in the kingdom indirectly belonged to him, including Naboth's garden. Ahab's anger was displayed by ignoring his wife, refusing food, and going to bed sulking like a child. Jezebel, being sensitive to her husband's emotions, knew he was declined an offer. King Ahab wept as he related to her about Naboth's blatant refusal to give him the garden in exchange for money or for another garden.

Jezebel's true character sprang to life as she rebuked her husband, telling him **kings weren't wimps. Kings in Israel exercised authority and had the final say. It was unacceptable to say no to the king.** *Taking matters into her own hands, she devised a plan.*

Late that night Jezebel went to the king's office and wrote a few letters. She then signed them in her husband's name and sealed them with his seal. The content of the letters were deadly and every government leader in the land received one. Since it bore the king's name, the command had to be carried out. A few days later Naboth was murdered.

That same day Jezebel and Ahab took possession of Naboth's garden. They celebrated their achievement for a long time. This was not their only evil act, as the duo committed scores of wicked actions, causing them to bring a curse upon their families. Their prolonged evil acts also brought their lives to a tragic end under terrible circumstances.

Evil people are revisited by evil deeds; whereas people who are blessed with the blessings of God are blessed for generations to come.

God was at work in the land through a great prophet called Elijah, who lived in the time of King Ahab and Jezebel; he was mightily used by God to perform many miracles.

- Barren women were able to have children.
- The dead were brought back to life.
- Three years of drought ended with a great downpour of rain as he commanded.

In a contest to show God's power, Elijah stood up against the enemies and prayed for God to perform great miracles. God sent fire down from heaven, burning a pile of wood heavily drenched in water in a pool. He challenged false worship by killing the prophets of Baal, a false god. Jezebel was deeply committed to the worship of false gods; she had a celebration party for eight hundred and fifty (850) prophets of Baal and Asherah who dined at her table.

Jezebel not only worshipped false gods and associated with false prophets, she practised witchcraft. Jezebel *hated* God and the prophets of God. She had Elijah running for his life by sending death threats to him. Elijah was an expert in the field of the miraculous. He was great at interceding for others; he also saw God do the impossible to defend His people. However, Elijah lost all self-confidence and all trust in the power of God. When threatened, he fled to a lonely place, desiring to die.

Jezebel disguised herself by painting her face and changing her hairstyle. She posed by her window since she felt her enemies would not recognise her. Her enemies approached the window and saw through her disguise. They ordered that Jezebel be thrown from her window. They were obedient since disobedience would result in consequences for the entire house. The servants threw her out of the window. A horse galloped by, trampling her. Her body was dismantled and some parts were never found.

Jezebel was mentioned in the book of Revelation as a spirit of sexual exploitation, idolatry, and godlessness. Those who possess the spirit of Jezebel were given time to recant from their evil or suffer and die if they continued in their evil ways.

What then makes Jezebel so influential and powerful?

She knew:

- *the authority of a king.* The evil letter that she wrote was distributed throughout the land. If she wrote a good letter, the same principle applied.
- *the power of a king* when her husband, who was the king, did not know his own power.
- *how to use the king's* approval, seal, and signature.

Jezebel knew the power and authority she possessed in the city of Jezreel. Her threatening messages to Elijah were piercing so he ran away, asking God to allow him to die. He felt he could not survive the queen's diabolical threat.

She displayed fearlessness, a characteristic God required of His people. Elijah knew God did many great miracles through him and God honoured his request. He acted in fear and never asked God to help him defeat Jezebel.

Jezebel was wicked but she used every godly principle that God has given to us. As God's people we have the king's letter, the word of God and His promises. We have the blood of Jesus and the Holy Spirit. We can give the word of God an assignment and see it work. The king's seal, which is the working of the Holy Spirit in our lives, entitles us to God's favour. King Ahab did not recognise who he was and what he had, his wife Jezebel knew the power and authority that kingship commands.

God's people suffer if they fail to realise who they are in Christ and the power or authority they possess when they step out on the word of God. Jezebel demonstrated in her domain, there was tremendous power in the spoken or written word.

The word of God is sharp and powerful. The spoken word of God will not return empty but it will accomplish great things. Elijah did not realise he was not meant to run away from Jezebel's wicked threat. He had the power to speak God's word, which was an antidote for Jezebel's diabolical plan.

She was a wicked leader; her example was duplicated by her children, who learnt about idolatry, greed, hate, and murder. Her lifestyle and actions were in total defiance of God's will and purpose, so the end of her life was shameful; being stripped of power, she died a gruesome death.

Modern-Day Reality: Evil and unrighteous deeds never profit.

CHAPTER 62

QUEEN ALTALIAH

(2 Kings 8:16–29; 9:1–29; 10:6–11; 11:1–20;
2 Chronicles 21:1–20; 22:1–12; 23:1–21)

Ungodly, evil upbringing often overpowers godly influence.

S he was indeed a chip off the old block. Her life, without a doubt, reflected the home from which she came. Her mother was Jezebel and her father was Ahab. Lust, malice, theft, gross wickedness, divisiveness, coup and bloodbaths are all characteristics of their reign. Altaliah was married to King Jehoram. However, it was paradoxical that much unlike Altaliah, Jeroham was raised by a godly family from a succession of righteous kings.

Jehoram:

- was the son of King Jehoshaphat, a God-fearing man from the tribe of Judah.

- was taught the ways of God by his godly father.
- received wealth, which included silver, gold, and lands from his father.
- was given the kingdom because he was the eldest son. However, he was influenced by the house of Ahab and became evil and selfish.

Jehoram turned his back on all the godly principles his father taught him and lived recklessly. He built places of worship to false gods in the hills of Judah and led God's people away from Him. One day he had a rude awakening when he received a letter from Elijah the prophet.

Dear Jehoram,

This is a message from God whom your father served. You did not follow the way of Jehoshaphat your father and Asa your grandfather, who were the two kings of Judah before you. You followed the kings of Israel. You lead the people of Judah and Jerusalem into sin just as Ahab and his family did. You killed your brothers, as they were better than you. So God will punish you severely. He will punish your wives, your children, and you will lose everything you own. You will suffer from a disease in your bowel and you will never get better but your bowels will fall out.

Shortly after that the Arabs and the Philistines seized all of King Jehoram's wealth, his sons and daughters. Only his youngest son Ahaziah was left alive. King Jehoram developed bowel problems and suffered for two years, as Elijah prophesied. He had excruciating pains, which was not relieved by any form of painkillers. He suffered until finally his bowels fell out and he died. At his death all the people were relieved of the burden brought by his wicked reign. No one was sad and there was no state funeral for this king.

After King Jehoram's death, his youngest son Ahaziah, whose mother was Altaliah, became king of Judah and Jerusalem. He was influenced by his mother's negativity and wrongdoings. He did evil and was numbered with those wicked kings. He completely forgot what happened to his father.

King Ahaziah reigned at the same time as his brother-in-law Joram, the king of Jezreel. There was a period of upheaval and King Joram was wounded in battle. When King Ahaziah got the news he thought King Joram would die; he went to Jezreel to visit his brother-in-law. Jehu, the son of Jehosphaphat, was anointed king of Israel. Jehu knew that the house of Ahab would be a threat to his kingdom, so before ascending to the throne he killed all of Ahab's family, including Ahaziah and his followers.

Altaliah realised that most of the men who were eligible to the throne were dead. She thought if she destroyed all eligible males she would become queen. So she pursued her plan, destroying all the male heirs to the kingdom, making herself queen of Judah by default. In the meantime Jehosheba, who was the daughter of Altaliah, realised that the males were going to be destroyed. She took her one-year-old nephew Joash, son of Ahaziah, and hid him from her cruel mother. She did this in order to spare his life, Joash and his nurse were taken to a private room in a secret location.

Jehosheba was the aunt of Joash and she was married to a priest whose name was Jehoiada. Jehosheba and her husband took Joash, hiding him in the temple until his seventh birthday. In those times, when someone's life was threatened they could go to the altar in the temple, the priest would protect them and make sure they were safe. While in the temple for safety, one's life was spared since blood shed was not allowed within the sanctity of the holy place. Altaliah became queen; after reigning for six years, she felt there was no threat to the monarchy. She ruled with confidence, thinking her corrupted actions were forgotten. Jehoiada decided that it was time for Joash to become king. He had a meeting with all the officers first, then he anointed Joash at age seven to be king.

Queen Altaliah did not know that her grandson was alive or the plans to crown him as king. She was busy, pre-occupied with her royal duties when she heard the trumpet blowing in the temple. She recognized the sound, as one of jubilance, so she went to investigate. Upon entering the temple she was flabbergasted by what she saw. Her seven-year-old grandson, whom she thought dead, was being crowned king. She tore her dress and shouted, **'Traitor! Traitor!'** The vengeful officers wanted to kill her immediately, but the sanctity of the temple demanded purity and no bloodshed. They waited until she came to the Horse Gate and killed her. There was a bigger celebration in Judah and Jerusalem, followed by peace.

Altaliah:

- was brought up in a palace.
- saw her parents' wickedness and knew that they died cruel deaths.
- was more evil than her ancestors.
- could not afford to stay away from power and was willing to massacre all of her relatives to ascend to the throne.

- did not live long to enjoy life in the palace.
- thought she would go completely unchallenged.

Queen Altaliah was coldhearted, power-hungry, self-centred, and had her eyes on the throne at the expense of the lives of her children and grandchildren. Sometimes children are a replica of their parents. She was evil and did not portray a good example of life and living. Altaliah's evil lifestyle was reflective of her upbringing. She was married to a young man who was raised in a godly environment. He became as corrupt as she was. Ungodly, evil upbringing, often overpowers godly influence.

Altaliah's story teaches us that evil never succeeds. Those who live evil lives, also die horrible deaths in the height of what seems as conquest and success. Wickedness and ungodliness along with wicked and ungodly people are short-lived. Altaliah had six years of fame as she ruled, not realising that her reign would come to an abrupt end.

However, goodness never goes unrecognised. If it's not rewarded in one's lifetime, it will pass on to future generations.

Modern-Day Reality: Willing to chart the most evil course to achieve temporary fame and power.

CHAPTER 63

Jehosheba

(2 Chronicles 22:10–12;
2 Kings 11:1–21; 12:1–20)

Determined to preserve a royal heir for the future.

Jehosheba was the sister of a king who was murdered and the daughter of evil Altaliah. In unusual circumstances, despite the indescribable grief and insurmountable pain, she switched from a natural response of brokenness to becoming proactive and life-saving.

Jehosheba:

- displayed unprecedented patriotism.
- snatched her baby nephew Joash, who was among the king's sons destined to be killed.
- was determined to preserve a royal heir for the future.

After her hideous actions of massacring all her sons, she made herself queen. It became apparent that Queen Altaliah would kill her grandson also as he was entitled to become the next king. Jehosheba hid Joash and his nurse in a bedroom in the temple, where they were safe. Joash lived in the temple for six years, a place free of cruelty, where he could not be harmed. Under Jewish culture, a person whose life was in danger must hold on to the horn of the altar and no harm could befall him or her. Joash living in the temple was equal to holding on to the horn of the altar to save his life since bloodshed could not occur within the temple walls.

On Joash's seventh birthday, the priest enlisted the loyalty of the centurion as he made Joash king. The centurion was expected to protect and defend the juvenile king. There was heavy security in the temple as Joash was crowned king. The priest anointed Joash and put the crown on his head. Noise from the jubilant celebration in the temple was heard from a distance as they blew the trumpet and shouted, 'Long live the king!'

The queen, not knowing what was happening, heard the celebration and wondered why she was excluded. She hurried to the temple; she almost collapsed in shock when she saw a young king and all present celebrating with exuberance. They blew the trumpet joyfully and shouted, 'Long live King Joash!'

The queen tore her clothes and screamed, 'Traitor, traitor!' as she was overthrown. Queen Altaliah and her followers were taken outside to be killed. There was peace in the land at the death of the wicked queen.

Joash's reign on the throne was more than purification from evil. He was the 'godliest' king in Israel since he spent six of his seven years living in the temple. For this meritorious achievement, Jehosheba kept a secret as she hid Joash in the temple, during the horrific reign of her mother. Jehosheba's brave actions saved the life of an heir to the throne. She must be credited for her boldness to counteract the plans of a notorious queen. Her bravery was remarkable, since she refused to be over whelmed by sorrow. The magnitude of sorrow she experienced, when all her brothers were murdered. She reacted as though she was completely anaesthetised to such genocide.

Jehosheba was the wife of Jehoiada, a godly priest, and was knowledgeable of the priestly role and life in the temple. She was a woman of prayer and knew how to advocate to God for His people. All the worshippers in the temple respected her.

Her benevolence to her nation was well known. She received accolades for charting a nation's course of history from doom and disaster to a pinnacle of success and victory. She must receive commendation and recognition for the sacrificial, selfless service rendered in her time; honouring God and her nation above herself.

Her intelligence and strategies for conquest must be recognised: she fought evil with good.

Modern-Day Reality: Patriotic, sacrificing self to save a nation.

CHAPTER 64

JABEZ'S MOTHER

(1 Chronicles 4:9–10)

... she chose a name that was an icon for the pains she experienced.

She was not a first-time mother and knew exactly what to expect in pregnancy and labour. This pregnancy was not different from her previous pregnancies, so her expectations were no different.

Jabez's mother:

- went into labour on the date expected and anticipated a quick delivery.
- was sadly mistaken.
- experienced the worst pain she ever had.

The pains of labour coupled with the prolonged duration had a weakening effect on her. She had only one wish, to get it over with and **die**. The pains she experienced in labour and childbirth were unbearable and she felt there was no other pain with such severity and intensity.

She:

- *was a descendant of Caleb of Judah. Judah was one of the twelve tribes of Israel. Her actual name is unknown. However, after her recovery from labour she held her son in her arms, giving him a name.*
- *wanted the meaning of his name to reflect the totality of her experience.*
- *wanted her experience engraved in her mind and the mind of others.*
- *was determined to relive her painful experience over and over again, she chose a name that was an icon for the pains she experienced. Therefore she named him **Jabez**, which meant **pain**.*

It must be taken into account that within the Jewish culture it was rather uncommon for names of sons to be given by mothers. This was a task performed by Jewish fathers. In her case she was the one who chose the name for her son Jabez. It is believed that she became a widow during her pregnancy. The intensity of her pains in labour could be a result of her effort to deal with overwhelming grief and sorrow. She was frustrated about raising her family as a single parent and the major adjustments she must make in her life. She envisaged the responsibility of taking on the roles of both parents and raising successful children as a mammoth task.

As a child, Jabez spent most of his time crying as he was constantly reminded that his name meant pain. He was hardly called by his real name.

The child felt he would never rise to be successful; he had low self-esteem. His mother did not realise that not only would she be reminded of the pains, but that her son would spend almost the rest of his life isolated and depressed because of his name. She later realised the error she had made when the damages were done. She had acted in complete ignorance. Her son became successful and wealthy when he asked God to change his disposition.

Jabez:

- was highly respected by all the people, more than all his brothers.
- was known in his community as a kind, caring, and humble person.
- wanted God to change the way people perceived him. He wanted his name to be synonymous with more than *pain*. His prayer was for God to change the negative concept associated with his name.
- cried out to God to bless him, give him wealth and protect him from evil. God heard his prayer and gave him his request.
- was the only one in his family who was referred to in the scripture.

She was a woman who feared God and taught her children the ways of God. Jabez knew he was disadvantaged and was determined to live above the expectations of society. His determination motivated him to draw closer to God and he became reputable. He allowed the teachings of his mother to develop in him as he became a mighty man in his time. His mother learnt from her mistake as she sought God's help. She stood in support of her son whose character changed from being wounded to well rounded.

Modern-Day Reality: Characteristics and confidence can also be found in a name.

CHAPTER 65

ABIJAH

(2 Kings 18:1–37)

In the midst of all this negativity there was a godly woman.

Not to feel left out or indifferent from the other nations around them, they became resolute and conformed to the ungodly practices. They did so by joining with the ungodly nations to worship false gods and offer sacrifices. God's people became utterly engrossed in their sacraments, burning their own children along with incense upon altars built to worship false gods. They had gone completely *away* from God's teachings. Their hearts became callous and unrepentant; they no longer worshipped the One and only God. Yet, in the midst of all this negativity there was Abijah, the daughter of Zechariah and the wife of King Ahaz. She was the wife of a godless king, but she became the mother of a godly king and champion called Hezekiah. His name was aptly chosen. It means *strength in God.*

The people of Israel were commanded by God to drive out the evil nations and get rid of their enemies, who were also the enemies of God.

However, these Israelites compromised and acted politically correct by saving the lives of their enemies. Their disobedience resulted in struggle with their enemies for hundreds of years. Their struggle was so immense that many, many kings ascended to the throne and lived reckless lives, like the ungodly nations around them. The lifestyle of the Israelites mimicked that of the nations, God had previously asked them to completely destroy. They forsook God's teachings and felt justified. As a result they were driven further and further away from God and became detached from the true God.

The kings led the people into unrighteousness by condoning idolatry, erecting altars and high places in honour of the many false gods.

Many years had passed. Numerous kings had reigned over Israel, yet God was not known as the Only God in Israel. There was a god for every purpose, occasion, and season; a god for protection, a god for prosperity, and a god for provision, etc.

A young Hezekiah succeeded his father Ahaz to the throne. It is believed that Hezekiah was greatly influenced by his mother. His father had failed to stamp out the ungodliness around him. The Israelites had served foreign gods for hundreds of years and the current generation knew only about worshipping false gods. Hezekiah removed the high places, demolished the sacred pillars, and cut down the wooden images. He got rid of the bronze serpent his ancestor Moses had made. He was one of the few kings recorded, in the history of the kings who did what was right.

Abijah, his mother, taught him Israel's history of the bronze serpent (Numbers 21:7–9). Israel had journeyed with this bronze serpent for many years. It was meant to be a symbol of God's faithfulness and never meant to be a replacement of God. However, Israel carried this symbol and worshiped it. Hezekiah remembered the First Commandment according to (Exodus 20:3–4), taught to him by his mother. God commanded Israel not to have any other God or to make any image with the semblance of creatures in heaven, on earth or in the seas.

Hezekiah's mother nurtured, guided, and instructed him in a godly manner, modelling godliness in her house. Abijah taught her son about Israel's history, including God giving them His laws.

'Hezie' as his parents called him was taught the *Ten Commandments*. They were displayed on the walls of his bedroom. Abijah saw greatness in her son and groomed him for the throne. Hezekiah however, saw faith in his mother and trusted the God of heaven. Hezekiah's reign was distinct; he purposed in his heart to be different. God was with him and prospered him. He stood up against kings who did not uphold God's word and conquered the Philistines. Israel's oppression was from the time of King David to Hezekiah's reign.

Abijah knew when she was pregnant, the son she was carrying would become a king. In Israel, quite often the first son succeeded his father on the throne. Abijah prayed for her son in her womb. She assigned him to solve the problem of godlessness in the nation of Israel. Abijah spoke positively over her son's life.

At his birth she pronounced blessings on him and encouraged every leadership potential in him. She spent time with Hezekiah in his formative years and helped him to build a godly foundation.

Hezekiah:

- completely eradicated years and years of history, traditions, culture and norms.
- trusted God and decreed a change.

- had strong opposition and death threats, but he stayed focused and resilient.
- Saw his enemies overthrown. 185,000 of them were massacred including the king of Assyria.

Hezekiah's father, Ahaz, was a good king, but Hezekiah was a great king. Hezekiah relied totally on the God of his mother. Abijah produced a son who was fearless and willing to trust God, even if it cost him his life. Producing a son of such caliber could only be possible with the prayer and influence of a godly and God-fearing mother. The saying holds true, behind every great man is a greater woman.

Modern-Day Reality: Raising godly children to assume royalty status is not automatic.

CHAPTER 66

HULDAH

(2 Kings 22:1–20; 1 Chronicles 6:13)

While everyone around her was in a state of apostasy,
she communicated with her God.

What a dilemma! Their most valuable document, the scroll, went missing. It seems unbelievable that the Israelites could not find all the laws and teachings. They had been through the worst demolition in their history. The magnificent edifice that governed and represented their fundamental belief was completely destroyed. To compound matters, none of the leaders had a copy of the laws. The Israelites forsook the word of God; they no longer read, taught, or obeyed it.

Huldah was one of the very few prophetesses at that time. She was married to Shallum, a priest from the tribe of Levi. Shallum's father was Tikvah, the son of Harhas (the keeper of the king's wardrobe). His job was to ensure that the king looked his best at all times.

*During this period of Israel's history, the people had gone **far away from God**. The people of Israel forsook God's law. The Israelites were* rebellious, disobedient and worshipped false gods; therefore God's wrath was evoked. They indulged in practices which contradicted God's nature, by erecting altars and burning incense to many false gods.

King Josiah was the leader at the time and was anxious about the evil around him. He knew that the people had forsaken God's law. Josiah consulted with Hilkiah, the priest, about the nation's apostasy. Hilkiah could not sleep; he went into the house of God to search for God's word. He searched until he rediscovered the book of the law in the house of the Lord. In his excitement he read it to all the people. Then he went back to the palace and read the book of the law to King Josiah. Josiah listened attentively; he became penitent and he tore his clothes and wept. The king could not comprehend the contents of the book, even though he felt it was not good news. So he sent Hilkiah to ask the Lord concerning the book that was found. King Josiah's action was one of humility; he repented, calling on the nation to return to God.

God always have a word for His people. Hilkiah was also unable to interpret the word God gave to the king and his people. He took a trip to Huldah, the prophetess who was God's spokeswoman in that era. Huldah was in contact with God and knew what God's plans were for His people. She had an intimate relationship with God and communicated with Him daily. She told the priest boldly to take this message back to King Josiah: 'God was unhappy with his people's actions, as they had gone far from His word. He would judge them and bring evil upon them until they were destroyed'. The priest was saddened by the words spoken by Huldah, but he took the word back to the king.

King Josiah took decisive actions by destroying the altars and putting away all the wicked people in the land. God sent another message, promising destruction on the land, but not during the reign of Josiah.

Huldah was different. Everyone around her was in a state of

apostasy, but she communicated with her God. God gave her messages for His people. She was used as God's powerful mouthpiece and spokeswoman, although it was not the norm for a woman. God is sovereign and He makes what seems impossible possible. At the most crucial moment in Israel's history, not even the priest knew God's plans for the nation, however God revealed Himself through Huldah.

Modern-Day Reality: To be used by God to accomplish His purpose requires availability.

CHAPTER 67

Vashti

(Esther 1:1–22; 2:1–4)

Never realised she was the prime example of what a wife should do.

Seemingly there was no greater honour in the land. She was elevated to the noblest place a woman could attain. Thousands of women vied for this high honour. Vashti was married to a king whose sphere of leadership spanned one hundred and twenty-seven countries. His kingdom stretched from India to Ethiopia in Africa, located in Shushan. It was normal for the king and his queen to entertain their workers and officers regularly.

The king and queen sponsored an exorbitant party in celebration of their third anniversary in the monarchy. All the important dignitaries in the lands were invited to the party, which lasted for six months.

When the six months was over, the king was well into the swing of partying and decided to have another six months of celebration in the palace garden. There were parties and celebrations within the palace grounds for the past twelve months, and the queen wanted the festivity to remain.

Queen Vashti organised a separate party for all the women who worked in the palace. There was music, dancing, lots of food, and the best wine.

The king:

- *became intoxicated.*
- *asked his servant to go and get his wife Queen Vashti; he wanted to pose with her. He also requested that she wear the most exquisite royal outfit and her crown.*
- *wanted her to come out and model for the crowd, displaying her beauty.*

Queen Vashti refused to model for the king. She thought this request was unreasonable, and sent a message back to her husband, declining his request.

The king became sober instantly when he realised that his wife refused to honour his request. He was humiliated, embarrassed, and insulted as no one in the kingdom disobeyed his orders. The party ended abruptly as the king sought advice from the wise men, his advisers.

The wise men:

- *told the king that Vashti's disobedience would be a bad precedent for all women.*
- *told the king that other women would hear about what Queen Vashti had done, thinking it was acceptable to disobey their husbands.*

- *advised the king to start looking for another queen, another wife who would be obedient.*

The king loved the advice and ended his relationship with Vashti immediately.

Vashti:

- *felt disgraced and devastated.*
- *never realised she was the prime example of what a wife should do.*
- *did not realise she would not be given another chance to be obedient to the king.*
- *was dethroned and the king started his search for a new bride, a queen who would love and honour him.*

Vashti was young and inexperienced; she took the advice of those who were not versed in royal protocol. She was ashamed and hid herself for months. She knew that everyone in the land would know of her folly.

Queen Vashti would certainly have acted wisely if she knew that her power, prestige, and position could be lost in a moment. She did not live up to her expectations, as one whose life must exemplify obedience to the king. Vashti displayed ignorance to royal protocol and an inability to live as a queen, she dishonoured her husband and was demoted.

Modern-Day Reality: Premature promotion without preparation leads to extinction.

CHAPTER 68

QUEEN ESTHER/HADASSAH

(Esther 2:1–7:10)

… they beamed with excitement at the opportunity of a lifetime…

Medians and Persians lived in a society bound by strict laws. Such laws were binding and impossible to change. Hadassah, otherwise known as Esther, was an orphan girl growing up in an era when law could only be changed by the king. Esther had royal ancestral links. She was a descendant of Kish, the father of King Saul, Israel's first king. Their origin was from the tribe of Benjamin, one of the twelve tribes of Israel.

She was adopted by her uncle Mordecai, in the times when Jews were slaves to the Medians and Persians. They lived among the people of Media and Persia for a very long time and their lifestyle reflected the nations that held them captive.

King Xerses was the reigning monarch at the time. He was in search of a new queen since his first wife operated outside of royal protocol and disgraced him. She blatantly refused *to model herself for her husband, his friends, and all the people of the land.*

The king asked his servant to advertise the position for a queen to replace his former queen. The criteria for a new wife stated *she must be a beautiful young virgin.* All of the young women in the land were beaming with excitement at the opportunity of a lifetime to become the next queen of Persia.

The atmosphere was illustrious as all the beautiful young virgins were bought to the king's palace. One of them would be selected as the next queen of Persia. The king did not want foul play, so he hired a eunuch (a man not interested in women) to screen the would-be queens. After a long and tedious search, Esther, an Israelite slave, was chosen. The king, not wishing for a repeat of Vashti's behaviour, ensured that Esther spent twelve months with the eunuch, who prepared her for royal status. In preparation for her new role, she had beauty treatments, special foods, and attended numerous counseling courses.

All the members of the king's team liked Esther; they felt she was the best person to become their next queen. Esther had all the characteristics of a queen. Her look and mannerism depicted royalty. Incidentally the king's crown was a perfect fit for her head. Twelve months later there was a beauty pageant and all the prospective queens modelled before the king. After the pageant the king made his choice. Esther went through the selection process and was successful. The king felt elated and was pleased with her more than any other contestant.

She was crowned queen and there was celebration throughout the land.

Esther was happy in her role as queen, making her husband proud. The king was also pleased with his kind, caring, and easygoing wife. However, elsewhere in the palace jealousy raged. Medians did not like the Jews. Someone secretly planned to kill Esther and all the Jews.

One day Esther was troubled as she heard about the plans made by the king's official. Esther knew she had to discuss the matter with the king, but she could not. The law of the land forbade anyone, including the queen, to approach the king without being invited. Esther knew royal protocol.

Esther chose to pray and fast for three days then go to see the king, whether or not there was an invitation. Disobeying the law was punishable by death, yet Esther was willing to die for her people. Haman, one of the king's officials, stirred up hatred for the Jews. He wanted the Jews killed and this included Esther.

When the fast ended, Esther hoped that the king would invite her to the palace. She was dressed in her royal attire, as she approached the king. The king smiled; he found her irresistible, and invited her in.

She seemed rather distressed as she related to the king about the plan made by the wicked official Haman. Infuriated and outraged, the king paced the palace floor in anger and shouted **that Haman must die**. He ordered another officer to kill Haman. Queen Esther and all her people finally escaped Haman's death plot. Haman was hanged instead.

Queen Esther changed the course of nature and saved a nation from death. Her adopted father, who was also her uncle, was promoted to be the king's official.

Esther's started from a lowly beginning, as an orphaned Jewish slave in Babylon.

God:

- used the heathen king to fulfil His purpose in Esther's life.
- is not confined to location and He changed Esther's story into a majestic end. Esther was earmarked to the kingdom for that time.
- used Esther's life to release His people, the Jews, from captivity. He gave them favour and promotion among their enemies.

Esther was young and inexperienced, but she overcame severe adversities by the wisdom and help of God. **She knew how to change her spiritual climate by petitioning God.** Her lesson of triumph hinged on the fact that neither fear nor doubt belonged to the vocabulary of God's people.

Modern-Day Reality: A warrior, putting her nation before herself.

CHAPTER 69

ZERESH

(Esther 3:1–7:10)

The second most powerful woman in the land.

The king in the land was elated since he had wed his young virgin. His jubilance compelled him to make all his officials happy. He promoted Haman, the Agagite, to chief officer. This promotion meant all the other servants would pay homage to him. Haman was proud and preoccupied with the thought of being in charge and second in command.

Haman:

- was a family man and would never make a decision without the valued opinion of his beloved wife Zeresh. She advised him how to act and assert himself in his new role.
- was the first person to arrive at the gates of the palace daily.

- did this so that all the other servants would bow down and revere him before they entered the palace.
- acted on the king's command and felt he was the most important subject in the land.

However, to Haman's surprise, Mordecai a Jew, refused to revere him at the gate. This made him angry.

Mordecai was expected by law to be obedient and to respect the king's authority through Haman. To disobey the king was a crime punishable by death. Other servants noticed Mordecai's defiance and the news spread quickly about his refusal to acknowledge Haman's authority. Haman discussed the matter with Zeresh before speaking with the king. It was the first week of his promotion. Zeresh expected her husband to be ecstatic, but he appeared withdrawn and indifferent. His lack of confidence was abnormal for a man of his calibre. Zeresh sat with Haman as they talked about his position in the palace and dealing with Mordecai's disrespect for authority. Haman was happy with his wife's suggestion. The plan was to kill all the Jews, which included Mordecai and Esther, the queen.

Haman was greatly influenced by Zeresh: his thought and conversations completely represented the view of his wife. He told the king about the Jewish people who refused to obey his command, and they (the Jews) could overthrow him and take leadership in his province. Haman's job was to notify the king of threats to the kingdom, so the king believed him. The king gave Haman his ring, which was a token of investment, favour, and authority. Haman was happy being promoted to the highest rank in the palace. He went home to Zeresh and broke the good news. She advised him to send letters to all the officers of the country, warning about the imminent destruction of the Jews. When Mordecai heard about it, he broke down and wept bitterly.

Haman's plan meant that Queen Esther, a Jew would also be

destroyed. She was saddened as she thought about the destruction of her people. Esther went to discuss the matter with her husband. She asked him to invite Haman to a banquet to talk about his **discriminative plans**. The king, driven by compassion, looked at the record and found that Mordecai had saved his life and was never honoured for such act of bravery. The king decided he would ask Haman to plan an honorary event for this bravery.

Haman went home boasting to his wife and friends. His ego was elated as he talked about his power in the country. He told them the king trusted him greatly and believed all the information he provided. He flaunted the king's ring as evidence that he was second in command. Zeresh felt she was also promoted to a place of prominence in the country. The next day, the royal courier stopped by with Haman's invitation to the banquet at the palace.

Haman had mixed emotions, overwhelmed with joy at the invite, yet he was still troubled that Mordecai the Jew refused to honour his authority. He discussed his concerns with Zeresh since he valued her opinion highly. Zeresh could no longer endure the distress of her husband and thought Mordecai and the Jewish people were enemies of the king and the kingdom. She was in favour of having Mordecai executed and the Jews completely destroyed. She proceeded to help Haman build a private execution chamber.

Overcome by pride, Haman entered the palace. He was welcomed as a guest of honour and escorted by the king's chamberlain into the banquet hall. As Haman was daintily sipping his aperitif, the king propositioned him about what to do for someone whom the king wishes to honour for bravery. Haman thought this was his big moment since he would be the only person deserving of honour.

In excitement, he told the king to **allow the person to wear the** *king's robe, ride on the king's chariot through the country, and let all the people in the country bow down to this person, shouting, 'He is the man whom the king is pleased to honour'. The king felt Haman's recommendation was excellent and asked him to go out and honour Mordecai. Haman stood in shock, he could hardly believe his ears. He could not defy the king's command so he reluctantly went out to honour Mordecai.*

While Haman embarked on the tour of honouring Mordecai, news reached the palace that Haman and his wife had built a private execution chamber to kill Mordecai. The king, fuming with anger, sent his officers to fetch Haman immediately. Haman was executed on the chamber he built for Mordecai.

Haman and his wife were self-centred, proud, and hungry for power, however they were united in purpose. Their devious motive precipitated Haman's untimely death.

Zeresh knew all the secrets, as she was her husband's confidante and advisor. She spent time discussing his plans, giving guidance in every decision-making process. The couple was initially highly respected, honoured and trusted by the king. They had the opportunity to ask the king for great wealth. Unknown to them it was their life-changing moment, but their desire for power consumed them. Their own self-centeredness coupled with an overpowering aspiration to take the utmost place of honour robbed them of the ability to live full and complete lives.

Zeresh:

- did not use her influence to positively impact the life of her husband and steer him away from evil, including murder.
- was also guilty of murder.

- failed to recognise the authority she had and the power of influence that she carried.
- was the second most powerful woman in the land; she had access to great wealth and prestige.
- had connection to the king and the decision-making processes in the land.

The morning she awoke filled with excitement, thinking that her noble status would increase, and she would be among the most influential dignitaries in the palace. It was the day she became a widow. She never thought the ecstatic, honorary heights were nothing less than momentous episodes of delusions. She discovered, her advice did not secure favour or cause her husband to assume a greater position. Instead, it was used against him, ending his life.

Zeresh most certainly would have acted differently, if she knew her decision would cost the life of her husband and all her entitlement. In Jewish culture it was probable that Zeresh was also killed with Haman, since families were seen as one unit. The king wishing to rid the land of evil would destroy the individual along with his/her family members. Zeresh was fuelled by individualism and greed. She did not display qualities of humility, nor learn to prefer others more than herself. She sanctioned the death of an innocent man. She believed, as a couple, they would secure greater prominence, but in the end, she was sadly mistaken.

Modern-Day Reality: Recognise your power of influence and affluence; make wise choices.

CHAPTER 70

CHILDLESS WOMAN

(Isaiah 54:1–17)

Mountains can crumble,
Hills may disappear,
But my love for you is pure,
My kindness and mercy remain.

Single and childless,
Her song makes people glad.
She never gave birth,
Yet a mother of many,
Her home is completely overcrowded.

All her children are governors and rulers.
They live in modern cities once destroyed.
She also lives in comfort,
And has nothing to fear.
She will never be ashamed or disgraced.

Single yet married,
Her husband is special,
His name is the Lord of Host.
When she feels unsure and insecure,
Her lover reassures her,
You are my pride and joy.

Still feeling uncertain she turns
Thinking her lover was gone.
She shouts
To her surprise, He responds
I will never leave you, darling, I am right here.

Mountains can crumble,
Hills may disappear,
But my love for you is pure.
My kindness and mercy remain.
I have made you beautiful and strong,
Preserving you from the evil one.

My protection always surrounds you.
Any evil plans against you
Cannot stand.
Unproductive speech is empty words.
It has no effect on you.
You will always receive good things,
And be victorious through it all.

Modern-Day Reality: Finding solace in Christ when no one understands.

CHAPTER 71

DAUGHTER OF ZION

(Isaiah 52:1–2; 62:1–12;
Zephaniah 3:14–20;
Zechariah 9:9; 10:1–12)

The enemy cannot rob you anymore.
You will have fame for your shame.
Many tongues will speak your name.

Wake up,
Shake off the dust,
Use your favourite fragrance,
Dress up, put on your best attire.
Free yourself from the bondage,
Your God has rescued you,
You will outshine the sun.
No one will refer to you in derogatory terms,

Your land will be fruitful,
It will be filled with good things.
You and your family will not lack,
The enemy cannot rob you anymore.

Set an example for all people.
The Lord, your master
Rewards your faithfulness.
You will be called redeemed and holy.

Many people will come searching for you.
Sing and shout,
Rejoice you daughter of Zion,
For God has destroyed your enemies.
Don't be afraid.
Evil will never rise again.

The mighty One is with you,
To heal your heartaches and pains,
He comes to restore all that was stolen from you.
You will have fame for your shame.
And many tongues will speak your name.

Get excited O daughter of Zion,
Shout for joy,
Your King is here.
Riding on a horse defeating iron chariots.

He speaks peace to those who are at war,
And His Kingdom is from
Nation to nation,
Coast to coast.

Modern-Day Reality: Be courageous and strong; be happy the King causes you to triumph over the enemy in every battle.

CHAPTER 72

VIRTUOUS WOMAN

(Proverbs 31:10–31)

Can anyone find a reputable woman?
Where is she?
Being reputable
Is not about outer beauty.

Can anyone find a reputable woman?
Where is she?
If you find her,
She is worth more than all the monies in the world.
She is the key to her husband's contentment.

She is self-fulfilling,
An economist, a strategist,
Working hard for every penny,
She puts her money to good use.

She doesn't believe in excessiveness; she wastes nothing.
She plants her food and doesn't believe in takeaway.
She makes sure her children and husband are warm and fed.
She goes to bed late at night, awakens before dawn.

She has great strength,
And lots of vigour and vitality.
She believes in social justice.
She talks about tomorrow as if it happened yesterday.

She is not idle or lazy,
She plans her day.
She does not whine or complain.
She gives sound advice.

Her husband is a distinguished gentleman.
She is respected by all,
She teaches others kindness and forgiveness.
Her husband and children appreciates her.
They tell her daily how special she is.

Reputability in a woman
Is not about outer beauty,
Since it depreciates with age.
Nor is it about nice words,
As they can be deceptive.

Her reputation is characterised by her great love for God.
Making her excel above them all.
She deserves to be **celebrated**
Twenty-four seven.

Modern-Day Reality: Integrity and being purpose-driven are at the core of her existence. She is sought after by all.

CHAPTER 73

ELIZABETH

(Luke 1:5–80)

She did not get the information firsthand from the angel of God,
yet she believed.

Their lives stood out as exemplary in their community and nation, in an era dominated by anarchy and corruption. She was the wife of the high priest. They were expected to be people of integrity, faith, and commitment. The fear of God made their lives exceptional, since no one could accuse them of any form of wrongdoing. Their love for God and His word compelled them to total obedience. Elizabeth faithfully supported her husband in his priestly duties. After many years of marriage the couple remained childless, making them devout since they prayed and fasted regularly.

Zacharias the priest was on duty in the temple, offering sacrifices to God for all the people. A bright light shone in the temple, this startled him. He lifted his head and was greeted by the presence of a gigantic creature dressed in pure white. It was an angel. Zacharias was petrified and utterly speechless. His entire body shook as if the earth beneath him quaked, the angel unfolded his wings, filling the room. The angel reassured Zacharias, 'Do not be afraid. I am Gabriel'. The angel announced good news to Zacharias, something he never expected: **your wife Elizabeth would become pregnant and she will give birth to a son—whom you must call John.**

*Zacharias was perplexed and confused; in complete disbelief, he told the angel, they were **too old** to have children. His complete lack of faith in what the angel had said impacted his life negatively; he became dumb instantly. When the angel left, Zacharias resumed his priestly duties. In his confusion he found himself repeating many of his tasks and wandering about in the special room. While this was happening the people were in the temple, waiting patiently for Zacharias to emerge. They became suspicious and thought he was dead.*

Zacharias arrived home and Elizabeth found his behaviour strange. She could not understand his signs as he tried to explain the angelic visit. Elizabeth had to deal with a speechless husband. She did not get the information firsthand from the angel of God, yet she believed.

Elizabeth became pregnant with no complications. The moment finally came for her delivery and she gave birth to a healthy baby boy. However, her husband remained dumb throughout the entire period of her pregnancy because of his unbelief. Elizabeth and her husband raised their only son John, teaching him godly principles including having faith in God. John was a mighty man of God, the forerunner of Jesus Christ. John mimicked Jesus' words and works insomuch that people mistook him for the promised Saviour.

Elizabeth must be commended as a woman of faith; she did not allow her past experiences, her age, or even a doubting husband to stop her from God's manifold blessings.

She was the cousin of Mary the mother of Jesus. She was much older than Mary and became her mentor. Elizabeth knew the scriptures and was expecting a King to be born in Bethlehem during her lifetime. Mary paid her a visit during her pregnancy. Mary greeted Elizabeth with enthusiasm and was overjoyed that her cousin was pregnant in her old age. The baby within Elizabeth's womb moved vigorously, a movement she had never experienced before. Elizabeth was filled with the Holy Spirit immediately and remarked, *'How blessed I am to be visited by the mother of my Lord'.*

Elizabeth was a prophetess, a woman who knew the plan of God. She was a woman filled with faith and anointed by God.

Modern-Day Reality: Situations can change; it is never too late.

CHAPTER 74

MARY THE MOTHER OF JESUS

(Matthew 1:16; 18–2:23;
Luke 1:26–56; 2:1–52)

*To be pregnant as a Jewish woman and not yet married was
a crime punishable by death.*

She was as any teenager, engaged to be married, probably preparing for her big day. Her fiancé was a tradesman from Nazareth. They were deeply committed in their relationship even though they had only recently become 'an item'. She was flabbergasted when suddenly her room illuminated; the sound heard was as though an army had invaded. Mary was in a state of shock, as the hair on her body raised. Her eye lips moved rapidly and involuntarily, her hands shook violently and her knees trembled. She tried to focus her gaze, on the huge creature towering over her. It was dressed in white, with its wings outstretched, filling the room. **An angelic encounter!** 'What does this mean?' She questioned puzzlingly, the angel then spoke, and every word was impressed on her mind: *Be brave. God has carefully selected you to have a baby who will be the son of God.* Mary had mixed feelings of humility and honour to be chosen as the mother of God's son. She considered the impossibility and asked the angel for clarity knowing she was an unmarried virgin.

The angel told her:

- *God's Holy Spirit will fill you and you shall become pregnant with a Holy seed. This child will be the son of God.*
- *Elizabeth, your cousin, is also pregnant.*

Mary's voice was heard as she shouted praises in exuberance to God. She was willing to use her womb to carry the baby Jesus.

The angel left her and she immediately rushed into the house. She packed her bag and was in utter astonishment at what the angel had said. Mary was overcome by emotions as she headed to the mountains of Judea to visit her cousin Elizabeth. Upon her arrival at Elizabeth's house, she stretched out her arm to hug her cousin when the baby in Elizabeth's womb **jumped for joy**. Mary had not told her cousin Elizabeth what happened. Elizabeth confirmed that Mary was blessed and privileged to be selected by the most High God to carry the son of God and be the mother of her Lord. Elizabeth felt Mary's visit was uncommon, but Mary stayed for three months. The pregnant women were baffled despite their variances in age and their personal circumstances: Elizabeth's barrenness and Mary's unmarried status. They were carefully selected by God to fulfil His divine purpose.

Mary then gave this special thanksgiving note to God:

**I adore you and give thanks. I am extra happy because of you,
O my Lord.
You have chosen me above all my contemporaries as your humble
servant. You have showed me how much you care for me. You have
put my name among great people, since from now on all people
will call me 'Mary the blessed one'.
You are so powerful, holy, and merciful.
You know how to deal with those who think so much of themselves.
You destroy those men who rule as though they were God, and you
lift up the humble.
The hungry get much to eat and the rich goes away with nothing.
God, you help those who believe in you.
God, you are true to your word, as you have fulfilled the promises
you made years ago to Abraham and many others.**

*As it became apparent that Mary was pregnant, she had to face
harsh realities. In Jewish culture, being pregnant and not yet married
was a crime punishable by death. Mary related to Joseph all that happened to her, finding boldness to tell him she was pregnant. Joseph was
even-tempered, and although he could not understand the mystery about
the pregnancy, he contemplated calling off the engagement privately. The
same angel visited Joseph, advising him against calling off the engagement. The angel informed Joseph that Mary was having a special child,
a Holy child, the son of the Most High God. Joseph was compliant; he
had a private wedding ceremony with his fiancée. They had no sexual
relationship until the baby was born.*

In the last trimester of her pregnancy, both Mary and Joseph travelled by donkey to Bethlehem. All roads to Bethlehem were uneven and unpaved, making the journey extremely uncomfortable for Mary. Joseph was careful with his pregnant wife, as the birth was imminent.

They made it safely to Bethlehem, and on their arrival they were completely shocked, to find that all the rooms in the hotels and guesthouses were taken. A crowd of people were visiting Bethlehem at the government's request. The government conducted a census to compile population statistics. It was the last days for this census, so many families had arrived in Bethlehem to register.

Although it was quite obvious that Mary was pregnant and in labour, there was no room available for her. The only place recommended for them was a farmhouse.

Mary:

- did not think this was not good enough for the special child she was carrying, the Son of God.
- did not consider the farm to be a place unfit for a King to be born.
- understood the purpose of His birth and that He would be the Messiah, the King who was expected for thousands of years.
- knew the scriptures, that the King would be born of a lowly beginning.

The child was only a few days old when the king of the land, Herod, threatened the life of this innocent baby. His parents secretly escaped to Egypt for a few years until the death of King Herod.

Jesus:

- *grew up ordinary yet amazing.*
- *was taught the word of God even though He was the word.*
- *was in the temple reasoning with the scholars and teaching them the scripture from age twelve.*

His parents, Mary and Joseph, had travelled for a few days without realising that Jesus was not with them. They turned back, found Him in the temple with all the teachers and leaders, debating the word of God with so much wisdom. As a child he was taught the word of God daily by his parents.

At Jesus' death, Mary followed closely. She painfully looked at the unbearable suffering of her son. Her heart bled as she stood by the cross. She found it difficult to come to terms with the suffering and death of her beloved son. Mary was well informed since Jesus often revealed His mission and the purpose of His birth. She was among the group of women who remained at Jesus' cross long after His death and also helped to embalm His body. The nights following His death were the most distressing. Early that Sunday morning, as she visited the tomb, she was plagued by thoughts of hope and optimism. There was a possibility that her son could be alive. Mary was overwhelmed as she peeped into the tomb, realising His clothing were neatly folded, but Jesus was missing. She jumped, screamed with joy and deliriously celebrated the resurrection of Jesus the Saviour.

Mary was an extraordinary teenager, distinguished among her peers. She knew the scriptures and willingly submitted to God's power. She was willing to risk her life by doing what was contrary to Jewish custom: being pregnant and unmarried. Mary had mixed emotions of shame and *apprehension. She was handpicked by God, her Creator to be the mother of Jesus, the Son of God. Jesus was the fulfillment of a promise made to the world thousands of years earlier. Mary had at least six other children. Jesus had four brothers and sisters (St. Matt 13:55 – 56; St Mark 6:3).*

Modern-Day Reality: Even though there are billions of people on the planet, God works through the individual.

CHAPTER 75

ANNA: THE PROPHETESS

(Genesis 46:17; 49:20; Luke 2:36–39)

She lived longer than the average person in those times;

S he existed in an era of ungodliness. Yet she was a prophetess and a faithful servant of God. The people in those times had no desire to serve God. The good news of a coming Messiah was heralded all over the land. Anna also heard about the coming of the Messiah, to rule the world in righteousness and justice. The people thought the Messiah would defeat the other nations by combat. He would become the supreme ruler on earth.

At age eighty-four, she had lived through the regime of many evil leaders, including Herod. She lived longer than the average person in those times; the life expectancy was seventy to eighty years.

Anna's ancestors were descendants of Asher, one of the twelve tribes of Israel. Thousands of years earlier Jacob the patriarch blessed all his sons before his death. The tribe of Asher received a blessing of production and abundance. Their lands would produce much bread and food for those living in the king's palace. Her ancestors were powerful leaders and outstanding warriors who knew about wars and conquest.

Anna:

- *knew the history of her tribe and fully understood war, conquest, invading and capturing territories.*
- *was able to draw parallels between physical and spiritual war.*
- *knew the words of God and looked forward with expectancy to the birth of a King who would teach men the laws of God by His life, death, and resurrection.*
- *understood spiritual mysteries and eagerly waited for the fulfilment of those scriptures.*

Anna was married, after seven years of marriage her husband died. Anna never remarried and devoted all of her time to praying, fasting, and worship in the temple of God. She was a godly woman who daily anticipated the birth of the Messiah.

Anna knew that:

- *Jesus' mission here on earth was to establish a heavenly Kingdom.*
- *He was expected to live, die and establish His mighty Empire.*

Anna heard about the virgin birth; she knew it was the fulfillment of the ancient prophesies. She prayed for long life since she wanted to see this special child. She was present in the temple to witness the ceremony *of Jesus' dedication. Anna had no doubt that this King would change the course of history by saving the world from sin and evil. She not only wanted to see the baby Jesus, but yearned to hold Him in her hands and bless Him before she died. Anna understood every prophetic utterances regarding the Christ Child Jesus. **The King who will be a shining light, His kingdom will pierce and completely destroy darkness.***

Anna understood the mysteries of God; she represents all those alive today, who gladly await the second advent of our Lord and Saviour Jesus Christ. She is a typology of the church; who through faith awaits the fulfilment of the prophecy of a coming Messiah (second coming).

Modern-Day Reality: God honours faith and expectancy.

CHAPTER 76

TEN SINGLE WOMEN

(Matthew 25:1–13)

Someone else's bridegroom is not worth staying up at night and waiting for indefinitely. Therefore, these ten girls were waiting for their own bridegroom.

When attending a wedding ceremony, the bride is often the centre of attraction and the focus of attention. Ten women decided to stay up late at night until their bridegroom arrived. They lived in an era when there was no electricity, so they had to use their portable light. This light was equal to modern-day satellite navigation. The ten girls could not find their bridegroom without the use of their portable light.

Someone else's bridegroom is not worth staying up at night and waiting for indefinitely. Therefore, these ten girls were waiting for their own bridegroom.

Many of the other girls in the country thought that it was foolish to dress as a bride and wait for a bridegroom, so they never tried. The detail of the wedding was sketchy since they didn't know the whereabouts of the bridegroom, nor the date or time of their own wedding. They decided to change their status from single to married, so the women tried the idea even though it was uncommon in their country.

There were lots of mental, physical, and emotional challenges. They were ready to wait as long as it took; they all arrived at the meeting place where their bridegroom would collect them.

He was no ordinary bridegroom, since he was planning the biggest surprise a woman could ever have. Time passed and no sign of the bridegroom. Some of the women were tired of waiting so they went to sleep. The others were dressed, alert and waiting expectantly.

THE BRIDEGROOM IS HERE!

They knew they had limited time for this grand moment. The girls jumped up and readied themselves for the moment he would enter. The tired women who went to sleep during the lengthy wait did not realise that their lights were not working. The others who stayed up had the brightest light and were ready. **'Help us fix our light'***, the impatient ones cried. But it was too late. Time was not on their side so they sought help elsewhere. The five wise girls went in with their bridegroom since they were waiting and fully prepared for their life-changing moment.*

It would be unheard of for a bride to miss her own wedding. The same sentiment is expressed for those who are unprepared for Christ's return. All ten girls were together, spending the initial time sharing what was common to them. They laughed and talked together. However, at the crucial moment of truth their differences were revealed. One group was ready, having all they needed to be with their bridegroom. The other group was unprepared for the purpose they originally came together to achieve.

Modern-Day Reality: The keys to success are steadfastness, determination, and consistency in the word of God.

CHAPTER 77

WOMAN OF SAMARIA

(John 4:1–39)

*The woman was puzzled since Jesus was a Jew and
she was a Samaritan.*

It was one of those hot summer days, with dense humidity; the stillness in the air was noted as the branches in the tree were completely stationary.

Jesus:

- arrived in Samaria at about midday.
- had travelled on foot from Judea and His final destination was Galilee.
- was tired, hungry, and overcome by the hot conditions.

Jesus had a moment of solitude: all His key workers had gone into town to buy food, as they were very hungry. Wandering around

Samaria, Jesus' ultimate plan was to visit the well, a famous land-mark built by the forefathers hundreds of years prior. It was one of the hotspots in Samaria, a place frequented by all the villagers. Jesus had walked many miles and was tired. He sat down knowing that a Samaritan would come by very soon to get water. The Jews and the people of Samaria were enemies and He appeared to be in the wrong place, perching at the well of the Samaritans.

A Samaritan woman approached the well. Her face lit up as she saw this handsome young man sitting by the well. The woman thought she might be in for a *'very good catch'*. She came to fetch water for domestic use, this was part of her daily routine. Jesus said to her, **'Do you mind getting me a drink of water?'**

The woman was puzzled since Jesus was a Jew and she was a Samaritan; the two groups never mingled. She felt weird as women were not seen communicating with men in public.

Jesus:

- *revealed all of her social background without mentioning her name. The woman did not know who this stranger was.*
- *said to the Samaritan woman that He could **give her water that would last forever**.*
- *told her that the area of her life she was trying to fulfil could only be fulfilled with what He had to offer.*

She wanted this living water. Jesus asked her to go home and fetch her husband so the entire family could share in the blessing. The woman replied she was single and uncommitted. She had a few men in her life, but none of them were her husband.

This Samaritan woman:

- *had good communication skills. No wonder Jesus found it easy to chat with her. All the men were drawn to her.*
- *was knowledgeable and knew the history of the well.*
- *felt that if she could have water and not return to the well every time that would solve a big problem in her life.*
- *remembered all the wrongs that she committed and wanted to make changes.*

She spoke with Jesus and had a divine revelation about who He was. She wanted all that He had to offer. She left her jar behind and ran home. She shouted. **'Come meet a man who knows all about me!'** *Her life was completely transformed.*

This place that was familiar seemed so strange.
All she ever knew now appeared distant and vague.
A place she visited so many times became a brand-new experience.
She got life and she started living.
She got water that quenched her thirst.
She was offered security and destiny.
She stopped searching and started sharing,
She stopped stealing and got her healing.
This woman was transformed instantaneously.
She had gone repeatedly without realising,
What she really needed was
THE WELL to visit her instead.

Modern-Day Reality: There is a brighter tomorrow; don't be hampered by a negative past.

CHAPTER 78

Jairus' Daughter

(Mark 5:21–43; Luke 8:40–56)

At twelve years of age she was well known and loved.
The entire village came out to cry and mourn for her.

The crowd camped out overnight outside Galilee, waiting for a glimpse to see who He was. This was not unusual, as people showed up everywhere He went. They heard much about Him and all the great miracles He did. The very thought of Him raised people's expectations for a miracle. Jesus was indeed the greatest celebrity of His time.

Jairus was desperate for a miracle as his twelve-year-old daughter was very sick. He believed Jesus could heal her. He walked from a nearby town to Galilee to see if Jesus would come to his house. His daughter's condition deteriorated and she failed to respond to treatment. The doctors reluctantly broke the sad news to her parents: *she would not survive*. Jairus was a wealthy spiritual leader. He knew that his only option was to get Jesus to come to his house and perform a miracle for his dying daughter.

Jesus was busy teaching the crowd and praying for all the sick persons who came to be healed. Jairus waited for a private moment to talk with Him. His request: **'Please come to my home to heal my dying daughter'.** At that same time one woman came through the crowd and touched Jesus' garment, expecting to be healed after bleeding for twelve years. This woman's health condition started the same year this girl was born.

Jairus' servant, overcome by grief, came running; there was a sense of loss. He knew that the servant's visit could mean only one thing: his daughter had died. Jairus wept loudly. Jesus was emotional, realising Jairus' daughter had just died. He assured Jairus if he believed, his daughter would be brought back to life. The crowd followed Jesus as they journeyed to Jairus' house. The sound of weeping and wailing was heard as friends, neighbours, and relatives gathered at Jairus' home. Jesus told the wailing crowd that the girl was **asleep**. They roared with laughter because Jesus had not seen the girl. *Is Jesus really saying we cannot tell the difference between someone who is sleeping and someone who is dead?*

Jesus then took five people with Him, two of whom were the girl's parents. The room where she laid was magnificent. This seemed insignificant in comparison to a young life that was cut short. They believed Jesus had the power to raise the dead. He took the girl by her hand, asking her to stand up. Immediately the girl stood up and was well again. Her funeral turned into a massive celebration with singing and dancing, death was overcome by life. Jesus raised Jairus' daughter from the dead, He returned her to all the people in her life, including the village.

At twelve years of age she was well known and loved. The entire *village came out to cry and mourn for her. Her death meant there was a void; something was missing. Everyone had felt the pain of this loss. She was a girl who brought joy and happiness to all. Her life was a testimony of the miracles Jesus performed. Everywhere she went she was referred to as **the girl who had the great miracle**. She was proof of the power in a God who could do the impossible—exceedingly abundant above all we ask or think. Her life was never the same. She lived, died, and lived again.*

Modern-Day Reality: When situations worsen, it is not the end. With Christ this is an opportunity for greater things.

CHAPTER 79

THE WOMAN WITH THE ISSUE OF BLOOD

(Mark 5:25–34)

In the twenty-first century she would have been diagnosed with
uterine fibroids or cervical cancer.

Since she was not known by her real name, very little was known about her true identity. She was known as the bleeding woman. Being known by her medical condition was not a great start for her. The fact that no one took the time to learn her name denotes her insignificance in that society. No official name or title was recorded in the story. In the twenty-first century she would have been diagnosed with *uterine fibroids* or *cervical cancer*. There was no free health care and no medical insurance. Twelve years of her life was spent with an incurable bleeding disorder. All her monies were spent on medical bills. Even the monies she saved for her burial was spent, since her long-standing condition worsened.

Although she saw the best gynaecologist there were no positive results. Blood samples, profile analysis, and ultrasound scans were not invented, so she had no diagnosis. She was not taken seriously and was prescribed medications that never worked. The woman lamented as her depleted savings ended up in someone else's pocket.

Culturally, she was viewed as unclean and not expected to visit any public places, in accordance with the law. She did not attend any weddings, funeral, birthday parties or church services for twelve years.

She was frail, weak, severely anaemic, and also depressed with no health, no wealth, and no friends. The woman heard about Jesus the healer and was determined to change her situation. She heard many accounts of Jesus healing the sick and raising the dead. Culturally, it was unacceptable to go out of her home or among the crowd when bleeding.

*She was disadvantaged, chronically exhausted, yet she made up her mind to head into town where Jesus was. She woke before dawn knowing she needed to wash and dress herself. She mustered enough strength, pulling herself from her sickbed. Her favourite dress hung on her weak, bony frame. It took her over two hours to walk the fifteen-minute journey. She pushed herself through barriers to get what she needed—**her healing**.*

She was strong in faith. The woman knew she must do something to receive her miracle or she would die. There was a war of emotions going on in her mind. Her circumstances were dire and her medical and social history was depressing.

There was much opposition, but she was determined to be healed. The woman was not short of excuses as she felt hopeless and weak. She first had to cut through the bureaucracy of the ceremonial law and contend with the crowd around Jesus.

Her mind was plagued with many negative thoughts. She got the result she anticipated because the conversations in her *spirit* were greater than the conversations in her mind. The woman did not spend what was left of her life worrying about what might happen and how negative her situation had become. She returned home healed, stronger and better. It was all done by faith. *Goodbye bleeding.* The woman embraced wholeness and well-being by faith.

She wanted to quietly touch the hem of Jesus' clothes and walk away healed and whole. Faith is not faith unless there is accompanying works. As she consciously made contact with Jesus' clothing, her bleeding stopped immediately.

It must be noted that the woman touched the hem of Jesus' garment. Priests wore a long garment and they were anointed from their head. This anointing oil flowed down to the skirt/hem of their garments. The hem was the most saturated part of the garment and would be the last part to dry out. This was why she stooped low and touched the hem. Stooping represented a place of selflessness, humility, reverence, and worship.

Jesus then asks who touched Him, with expectation.
Who touched Him, putting a demand on the anointing?
Who touched Him, knowing that this touch is their last resort
and it will change their situation.

The woman admitted that she had touched in expectation, knowing that Jesus was greater than any doctor she had visited, and He could heal her. She had made up her mind that this was the last day this plague would torment her. She knew God's power was available to heal her.

Jesus referred to her as 'daughter'; both her circumstances and her name *changed instantaneously*. Her faith saved her and made her a daughter of the Most High God. This woman was a great example of how to touch Jesus for a miracle. Many people learned that they can touch Jesus by faith and be healed. Jesus in town can make that difference. He gives hope in a hopeless situation. He gives life in a lifeless situation and peace when there is nothing else but trouble. This woman who spent more than a decade in ill health and poverty experienced the biggest change in her life. She looked away from her situation and looked to the God of the impossible.

With great reflection up to this day, this woman is still known by her medical condition even after she experienced healing and wholeness. She is referred to as the **woman with the issue of blood**. The woman became so much more than her previous status: she was converted to a daughter of the Most High God.

Modern-Day Reality: Better days are coming even though all seems lost.

CHAPTER 80

THE ADULTEROUS WOMAN, FORGIVEN BY JESUS

(John 8:1–11)

This woman knew that at the end of this ordeal,
being stoned to death was inevitable.

Society was much more tolerable with men cheating on their wives in biblical times. However, for a woman to cheat on her husband would mean she was deserving of the death penalty.

Her marriage had so many challenges when romance dwindled and the river of love stopped flowing. Admitting to no longer loving her husband, she could not live without a man in her life. Although she did not separate from her husband, she had another man visiting her home when her husband went out to work. The woman sought marital counsel; the church leaders knew she was struggling in her marriage.

The leaders:

- were deceptive and didn't protect her confidentiality.
- took the information as ammunition and were determined to catch her and bring her to justice.
- knew that the Law of Moses stated that ***cheaters, whether they were men or women, should be stoned to death*** (Deuteronomy 22:22).
- planned to catch her and were prepared to have her stoned to death.
- secretly climbed up on her roof, spying on her and waiting for the moment.

It today's society, it would have been captured on social media.

These religious leaders, behaved as though adultery was only a woman's sin. They justified their actions as they convinced themselves how godly they were. They showed mercy to the man and spared his life, without thinking they had broken the law, by allowing him to go free. Just imagine a man committing adultery being let off the hook. This woman knew that at the end of this ordeal, being stoned to death was inevitable. It could only be imagined, with such aura of superiority, these men felt they were acting in defence of the law of God; they were defending her husband who was not aware that she was cheating. **Surely Jesus would agree with us and get rid of her for committing a sinful act**, *the men thought to themselves.*

*Jesus listened to the leaders without speaking. He knelt down and could have written, '**Where is the man? She could not commit adultery on her own. You are all as guilty as he is**'. Jesus asked the perfect one to stone her to death. He continue to write information which disqualified* *them from the innocence status they tried to display. They were ashamed. The men disappeared, from the most senior to the youngest. Jesus turned to the woman who was willing to put the past behind and make a change in her life. He said to her that He **did not sentence her to death, but if she would go and turn away from her wrongdoing, she will live.***

Although her name was never recorded, her status and lifestyle changed when she met Jesus and confessed her sins.

Modern-Day Reality: It is never too late for a change.

CHAPTER 81

Daughter of Abraham

(Luke 13:10–17)

For the first time in her life she heard words of love and
felt someone cared.

No one could tell her actual age, since her body showed signs of aging beyond her literal years. She was depressed and isolated; she lost purpose and the will to live. When she stood up, she appeared to shrink to half of her normal height. For eighteen years she experienced this prison of ill health and demonic powers controlling her mind.

Abraham's daughter:

- had spinal disfigurement (loss of height). Her gaze was always towards the ground as she could barely hold her head up.
- hardly went outside.

- was conscious that people were staring at her even when she could not see them. She was treated as an outcast.

Her relatives were not interested in her. She was lonely and desperate.

Abraham's daughter:

- *was a Jew.*
- *forced herself out of bed to go to the temple.*
- *was asked to sit in a corner.*
- *was treated with indifference.*
- *was isolated; her emotional pains were more than her physical pains.*

Jesus saw her and with His hand He gestured for her to come over to where He was standing. Jesus spoke to this woman. For the first time in her life she heard words of love and felt someone cared. When Jesus touched her, the curvatures on her spine immediately straightened. She stood up at over five feet and shouted praises to God. She was healed, delivered and whole on a Sabbath day.

*The leaders in the temple were outraged because Jesus healed a woman on the Sabbath day. Jesus told the leaders that they untied their animals and took them for water on the Sabbath day. However, a Jewish woman was in bondage for eighteen years and had not drunk of the **Water of Life** for all those years. This was a joyous occasion as this woman had been loosed so she could freely drink of the Living Water. They had more regard and value for their animals than this sick woman. Jesus reminded* *the religious leaders that she was also a daughter of Abraham and that she deserved to be free.*

This woman did not comprehend the power of God, until she got a glimpse of a covenant relationship with Christ. She experienced suffering based on man-made laws. She recognised that many non-Jews were privileged to the healing power of God, so she was determined to have her life story rewritten. Abraham's daughter became radical in her faith, pursuing her dreams. Her faith made her completely whole.

Modern-Day Reality: The end is better than the beginning.

CHAPTER 82

THE WIDOW WITH
HER TWO MITES

(Mark 12:41–44)

*They were anticipating a pat on the shoulders from Jesus
for their overly generous giving.*

A faithful church attendee, she was familiar with all the ceremonies that occurred. Putting money into the church offering bowl was not a new ritual. Churchgoers went to church with monetary gifts and prepared to present them. This day in particular, giving monetary gifts was not private since Jesus was there. The givers were making the ceremony spectacular in an effort to *impress* Him. As the church attendees gave their monies, Jesus stood next to the offering bowl, observing both the givers and the gifts. The wealthy givers took out their purses, giving two or three times their normal gifts as they sought to show Jesus how good they were. Their actions were in slow motion, drawing attention to themselves and their gifts. They created a public display putting multiple denarii (the largest Roman coin) into the offering bowl.

*They were anticipating a pat on the shoulders from Jesus for their overly generous giving. However, a little widow came to give her gifts; Jesus' attention was drawn to her and her gift. The woman had no children and no source of income. She depended on welfare. This was all that was known about her identity. Taking her handbag and shaking it into the offering bowl, out of her bag fell two mites. A mites was the **smallest** Roman coin that existed. It is the equivalent to a penny today.*

The Bible commanded a welfare system that would take care of the widows and fatherless. She did not have a pension or any savings. She gave sacrificially out of her love for God and not merely to impress others.

Jesus did not have a conversation with the widow, but He knew that she gave her all. Jesus asked the widow to stand next to Him until everyone had put their offering into the bowl. He knew what each one gave and what they had left over. He then commended the widow for giving one hundred percent of what she had. Jesus saw her giving as an act of **great faith**. She understood that God deserves her all, and she knew the purpose of gifts in her life, even her money.

She was the only woman recorded in the bible to give one hundred percent of her money. This woman trusted God to provide, as she was unemployed. She lived a selfless life, not consumed by money or wealth.

Modern-Day Reality: Willing to sacrifice the little to gain great wealth in Christ.

CHAPTER 83

THE SYRO-PHOENICIAN WOMAN

(Mark 7:24–30)

A scene straight out of a HORROR MOVIE.

B orn in Syria (Phoenicia), she was obviously not a Jew. As she followed the life and times of Jesus, she longed for the news of His
arrival in Syria. That moment finally came: **JESUS' ARRIVAL!**

She followed every account in detail of Jesus' life and miracles, and
wanted to see Him. This was not the only reason why she wanted to see
Him, as her young daughter was seriously ill and she felt that only Jesus
could heal her. Her symptoms were **strange dreams, nightmares,** and
hallucinations. Night-times were the worst since her behaviour was
inappropriate and abnormal. Her mother felt as though she had experienced a scene *straight out of a* HORROR MOVIE. The little girl's life was
lonely and sad; she could not attend school and did not have friends.
The desperate mother searched anxiously for answers. The best paedi-
atrician referred her to a neurologist, who also offered little help.

The woman knew that she was not entitled to claim 'Jewish

Blessings' since she was not a Jew. In her desperation she decided to try Jesus the miracle worker. She set aside cultural differences and was willing to pursue a cure for her child despite the cost.

Jesus had not yet arrived in her town, but was visiting the home of one of His followers in the neighbouring village. She was not acquainted with the home owner, nor was she an invited guest, yet she barged into the house.

Jesus:

- *knew exactly why she took such desperate measures.*
- *continued His teachings about love for others and love for God, when she told Him that her daughter was very ill and needed a miracle.*
- *stopped His lessons, and as though He was insulted, He told her that **He could not give the children's food to dogs, after the children had eaten, if any food was left, then the dogs could eat.***

*She knew what Jesus meant. He could not give away miracles to anyone who was an unbeliever. Non-Jews were considered dogs. The woman replied that **the dogs would go under the table and wait for any food that fell from the table, then the dogs would eat whatever fell to the floor**. She knew she was rightfully seeking that which the Jewish people had every entitlement to claim. This woman understood that societal rules couldn't hinder her from getting to God. The eternal plans and purposes of God were to give His blessings to **anyone** who seeks after it: Jew or non-Jew, rich or poor, male or female. Jesus was impressed by the faith and demands she placed on Him. She expected miracles and she received it.*

Jesus said to her 'go home, your faith would heal your daughter'.
She hurried home with excitement; she envisaged her daughter would
be healed and normal again. She raced home gasping for breath; the
sound of her heart beat was audible. She was surprised as her daughter
was also running to meet her for the first time.

The Syro-Phoenician woman:

- heard about the King of the Jews who came to reign over
  every situation.
- had great faith; she did not allow circumstances to dictate
  what happened next.
- did not take a position of inferiority since she was not a Jew.

This woman knew exactly who she was, not a Syro-Phoenician,
nor an outcast, but a daughter of the Living God. She stepped up to
the sphere of great expectancy, realising there was nothing standing
between her and Christ. The cultural impediments were thrown from
her mind; she exercised faith, bringing about her miracle as she stood
in the gap for her daughter. After her miraculous encounter, her life
demonstrated to all non-Jews that there was no limitation in Christ.
Her life and testimony fulfilled scripture: there are no barriers in
Christ, no Jews or Gentiles, no rich or poor, or slave and master—all
become one by faith in Christ.

Modern-Day Reality: The blessings of God are for **anyone** who sin-
cerely seeks after them.

CHAPTER 84

THE WIDOW AND THE UNJUST JUDGE

(Luke 18:1–8)

The judge had no intention to help her.
He anticipated what time she was coming and tried to avoid her.

A victimised woman seeks justice. Her neighbour had terrorised her, refusing to repay numerous loans. She thought about her recent past, when she lived peacefully in her home and the moment it ended. Without having a husband or an advocate, her adversaries mocked her. Life in her neighbourhood was hell on earth. She took her case before the judge in the land despite all the rumours about him. He was accused of being unsympathetic, uncaring, and not an advocate for the poor and disadvantaged. The woman had faith in the judge so she did not believe the rumours she heard about him.

She was deeply distressed as she went to the judge to present her grievance, showing current evidence to support her case. Evidence was given to prove that monies were owed to her. The judge promised her that he would bring her adversary to justice quickly. Unlike all that she had heard about the judge, she felt he listened and was interested in her plight. The widow left his office feeling vindicated.

The widow went home joyfully as she anticipated the verdict of the judge to rule in her favour. Weeks passed without a word from the judge. In the meantime her enemies continued to pester her. When she went back to the judge, he apologised and promised her that he would contact her adversaries. Again he did **nothing**. The enemies harassed her incessantly, and every time, she would take her concern to the judge for justice.

After visiting the judge numerous times, she stopped counting. The judge had no intention to help her. He anticipated what time she was coming and tried to avoid her. Making an appointment did not change her situation, as the woman was told he was not in his office. Deciding to vary her visiting times, she continued to visit the judge.

Years passed and still no justice for the widow. He became wearied by her constant bombardment and decided that it was time to act. One morning the judge awoke out of sleep earlier than usual, he thought about the woman who had visited his office nonstop. The judge felt that he had heard her story, which was consistent. The judge reflected on her persistence and felt she had exhausted him, so he had no choice but to bring her enemies to justice swiftly.

The judge did not honour God, nor did he care about people. He thought God must hear the cry of His people who prayed to Him night and day. God would answer their prayers quickly and make sure His people received justice.

The woman's action made the judge uncomfortable. Her persistence caused the judge to reflect on the greatest judge, God. He knew that God was not like him. He is a caring, compassionate God and cannot be equated with man.

This woman influenced a wicked judge's decision. His merciless attitude towards the juridical system changed as he encountered and emulated God as a judge. This was only possible because this woman allowed herself to be denied of her rights and was willing to wait for her miracle.

Modern-Day Reality: Persistence, consistency, and long-suffering; knowing that God will answer.

CHAPTER 85

MARY: SISTER OF MARTHA AND LAZARUS

(John 11:1–45; 12:1–11; Mark 14:3–9; Luke 7:36–50; Luke 8:2–3)

She seized the moment to ask Jesus questions...

Bethany was a small village located on the highlands en route to Jerusalem, via Jordan and Jericho. *Bible scholars believe it was located higher up the Mount of Olives, close to Bethpage where Jesus' ascension occurred.*

Their family home was in Bethany, where she lived for all of her life with her siblings. Her brother was a personal friend of Jesus. This made the entire family fond of Him since they knew of His Mighty power and all the wonders He did. She undoubtedly had encountered Jesus before, on a personal basis. She had experienced His outflow of love and forgiveness and wanted to express her thankfulness to Him.

One day as Jesus was dinning at Simon's house with His followers and many invited guest. *A woman rushed in from off the street unannounced, with the most expensive perfume to offer as a gift to Christ. The cost of this perfume was equal to one's year salary. Mary knew about different types of perfumes and their value. She wanted to extravagantly express her love for Jesus who loved her first. Mary carried the perfume to Simon's house intending to break the bottle and pour it all on Jesus. She wept senselessly, holding on to Jesus' feet, washing them with the tears she had collected in a bowl. Her hair was used as a towel to dry His feet. She broke her bottle of expensive perfume and anointed Jesus' head and feet; this was her act of worship. It was significant that Mary's expression of gratitude coincided with the big feast called Passover.*

She was undoubtedly grateful that Jesus was willing to have compassion on her, forgiving her of all her sins. Mary's act of anointing Jesus' body signified that His body would be preserved in the tomb since the Sunday after His crucifixion; the women arrived too late to anoint His body. Jesus' disciple and the onlooker witnessing her act of generosity thought it was wasted since the perfume was very expensive.

Those invited to the meal were shocked since they knew about all the wrong things this woman did in her past. They could not forgive her. They were petrified that Jesus allowed her to touch Him. Jesus saw their amazement, addressing their curiosity.

He told Simon that he had slipped up on cultural practice; Simon failed to wash Jesus' feet when He entered the house.

Jesus addressed the crowd by telling them a story. Two people owed a debt; one owed a small debt and the other a very large debt. They were unable to find the money to pay the debt and were both forgiven. Jesus asked them which of the debtors would be more grateful.

They answered the one who owed more. Jesus said this woman was expressing her gratitude for a large debt she was forgiven.

He reassured those who witnessed Mary's elaborate gesture that the perfume was not wasted, but Mary understood His teachings more than those who were close to Him. She was preparing Him for His death and burial. Jesus commended her, since His twelve followers who were close to Him for approximately three years, did not understand what was going to happen to Him.

It was few weeks before this, her brother Lazarus complained of feeling unwell, he screamed loudly, and went to his bed. Initial thoughts of panic were subdued when Mary and her sister thought about Jesus the healer. The servant was summoned to fetch Jesus quickly. Jesus received the message, but could not get to their home in Bethany for another four days. He was greatly involved in ministry to the people. During that time Lazarus's condition deteriorated, and sadly he died. The neighbours and many people from Bethany came to console Mary and her sister Martha, as they wept inconsolably. Lazarus' body was prepared in accordance with Jewish custom. A dead body was preserved with spices and wrapped in special cloth then laid in a tomb.

Mary believed Jesus was en route to visit Lazarus and thought it was not necessary since her brother was dead. She put on her mourning garment and went to meet Him. She was overcome with grief and met Jesus outside the city, falling at His feet. She sobbed and wept then she said, **'Lord if you had come four days ago when we sent for you, my brother would not have died'.**

The extent of Mary's faith, was only for the healing of her brother Lazarus. Jesus still visited their home, as was His original intention. At their home in Bethany all the neighbours, friends, and relatives were weeping for Lazarus. Jesus asked where Lazarus' body was. Jesus went to *the tomb and the crowd followed Him. Many of the people thought Jesus was going to say His last goodbye. They arrived at the tomb and there was an offensive odour; the body of Lazarus had deteriorated. Many villagers were weeping for the dead. Jesus asked them to remove the stone, then He prayed to His Father, as He wanted the crowd to believe that He is the Son of God. Jesus shouted, '**Lazarus, come out from among the dead**'. Lazarus heard the voice of Jesus and responded. Immediately he came back to life. There were screams of excitement heard in the midst of what was formerly a grief-stricken situation. The moment of chaos changed as the cemetery was no longer a place of sadness, but a place of jubilation.*

In an act of spontaneity Mary became a missionary, a woman of great faith, telling all the Jewish leaders and the people who did not believe in Jesus, about His miracles. It was not commonplace for a woman to debate scripture with Jewish leaders/men. Mary broke with the traditions of her time, realising that the power of God transcends culture and tradition.

Mary was not impeded by the cultural norms of her time. She seized the moment to ask Jesus questions about His purpose on earth. She sat at His feet, puzzled, in an effort to unravel the mysteries of God. Mary became increasingly cognizant of her deep inner needs. Physical food could not satisfy her cravings. She was able to put her life into perspective; knowing that only eternal things are lasting.

Modern-Day Reality: Faith grows by seeking after God.

CHAPTER 86

MARTHA

(John 11:1–45; 12:1–11)

She was in the presence of greatness and did not recognise it.

Martha, Mary, and Lazarus were well known in Bethany. Their Jewish upbringing meant they heard a lot about Jesus. They were among the crowd that followed Jesus and saw His mighty miracles. Jesus was quite fond of this family, spending quality time with them. This was a worthy position, and many families in Bethany envied them. Martha was an exceptional cook. She loved experimenting in the kitchen, creating new recipes.

*Martha felt it was the time to display all her cooking and entertainment proficiencies. She was **busy** with all the preparation of a sumptuous banquet for their special guest. While Martha was occupied with getting the meal ready on time, her sister Mary sat at Jesus' feet, totally engrossed. Mary listened attentively to Jesus as he related all about His life, His mission, His purpose, and His future. Martha's displeasure was audible from the sound of kitchen equipment being tossed about. Then* *her voice was heard as she complained about all the preparation she had to do on her own. She finally perked up the courage and asked Jesus,* **'Don't you care that I am here in the kitchen working so hard to put this four-course meal together and my sister is doing nothing?'** *Jesus replied, 'A cooked meal is good and important, but Mary has chosen spiritual food, which is essential'.*

Martha did not realise she had a meal already prepared for her by the King of kings and Lord of lords. All she had to do was sit and feast.

She:

- *did not realise she could switch off the oven and eat from the Bread of Life.*
- *was busy trying to be the perfect hostess, which was good; however, Martha lacked spiritual insight that there was something better.*
- *made a good choice at the wrong moment.*
- *did not seize the opportunity to be taught by the greatest teacher.*
- *did not stop to recognise the presence of Divinity; she only saw Jesus' humanity.*
- *saw a hungry Jesus. She was not connected to the Christ, the Son of the Living God and the Bread of life.*

Martha thought she was preparing food to feed Jesus. She did not realise that Jesus had the food that she needed.

The lack of spiritual insight negatively impacted Martha's faith months later when her brother Lazarus died. She said to Jesus, **'Lord, if you had been here, my brother would not have died'.** Martha had faith for yesterday and tomorrow. She said Jesus would raise her brother who was dead, to life in the last day; this was demonstrating faith for the future. Jesus reminded her, 'I AM the Resurrection and the Life. I AM right now, not I WILL BE in the future'. Martha again did not recognise Jesus for who He was. To misrecognise is to mistreat. She was in the presence of greatness and did not recognise it; therefore, she lacked divine revelation to appreciate and celebrate God's power and Majesty.

Martha felt ashamed. Although she spent so much time with Jesus and saw all the great miracles, yet she did not know Him. She reviewed her position of faith and confessed that she was spiritually short-sighted, asking for forgiveness. She turned from doubt, disbelief, and faithlessness as she experienced the resurrection power at work in her life. From that moment onwards Martha was never the same.

Modern-Day Reality: The priority pendulum shifts as one draws closer to Christ.

CHAPTER 87

Salome

(Matthew 4:21–22; 20:20–24; 27:55–56;
Mark 1:19–20; 3:17; 15:40–41; 16:1–8;
Luke 8:2–3; 9:51–55; 23:49–56; 24:1–9)

Salome did not realise that in Jesus' Kingdom there is no left hand;
all must be on the same level at the same place, His right hand.

Salome and her husband were popular and influential characters in Galilee. They owned great wealth, including many fishing boats with nets. Her two boys—James, the eldest son, and his younger brother John—were also involved in the fishing trade. One day Jesus walked by the Sea of Galilee looking for men to train to be His special followers. He loved those who were exposed to the elements—**the sun, the sea, the wind, and the waves.** James and John were selected while they were with their father getting ready to go fishing. The brothers immediately left their father, their boats, and followed Jesus. They left the security of their livelihood to follow Christ.

*Salome and her husband Zebedee loved God and knew the scriptures that a Saviour would come to redeem Israel. They taught their sons the word of God. The couple was honoured to have their two boys among the special followers of Jesus. The boys, filled with zeal and passion for Jesus, were offended by those who rejected Him. They then asked Jesus for permission to call down fire from heaven and destroy those who rejected Him. After this episode Jesus called them Boanerges, which meant **sons of thunder**.*

John the son of Salome:

- *developed a very close relationship with Jesus and was also known as the beloved or he whom Jesus loved.*
- *witnessed Jesus being transfigured or (taking on the radiance of the Father) on the mountain.*
- *wrote the gospel of John and four other books in the New Testament, including the book of Revelation.*

Salome was very much involved in her sons' lives even though they were grown men. She brought her sons to Jesus, asking Him to put one son on the right hand and the other son on the left hand in His Kingdom. Did Salome mean for James to go on the right hand, the position of authority, since he was the eldest son and this was the custom? Or did she mean for John to be elevated to a place of power on Jesus' right hand, as he was already close to Jesus and had worked hard enough to attain a place of authority?

To elevate James the eldest son would be a type of grace, an entitled right by virtue of being the firstborn, whereas to elevate John would be a type of law, an entitlement based on works.

*Salome did not realise that in Jesus' Kingdom there is no left hand; all must be on the same level at the same place, **His right hand**. Salome's request of positioning her sons in the Kingdom of God highlighted many examples of what positioning means.*

Jesus illustrated this in two accounts:

The sheep on the right hand and the goat on the left He will say to the sheep come and inherit the kingdom prepared for you from the foundation of the world. Then he will say to the goat on the left hand depart from me, I never knew you (Matthew 25:33).

At the crucifixion, the thieves on the cross were placed on Jesus' right and on His left. One thief realised that his physical position on Jesus' right hand had spiritual implications, so he cried out, 'Remember me when you come into your Kingdom'. Jesus responded, 'Today you shall be with me in paradise'. He realised he was not in a place of condemnation or damnation; he was at *Jesus' right hand*, a position of authority and power.

Salome:

- *was involved in the life and ministry of Jesus.*
- *used her own resources as she cared for Jesus while He ministered to the crowd.*
- *was in the company of Mary Magdalene, Mary the mother of Jesus, and Mary the wife of Clopas; they travelled from Galilee to Jerusalem.*
- *witnessed the many miracles that Jesus did.*
- *saw many people being healed and delivered from demons.*

- *witnessed the arrest of Jesus and the painful beatings.*
- *and many other women witnessed the crucifixion. They waited to see where Jesus' body would be placed.*

Salome kept a night vigil when Jesus was crucified. It was incomprehensible that Jesus the perfect One was placed in the tomb. Even though she was doubtful at times, Salome still had faith that Jesus' story was true. She often wondered how He could raise himself up from the grave. At the dawn of the first day of the week she sneaked out to take the spices she had prepared, to the tomb to embalm Jesus' body.

Salome:

- and the other women found the large stone at the entrance of the tomb removed, so they went into the tomb. Much to their amazement and shock, Jesus' body was not there.
- screamed with excitement as they had a second glance.
- saw the angels in the tomb, who spoke with them. The angels confirmed that Jesus was raised from the dead.
- ran with the other women to tell the apostles the good news.
- was a disciple of Jesus.
- was with the one hundred and twenty (women were not counted) in the upper room, waiting for the Holy Spirit forty days later. She witnessed the sound of the rushing mighty wind, the tongues of fire, and the coming of the Holy Spirit as Jesus promised.
- was filled with the Spirit and had lived through two major eras: the period of Jesus on earth and the period of the Holy Spirit on earth.

Salome cared about her family, but was initially preoccupied with status. She quickly learnt how to think like Christ, seeing things with eternal value. Her sons James and John were two of those privileged disciples to witness the transfiguration of Jesus Christ. They were with Jesus in Gethsemane. Her boys were among the Bible writers who penned a few of the New Testament books. She raised credible children who were disciples, and she spent her life ministering to Jesus during the short period of His public life.

Modern-Day Reality: Striving for excellence.

CHAPTER 88

MARY MAGDALENE

*(Matthew 27:55–61; 28:1–11; Mark 14:3–9;
15:40–41; 16:1–13; Luke 7:36–50; 8:2–3;
23:50–56; 24:10; John 20:1–18)*

*Spent most of her life engaged in sinful practices, she encountered Jesus
and understood the message He was trying to convey to His disciples.*

These extraordinary events must have made an indelible impression on all those witnessing them. All four gospels writers were explicit in their account of Christ's death, burial, and resurrection.

She met Jesus who recognised what her problem was. Mary Magdalene was possessed by seven devils. It is believed that she lead a promiscuous life, causing her to become destructive to many families and marriages. She most likely would have tried to stop herself engaging in such shameful practices, however she became worse and continued to engage in those immoral practices. Most women hated her because she was a threat to their marriage. Jesus commanded the devils to leave her and she was instantly delivered.

Feeling remorseful and embarrassed, Mary Magdalene's encounter with Jesus brought about significant changes in her life. Her outlook on life was different as she was able to value her own life and the lives of those around her. She loved Jesus' teachings, so she followed Him and ministered to Him with many other women. Wealth was not her portion, but she thought about how she could show her love to Jesus who forgave her from the burden of sin, guilt, and shame.

Mary:

- realised the purpose for which Jesus came.
- was prepared to anoint Jesus' body while He was in the tomb.
- believed that the spices she bought to the tomb would preserve Jesus' body however His body did not need to be embalmed. He was alive.
- knew that Jesus had power to defeat death, as He is the resurrection and the life.

A woman who spent most of her life engaged in sinful practices, encountered Jesus and understood the message He was trying to convey to His disciples. She boldly and confidently followed Jesus, and those who knew her past were amazed at her completely transformed life. She lived a life with meaning, she became focused and purposes driven, ministering to Jesus and His disciples. She witnessed the miraculous power of God working in other people and had no reason to doubt whether Jesus was the Son of God.

Mary Magdalene:

- was there at the cross, witnessing the crucifixion.
- was among the women leaving the tomb late that night.
- was among the first women to visit Jesus on resurrection day.
- was among those women who told the whole village that Jesus was alive.
- saw Jesus personally as He revealed himself to her after His resurrection.

Mary Magdalene was part of a group of women, including Jesus' mother, who cared for Him. She followed Jesus from the moment she encountered Him until His ascension to heaven. Her life demonstrated to all those who were sinners that Christ is able to deliver them. She proved to them that no one is beyond God's grace and that Christ came to make the wounded whole.

Modern-Day Reality: When life appears insignificant and disreputable, one encounter with Christ can add true meaning and purpose.

CHAPTER 89

Mrs. Pilate

(Matthew 27:1–28)

Told her husband about the dream she had the previous night,
the pains she had suffered because of all that was happening to Jesus.

The annual national feast approached. One of the highlights of the feast, a condemned prisoner would be freed. Pilate had the ominous job of putting prisoners to death, as well as the power to release them. He valued the opinion of the crowd in his choice of the prisoner to be released. Barnabas, a notorious prisoner, was among the dangerous criminals. The crowd was asked who they thought should be freed. In unison the mob shouted, **'Give us Barnabas and kill Jesus'**.

At that moment all the chief priests and the religious leaders decided to falsely accuse Jesus of making himself King and calling Himself God. The accusers came to Pilate, the governor of the land, bringing charges against Jesus and the prescribed punishment for the crime. After a lengthy period of listening to the accusers, Pilate stood baffled. Jesus was quiet in court; he saw this as Jesus' inability to defend himself.

Mrs. Pilate:

- was with her husband as they sat on the judgement seat.
- nudged her husband, telling him to have nothing to do with this case since Jesus was righteous.
- begged her husband to wash his hands from all this injustice.
- told her husband about the dream she had the previous night, the pains she had suffered because of all that was happening to Jesus.

*Pilate's wife was not moved by the chanting of the crowd. She was not influenced by the masses; she wanted justice. Her husband did not listen to what she had to say. However, she stood alone in advocating **justice for Jesus**. Pilate released Barnabas and sentenced Jesus to death. Jesus was fulfilling prophecy, since His purpose of coming to earth was to die. He came to redeem the whole world through His death. Pilate's actions were the fulfilment of God's word.*

Mrs. Pilate loved God and sought after justice. She had an unshakeable faith and was going to serve God even though her husband and a whole nation rejected Him. Barnabas was guilty and deserved to die, but the entire city wanted him freed, as they hated Jesus and all that He stood for.

Her name was never mentioned in scriptures. She was the person God visited in a dream. Her heart was connected to God as she believed and stood for justice. She shared her dream with her husband, he wasn't persuaded. Mrs. Pilate stood alone on her conviction, demonstrating that each person is responsible for his/her actions before God. She became aware that serving God is an individual choice.

Modern-Day Reality: In the midst of injustice, God will find someone to declare who He is.

CHAPTER 90

SERVANT GIRL

(Matthew 26:69–72; Luke 22:54–57)

Her presence in the company of men was not unnoticed
at Jesus' arrest…

S he was the kind of girl who was in the know; she could give an
account of the activities of Jesus and His disciples. She took time
to study Christ's teachings and fully understood that the lessons were
inundated with godly mysteries that the natural mind could not unravel.

She:

- could have heard the account at a wedding party and Jesus
  requesting that large water bottles be filled with water.
- knew about a neighbour or a friend who lived in her city
  whom Jesus had healed from physical sickness or diseases.
- knew that for the past three and a half years, Jesus had twelve

men with Him and they went everywhere, proclaiming the word of God.

- knew that Jesus and His men walked from Galilee through Samaria to Jerusalem, stopping to perform miracles along the way, and He visited the temple, teaching the word of God.
- was in the crowd when some of the healings occurred.

Events had changed in the life of Jesus; there was a presence of heavy security as the soldiers swooped into the crowd, arresting Him late that evening. His followers scampered for their lives, fearing they would also be killed. Outside was damp and cold as the night approached. The soldier did not notice Peter as he slipped into their company, trying to disguise himself. All the conversations were about the events of the day, and many were speculating what would happen to Jesus' disciples.

Peter pretended he never knew who Jesus was. None of the others in the crowd knew Peter, but the servant girl recognised his voice. She became much more curious, as she moved closer to the soldier. She was able to identify Peter. She could not fully understand why he now wanted to totally disassociate himself with his leader.

The servant girl:

- *worked faithfully for her mistress many years. Her mistress was kind, allowing her flexible working hours upon request.*
- *made special requests when Jesus was in town with His disciples.*
- *had firsthand knowledge of some of the miracles.*
- *knew all the disciples by name; she was also a **secret** follower of Jesus.*

*It was rather unusual for women to be in the company of men, but she was part of the male-dominated gathering when Jesus was arrested. Her presence in the company of **men** was not unnoticed at Jesus' arrest; she had great significance. She communicated with the soldiers, giving them vital information. Her actions demonstrated the message Christ came to teach: removal of barriers. A message of hope and reconciliation, oneness in Christ, there is no cultural inhibitions, no gender, no race, no class; we are all one in Christ.*

*Peter could no longer hide, since two other persons identified him. He denied any knowledge of Jesus. Months before Jesus was arrested He had numerous conversations with His followers, informing them what actions they would take when He was arrested. He told Peter, '**On three occasions you will say that you don't know me before the rooster crows**'. The events happened exactly as Jesus predicted.*

The servant girl was the only person in the crowd who knew Jesus' disciples and could identify them. She knew the prophecies of Christ, as she lived expecting their fulfilment in her lifetime.

Modern-Day Reality: Knowledgeable and brave.

CHAPTER 91

JOANNA

(Luke 8:1–3; 23:50–56; 24:10)

Joanna and her husband had a choice
between loyalty to Herod... or Christ.

B ible commentators believe her husband was an intelligent man who rose to the position of administrator in Herod's household. Joanna and her husband, had access to the king's palace. She was a messenger, as she shared the news about Jesus' miracles with Herod's servants.

Joanna was the wife of Mr. Chuza, an employee of King Herod.

Joanna:

- *had firsthand knowledge of the power of Christ.*
- *gave of her money and material wealth to maintain the work of Christ.*
- *was among the company of Mary Magdalene, Salome, and*

Mary the mother of Jesus and witnessed the many miracles in Jesus' ministry.

- *was a devoted disciple of Jesus and spent her life caring for Him and His twelve apostles.*
- *saw Jesus being tortured and interrogated. She witnessed his pain, anguish, beatings, and death on the cross.*

Herod was confused as he thought Jesus was the reincarnation of John the Baptist. It was possible that Chuza lost his position as Herod's accountant because of Joanna's faith and position in Christ. Joanna and her husband had a choice between loyalty to Herod, who represented an earthly kingdom, or Christ, who represented a heavenly Kingdom. They chose the latter.

Joanna mourned for Jesus after His death. She awoke early Sunday morning and joined many other women as they visited the tomb. Their sole purpose of visiting was to make sure his body was still there, and to embalm Him. Joanna was totally amazed, Jesus' body was missing and the tomb was empty. Fear and panic immediately followed until she remembered the teachings of Jesus: He would die and rise again from the dead on the third day. His missing body could only enforce one reality: He was alive. Overjoyed by the resurrection of Jesus, she became a much stronger witness for Christ. She was willing to challenge anyone who disbelieved in Him.

She was among those women who followed Jesus closely. Could the mention of her name in scripture bear significance regarding her status in her society? Joanna knew that her choice was a threat to their livelihood and allegiances to King Herod, but she chose what was costly; the Kingdom of God.

Modern-Day Reality: Heavenly royalty surpasses earthy royalty.

CHAPTER 92

SUSANNA

(Luke 23:49–56; 24:1–12)

The angel conversed with the women,
reassuring them that Christ had risen.

She devoted her time and her life to Christ's ministry and was known as a disciple of Jesus Christ. There were not many female disciples in her era, and this position, elevated women to a place of esteem and worth. A *follower* is a student, or one who follows the moral teachings of someone. This must not be confused with the term *apostle*, who were men selected by Jesus.

Susanna:

- knew the word of Christ.
- was a teacher of the word of God.
- displayed Christ-likeness and a godly example; her life fully demonstrated the teachings of Christ.

Susanna was most probably unmarried because she gave of herself, following Christ from village to village. She followed Christ, which was primarily a pursuit for eternal treasure and not for recognition on earth.

Susanna:

- was among the group of women who ministered unto Jesus.
- gave her money and her time ensuring Jesus and His apostle were cared for.
- was one of those persons who caringly provided all the necessities for Jesus and His apostles. She stood out as part of the *backbone* to Jesus' earthly ministry.

She was with Jesus and His ministry team in Galilee. They travelled to Jerusalem, which took several days on foot. Susanna was not selected by Jesus as an apostle, but she volunteered to be in the company of Jesus and in the presence of greatness.

Susanna had firsthand knowledge of the many mighty miracles that Jesus performed. She knew the teachings of Jesus, including His death as a martyr. As a devoted follower she was among the women who could not sleep because Jesus had suffered a slow and painful death on the cross.

Susanna:

- *was prepared to follow Jesus to the end, and was among the special group of women bringing spices to the tomb to embalm Him after the Sabbath.*
- *was in a company of like-minded women who panicked as they arrived at the tomb and found it empty. Susanna and the*

company of women were privileged, having witnessed the angel who guarded the empty tomb, firsthand. The angel conversed with the women, reassuring them that Christ had risen.

- *was ministered to by angels when the apostles never experienced such visitation of angels.*
- *served Christ with her whole heart and made a valuable contribution in the early church after Christ's ascension.*

Her name was mentioned among the group of women who ministered to Jesus when approximately half of this group was not mentioned. Her commitment, sacrifice, and dedication were extraordinary. As a single woman she devoted her life to her cause, the work of Christ. She no doubt waited for the Messiah. Susanna embraced the doctrines of Christ and believed in Jesus and His mission on earth. Her actions were unprecedented, when reflecting on the cultural element of her times, since married women (Jews) were taught by their husbands. However, she taught herself the scriptures and was called by Christ to become one of His workers.

Modern-Day Reality: Wholeheartedly seeking after Christ.

CHAPTER 93

SAPPHIRA

(Acts 5:1–11)

God-driven unity and purpose bring about a deserved harvest.

Their marriage was one made in heaven. They were very wealthy and extremely reliable. Their assets included lots of land, houses, and a substantial amount of money. Sapphira and her husband Ananias were devoted to their church. They were generous givers, making numerous financial contributions for the upkeep of the church.

News about the church was published; people who practised witchcraft and those who were involved in evil acts gave up their deviant lifestyle and became committed church members. Churchgoers were excited and felt more committed to ensure the work of the church continued. The owners of extra properties were handing the keys over to the church leaders. Others sold their land, bringing all proceeds from the sales to the church, so that the monies would be used to spread the gospel.

Joses from Cyprus was a landowner. He sold his property and

brought all proceeds to the apostle. Sapphira and her husband were in church that day and witnessed what Joses had done. They thought since Joses owned fewer assets, they could make a similar contribution.

Sapphira and Ananias:

- went home and discussed it.
- felt they wanted to sell their lands.
- valued the opinion of the other churchgoers and felt that people would think they were greedy for not selling their lands.
- decided on a price for the property; however, they received much more monies than expected.
- took the extra amount and opened another joint account. There was no disagreement over this. That night they slept peacefully.

Very early in the morning Ananias left home with some of the monies from the sale of the properties. He went into the temple and presented the monies to Apostle Paul. God's Spirit spoke through Paul as he questioned Ananias whether the amount of money he brought into the church was the price of the land. He agreed that this was so, after which he fell down dead.

Sapphira was at home expecting her husband to return, a few hours earlier, but he failed to show up. The couple never spent any long time apart from each other. She became weary looking out the window for Ananias. She did what a loving, caring wife would. She went to the temple to look for him. She had no prior knowledge of what happened to Ananias, she also told Paul the same lie. As a result she died instantly.

Ananias and Sapphira were united in purpose and spoke with one voice. It was sad that the purpose was wrong. Sapphira was a caring wife; she took time to discuss with her husband before making decisions. Their private and public life were in unison. They had a choice to be truthful, which would have saved their lives. It was plausible to offer a sacrifice to God, this was an external act. However God takes pleasure in internal actions, attitude and honesty. God-driven unity and purpose bring about a deserved harvest.

Modern-Day Reality: The principle of unity works for both good and evil. Choose to be unified in the good.

CHAPTER 94

DORCAS [TABITHA]

(Acts 9:36–43)

The only seamstress in Joppa, she was an exceptional designer.

D orcas was a remarkable businesswoman with a lucrative trade keeping her extremely busy. This woman was known as the best designer and the only seamstress in Joppa. The large room in her house was used to showcase her products. She employed many other women who spun cotton into yarn. This yarn was used to create tailor-made garments for people living in Joppa and all the surrounding villages. Dorcas was an expert in her trade and known by many in Joppa and Lydda as **Seamstress Dorcas**. She sewed clothing for citizens of every status—peasants and royalty alike. Her workers were paid well and she used the extra money from her business to help the poor, needy, and homeless. She no doubt displayed the gifts of help; she loved the Lord and wanted to please God in all that she did. She lived a life that exemplified Christ, and demonstrated love and kindness to her workers. The apostle Paul in scriptures referred to her as a female disciple of Jesus.

The terms *disciple* and *apostle* are sometimes used synonymously. Men like Peter, Matthew, Luke, John, James, and Judas are familiar names referred to as disciples of Jesus. However, they were *apostles*. A disciple is a follower of Jesus. The scripture records Jesus having many disciples, and she was one of those disciples.

*One morning Dorcas awoke very early and prayed. She then started her trade, business as usual. Complaining of having a headache and feeling terribly unwell, she took herself back to bed as she thought her illness was transient. An hour later, one of the workers went to check on her. The worker returned breathless and speechless. Dorcas' body was lifeless. The news spread **all over** Joppa and Lydda. The entire village flocked to Dorcas' home when they heard of her death. They wept and wailed; it was indeed the saddest day in Joppa.*

Two men who were relatives of Dorcas ran to the city close to Lydda to get Peter, the preacher. They believed Peter was a man of God and would be able to help. Peter knew Dorcas very well so he raced to her home. On his arrival he saw many of the villagers weeping and wailing for Dorcas. Peter knew that she was greatly loved. They showed Peter all the clothes Dorcas had made. He was amazed at the display of such great talents. What a unique legacy she left behind.

*Her body was wrapped in new material that she made before her death. Peter went close to where her body lay, praying, '**Tabitha, arise**'. Dorcas opened her eyes and sneezed, recognizing Peter, she sat upright immediately. Peter took her by the hand and she stood up. Dorcas, who was dead, responded to the prayer of Peter; her spirit came alive again. God manifested His mighty power in her life. The entire village commenced a celebration of life with feasting, music, and dancing. Many people were converted to Christ because of this great miracle.*

Dorcas was multitalented and used all her gifts and abilities to help her society. She was greatly loved as she touched the hearts of both the young and old with care and hospitality.

It must be noted that good deeds, good life, and good works does not immune a Christian from sickness and death. However, death is not the end.

God's power can raise the dead. The scripture teaches that we who were dead in our transgressions, sins, and wrongdoings had been raised up by God from the dead to be elevated, to a place of honour and glory. The Bible also teaches that our weak, frail bodies will be changed to that which is immortal and we will be raised up whether dead or alive to live in the presence of a Holy God.

Dorcas' life was pleasing to God and her experience of death was not the end. God allowed her experience so His message could be heard and His power manifested.

Modern-Day Reality: Our God specialises in miracles and the miraculous.

CHAPTER 95

RHODA

(Acts 12:1–17)

Her faith was high as she lived in expectancy.

Church leaders were martyred; the followers were dispersed and hiding for their lives. Those who followed Christendom could not convene for fellowship in the normal place or they would be dragged before the council to be put into prison or to death. Peter, an apostle, was put in prison for teaching the people about God. So the fearful followers gathered at the house of Mary, a widow, to hide from their persecutors. Realising that there were fewer options remaining, they thought it was best to cry out to God to rescue them, so a prayer meeting started.

The focus of their prayers was for their safety and the release of Peter. They did not realise it was past midnight. Rhoda, the slave girl at Mary's house, relinquished her duties to attend the prayer meeting also. Her duties were never measured in time, but were based on demand. She worked for long hours from early morning to late at night. They were careful as they knew if the sound of their prayers were heard outside of the four walls of Mary's house, they would all be sentenced to prison like Peter.

Although it was after midnight, Rhoda was attentive; she heard a knock at the door. Rushing to the door she noticed Peter, breathless and exhausted, as if he had been running for miles. She was stunned yet overwhelmed with joy. She did not open the door right away, but ran back to the meeting place with exuberance. Her speech was slurred with excitement as she informed those present that their prayers were answered and Peter was standing at the door. None of them believed her. They thought she was insane, dismissing the idea that Peter was at the gate; they said it was his angel. Rhoda's insistence brought the prayer meeting to an abrupt end. Rhoda, along with few of the followers, went to the gate and found Peter standing there. The house gathering became a late-night celebration as the crowd rejoiced over Peter's release from prison. Rhoda now had to prepare a sumptuous meal for all her guests as they celebrated the release of Peter.

Rhoda was a devoted and committed slave girl who performed her duties without fail. She was a follower of Christ who believed in the power of prayer. She was keen and alert to Peter's knock, recognising him in the dark of the night. Rhoda did not doubt what she saw, or think she had seen an angel or a 'spirit'. She had great expectations as she visualised a breakthrough for Peter. The other Christians doubted and did not believe God could answer prayers instantly. She faithfully served God and her fellow men.

Modern-Day Reality: A life of complete service and sacrifice.

CHAPTER 96

LOIS

(2 Timothy 1:5)

Paul the apostle described the word of God in Lois as a unique kind of faith.

Lois secured two godly generations 'under her belt' as she taught them the ways of God. She did that which was abnormal since men were predominantly teachers of the word, this contradicted Jewish culture. In this account there was no mention of her husband, although she was most likely married. Lois did not wait for her husband to teach the word, but familiarised herself with the word and became the prime teacher. She knew God, and was willing to pass on the teachings of Christ to her offspring. Within the Jewish culture reference would be made to a son, therefore it was most likely that she did not have a son. However, she imparted the word of God to her daughter.

Lois felt the word of God was not limited to gender, as the word of God in a man or a woman is a powerful tool. Once the word of

God is delivered, it will accomplish much. She knew the importance of teaching.

Paul the apostle described the word of God in Lois as a unique kind of faith. It was described as an unwavering faith, which believes God for the impossible. It also touches generations, withstands hardship and persecution. Lois proudly and boldly passed on her faith, declaring the manifold greatness of God. Her faith produced great results for two generations. Lois' action was like Joshua in the Old Testament, boldly declaring, 'as for me and my house (*my children and children's children*), we will serve the Lord' (Joshua 24:15).

Lois did not live in isolation and was tested in her faith. It is believed that life was challenging, but she taught her daughter how to love those who hated her and how to reward good for evil. Lois was a woman of great wisdom, seeking God to produce fruit through her knowledge and faith.

It is possible that the word of God was in this family for over one hundred years. Assuming at eighteen years of age Lois had her daughter Eunice, and her daughter was eighteen years old when she had her son Timothy. And if Timothy was eighteen years old when the book of Timothy was written, that would be 108 years of faith in this family.

Lois as a mother and a grandmother valued the faith in her daughter and her grandson as the richest legacy they could inherit. Knowing that anything else she would give her family would depreciate, she wanted to filter down something that became more valuable with time. Lois was filled with grace and godly influence; she was a mother and grandmother with an unshakeable faith.

Modern-Day Reality: The greatest family legacy is God's word.

CHAPTER 97

EUNICE

(Acts 16:1–5; 2 Timothy 1:5)

Timothy was encouraged to be steadfast in the faith, the same faith that was unwavering in his mother Eunice...

A young girl adopted her mother's model for life until she became a replica of all that her mother was and more. Eunice became **mini** Lois. She had the most impressionable exposure of godliness and righteousness demonstrated by her mother. There was a special place in their house called the family altar—a place of prayer and worship.

She keenly observed her mother dealing with disappointment and injustice. Eunice's mother became her best friend, counsellor, confidante, and teacher. Eunice was so deeply impacted by such godly life that she grew up and purposed to emulate her mother. She made a conscious decision to pass on this rich legacy to her child/children. Eunice became strong in faith, being constantly sharpened by the faith of her mother in example and words.

Eunice learned about the great heroes from her mother Lois. These heroes served God and were willing to sacrifice their lives. Eunice learned what made these heroes stood out in their faith. She also learned about faith; the reality of those things not yet tangible, but seen in the eyes of the spirit. Faith comes directly through exposure to God's word. Eunice meditated on the word of God, producing great faith.

It is believed that Eunice a Jewish woman, was married to a Greek. They had a son whom the father named Timothy; this name carried a Greek influence. Not much is known of Timothy's father apart from the fact that he was Greek. He was not a proselyte, but had much influence in Timothy's upbringing, since he was not circumcised. It is believed that Timothy's father was not a believer, as the scripture did not mention about his faith in God. Eunice's role as a mother was commendable as she taught her son the word of God. She passed on the teachings of her mother, through godly examples and words.

Timothy's focus in life was not divided between his mother as a Jewish believer and his father, who was probably an unbelieving Greek. Timothy understood that faith is personal; he resorted to develop a strong faith in God, as his mother Eunice and his grandmother Lois.

The apostle Paul, one of the greatest heroes of the faith in the New Testament, chose Timothy as his companion. Paul wrote to Timothy from prison, encouraging him to be **steadfast** in his faith. Paul told Timothy in the letter to stir up the faith he was given, the same unwavering faith that was in Eunice and Lois. Paul's desire for Timothy that his faith would flourish and excel so that his gifts would be manifested. He encouraged Timothy to allow the sharp and dynamic word of God within him to grow and multiply in the face of conflict and persecution.

Paul reminded Timothy that God has undoubtedly blessed him through his mother and grandmother. They were living examples and teachers of God's word. He emphasised to Timothy that the word of

God is limitless and transcends times; the word is always appropriate to any generation. It was completely relevant to his grandmother's generation, his mother's generation, and his generation.

Eunice was pleased to see her son Timothy live a life of faith and confidence in God. She taught him selflessness, sacrifice and service to God. Eunice's secret desires were achieved as Timothy chose to become a minister of the word and a companion of Paul.

Modern-Day Reality: A model of godliness; producing righteous fruits.

CHAPTER 98

PHOEBE AND JULIA

(Romans 16:1–2; 15)

In those times the cultural savoury for spiritual leaders in the life
of the church was a masculine imagery.

From scenic Corinth, probably from Greece, a wealthy city on par
with Athens, he wrote this book to the Christians living in Rome.
Paul knew that Jewish dominance would easily push these women further into the background. He commended Julia and Phoebe as female
leaders within the church in Rome. Paul enforced that there was *neither*
male nor female, bonded nor freed, Jew or Gentile in God's kingdom. He
always commended and appreciated all the faithful ministers, whether
male or female.

He addressed areas of church life and maturity in the Christian
faith. Paul concluded his writings, by honouring Christian leaders,
a reminder that they were not forgotten. Only a few women were
serving in public ministry in those times. Phoebe and Julia were

exemplary characters of faith. The Apostle Paul, who wrote several of the New Testament books, lavished gratitude on both women for their work in ministry. In concluding his writings to the church in Rome, he bestowed great appreciation and commendation for Julia and Philologus, her husband who played an active part in ministry. They worked tirelessly in the church, teaching and encouraging the body of Christ.

Apostle Paul addressed cultural diversities and variances as they crept into the church to replace spiritual belief and sound doctrine. The church in Rome was no exception. Paul penned a letter from his humble abode in Corinth to address those issues that were affecting the church in Rome.

Paul:

- addressed matters of faith to the church in Rome.
- told them that Salvation is a *work of God's Spirit* and that no one can work for their salvation.
- admonished them that Christ's work on the cross was full, complete, and not exclusive to the Jews.
- informed them that the Gentiles were welcome to God's plan of salvation, just as the Jews.

Paul, as he concluded the book of Romans, made several recommendations to the church.

He recommended and dispatched Phoebe from Cenchrea, a **humble servant**, a sister in Christ, with the book that he wrote to the Romans. Paul referred to her as one who was well loved and trusted.

He asked the church members to welcome her as a Christian and a minister of Christ. Phoebe, however, had made numerous sacrifices in previous years. She ensured that Paul and many other ministers did not lack the necessities they required to fulfil the work of the Lord. Paul was forceful. He beseeched the church to financially support Phoebe, ensuring that she lack nothing. Phoebe was a full-time worker, deaconess and helper, when few women were actively involved in the work of the Lord.

Phoebe:

- communicated with Paul while he was in Corinth and visited him.
- could have been the courier used to deliver the writings to the church in Rome; therefore, she was the first to handle the Holy Scripture after it was written.
- was trustworthy. Paul trusted her with the book of Romans.

The book of Romans was written to combat doctrinal struggles within the church. Its inclusion in the scripture as canonical testified to the fact that Phoebe took extra-special care in handling the word. The early church could not accept salvation as a completed work of Christ. They wanted to work for their salvation. This letter addressed to Rome, corrected all these concerns within the church.

In those times, the cultural savoury for spiritual leaders in the life of the church was a masculine imagery. Paul encouraged these women to keep up the work of ministry as worthy servants of the Living God.

Women were not known to serve in such positions of leadership at that time. Therefore, the status of these women within the church, was one to which many woman aspired.

Modern-Day Reality: Sacrifices never go unnoticed.

CHAPTER 99

CHLOE

(1 Corinthians 1:11–13)

The Christians in Chloe's household were greatly influenced by her.

When misunderstandings are allowed to fester and not resolved in a timely manner, they lead to division and rift even in the church. The church in Corinth experienced doctrinal *fallout*, creating power struggles and discouragement to some of its followers. It would appear that the male leaders within the church were content in their position, accepting schism within the church as normal. They were happy to carry on leading once the parishioners were committed to acknowledging their positions within the church. They were not disturbed by the disharmony.

Matured, spirit-filled Christians like Chloe were burdened for the work of Christ; she prayed and fasted, seeking God for wisdom to address the issues within the church. She did not think it was gossip or mischievous, but was driven by a desire for oneness within the body of

Christ. Chloe contacted Paul, highlighting all the confusion within the church causing such rift and damaging effects.

Paul wrote to the church, informing them that the house of Chloe contacted him. Paul's letter to the church highlighted the division and confusion within the church. He addressed the problems, appealing to the church to put away their differences and to unify the body of Christ.

Chloe:

- was a woman of God who refused to be intimidated by anyone within the church as she stood for truth.
- showed pride in the fact that she contacted Paul to let him know that the church was divided and needed to be remedied.
- chose not to remain anonymous.
- influenced her household to stand for unity.

The book of Corinthians was written by Paul to deal with the division and disunity among the believers in the church.

Issues that needed to be dealt with:

- The church had become divided over leadership, and over doctrines or teachings.
- Church members were elevating one leader over another.

The confusion within the church did not attest to their faith as Christians. Some churchgoers attended only to support the preacher they loved, causing chaos within the church. Paul was persuasive in addressing the issue of discord within the church, pleading with the believers to be united, as Christ is one.

Chloe was not the person Paul left in charge of the church in Corinth, but she was fully aware of the toil and sacrifice that Christ made to redeem the lost. She was totally committed to the work of Christ, therefore she communicated with the apostle Paul, informing him of the problems within the church. She often updated Paul of spiritual progress within the church.

She was a trusted and godly woman, and was known personally by the Apostle Paul. He praised her for such openness and Christian maturity. Chloe's husband was never mentioned, and since she had a family, it is suggestive that she could have been a widow. She dedicated her life and time to the ministry. She impacted all those living within her house. They were taught to avoid disunity within the church and elevate Christ in their lives. The church members became God-fearing Christians and emulated Chloe's life above those of the leaders in the church in Corinth. She was a remarkable woman whose life was reputable and outstanding.

Modern-Day Reality: Stand for unity. Know when to seek out help.

CHAPTER 100

BERNICE

(Acts 24:22–27; 25:1–27; 26:1–32)

Born into great wealth and honour... a princess.

B ernice was a magistrate, a noble role she performed along with her brother, King Agrippa. They sat on the panel of judges to make decisions based on a preponderance of evidence whether or not the apostle Paul was guilty of the charges laid against him—crimes punishable by execution. Bernice was the daughter of Herod Agrippa 1 (AD 38–45). She was married many times. It is believed, one of her husbands was her uncle Herod.

Paul was brought before Judge Felix, who was convinced that Paul was innocent. He was hesitant in concluding the sentencing since he felt obligated to please the crowd who brought the accusation. Felix, fuelled by greed, wanted a bribe from Paul. He refused to pay the bribe and was sent to prison for two years. Paul had a hearing two years later and was brought before Festus this time. The apostle Paul was tried by Festus, since there was insufficient evidence to convict him of the crime committed, the verdict was, Paul should be freed. In the absence of vital evidence, he felt Paul was innocent of the charges laid against him. Festus became increasingly fearful, given the state of anarchy within the country, if Paul was freed, the people would kill him. King Agrippa and Bernice were guests of Festus and, although they heard about the case, they did not know who Paul was. They begged Festus to allow them to see him.

Paul had previously appealed to the Roman authority and was due to be heard by Caesar Augustus (the highest court in his time).

Bernice and her brother, King Agrippa, visited Festus from Rome. They heard about this high-profile case against Paul so they begged Festus to allow them to preside over the matter. Festus felt relieved and gladly handed over 'the problem'.

Paul:

- *was elated, as it was another opportunity to have the king and his sister Bernice listen to his defence. Bernice was the first female judge to preside over Paul's matter.*
- *felt Bernice would be empathetic.*
- *knew that he was innocent of all the charges.*
- *stood up and defended himself.*

The king was touched by Paul's speech, to the extent that he was about to kneel down and pray for forgiveness. King Agrippa felt Paul was innocent and should be freed of all charges, as he did nothing worthy of death.

Bernice was:

- *born into great wealth and honour as a privileged part of the royal dynasty.*
- *a princess, the daughter of King Herod. She knew all about the monarchy since her father and all her brothers reigned on the throne.*
- *quite influential in her family and worked closely with her brothers.*
- *exposed to the juridical system and presided over many criminal cases.*
- *among the judges of the land; however, her heart was hardened since she was unmoved by Paul's plea for justice.*

She had become callous and corrupted, leading a reckless life and getting involved in promiscuity, which was contrary to the teachings of Paul. It is widely believed that she had an incestuous relationship with one of her brothers. Bernice was not ordinary. Her entitlement as a princess meant that she was a powerful and influential woman. Her prestigious position as a member of the monarchy does not grant automatic rights to morality since she was amoral. She revelled with her sister Drusilla as they both led reckless, ungodly lives.

Bernice heard those powerful words of God through Paul. He explained his own conversion from a murderer to a preacher. He spoke about his corrupt life, murdering God's people, but an encounter with Christ changed his life. She had a life-changing opportunity as Paul introduced her to the same Life Changer, however it was her choice to remain an unbeliever. She knew that it was time to walk in integrity and morality, but she chose to hold on to her self-destructive way of life.

Modern-Day Reality: Power and position are unprofitable unless used for good purposes.

CHAPTER 101

DRUSILLA

(Acts 24:22–27)

She conceded with her husband and did not use her power of influence positively.

In her era, preaching and teaching false doctrine was a major crime punishable by death. Christians were stoned, imprisoned, and murdered for their faith. Apostle Paul proclaimed the good news of salvation in Christ, this was different to traditional Jewish teachings. His accusers, opposing the teachings of Christ, brought him before every judge in the land. Paul was first tried by the Council, declaring him innocent of the charges laid against him. His accusers were determined to have him put to death. In unison they referred him to the highest judicial court in the land. He appeared before Felix, the most excellent governor of Caesarea. Felix was married to Drusilla, a princess, the sister of King Agrippa and Bernice. She was also Jewish and a judge.

The centurion sent letters to Caesarea ahead of Paul's visit, detailing the charges laid against him. Felix and Drusilla sat in the judgement hall and read the letter. They were not swayed by the contents of the letter, but anticipated Paul's visit. They eagerly awaited the accusers to put their case forward.

The plaintiff consisted of Ananias, the chief priest, along with some of the elders and Tertulus, who was an excellent spokesman. They appeared in court standing before the judge, the Most Honourable Felix and Judge Drusilla.

Paul was accused of:

- lawlessness.
- recklessness.
- inciting revolt.

Drusilla and Felix turned to Paul as he stood in the witness box to state his defence for the charges. Paul boldly and confidently laid his claim in defence of his Christian faith. The judges listened attentively. Paul passionately made his address, while Drusilla and her husband sat in the judges' chair, overcome by fear and emotions. Felix was deeply touched, being rather unsure of himself he asked Paul to go away.

Felix loved bribery and thought Paul would give him money to be set free. A disappointed Felix contradicted his own conscience, sending Paul back to prison where he spent two years. After that time an appeal was made for Paul's release. Drusilla and Felix hardened their hearts and kept Paul in prison longer, to please his accusers.

Drusilla had:

- *the opportunity to judge the greatest apostle.*
- *the power to revoke the accusations against the apostle Paul, but failed to do so.*

Drusilla failed to positively influence the prison sentence, which would allow an innocent man to be freed. She conceded with her husband and did not use her power to acquit the innocent. It was sad that Drusilla and her sister Bernice were demi-monde. Both were known in Rome as the most corrupt and shameless women in their time because of their adulterous and deceptive lifestyle. Their lifestyle was not only abominable within a Jewish culture, but it also contradicted the word of God and the teachings of Paul.

Modern-Day Reality: Never try to evade the power of conscience.

CHAPTER 102

PRISCILLA

(Acts 18:1–28; Romans 16:3;
1 Corinthians 16:19; 2 Timothy 4:19)

Priscilla worked hard in the ministry with him, and was willing to
risk her own life to save his life.

She must undoubtedly be the first lady of the New Testament, although she was not the wife of the great apostle, however she was referred to repeatedly by Apostle Paul in his writings. Aquila and his wife Priscilla originated from Pontus; they lived in Italy for a long time. They were forced out of their homes by Claudius, who expelled all Jews from Rome. Christianity and the Jewish religion were rapidly spreading all over Rome, much to the dissatisfaction of the Roman emperor. In an effort to control the religious sect, Emperor Claudius banished all the Jews living in Rome. The couple left Rome under these circumstances, heading for Corinth. They spent their time living a nomadic life as missionaries. Paul arrived at Corinth and connecting immediately with Priscilla and Aquila because of their commonalities in trade, as tent-makers and teachers/preachers of the word of God. Priscilla and her husband were Paul's personal friends, playing a crucial role in his life and ministry.

Hundreds of Jews and Gentiles were converted to Christianity. Priscilla and her husband were convinced God was working greatly through Paul; hence, they pledged to fully support him. They accompanied Paul as he travelled from Corinth to Syria and Ephesus, sharing the word of God.

Priscilla and Aquila met Apollos, who was also a Jew from Alexandria. Apollos was zealous for God, but was not sound in his theological discourse. He loved God and was an eloquent speaker. Priscilla and Aquila taught Apollos the word of God, showing him how to be effective in ministry. Apollos submitted himself and was schooled by these veterans. He became a mighty man of God, unshaken in faith as he preached with conviction.

Priscilla:

- was a godly woman.
- worked closely with her husband as a missionary and often travelled with Paul to many cities where Christ was not known.
- experienced God at work in powerful and unusual ways.
- gave up her home for ministry, and a thriving, vibrant congregation met in her front room regularly.
- was a very dynamic preacher who knew the word of God and the God of the word.

Paul repeatedly sent greetings to all those who were involved in the work of God. He sent more greetings to Priscilla than any other woman involved in ministry in the New Testament. Priscilla worked hard in the ministry with him, and was willing to risk her own life to save his life. In Asia, Paul was accompanied by Priscilla and Aquila; he remembered to convey greetings from them in his writings to the Corinthians. She was not only known by Paul, but her association was widespread. Her popularity in the New Testament churches is based on the fact that she was a companion of Paul and widely travelled. Timothy also conveyed greetings to her, from the Apostle Paul.

Pricilla was an outstanding servant of God and sacrificed all she had, to do the work of Christ. She made a remarkable impact in the work of God, more than many unmarried women in her time. She was sold out and committed to her cause, the cause of Christ.

Modern-Day Reality: Total commitment to a cause.

CHAPTER 103

Euodia

(Philippians 4:1-3)

She showed forgiveness and the fear of God, and a willingness to give up her rights and privileges to others.

Founders and pioneers exercise caution when handing over their work to other people. They are meticulous in seeking trustworthy persons. The apostle Paul, as the pioneer of the church in Philippi, would have done the same. He later dedicated a book in the New Testament in honour of this church in Philippi . Paul undoubted knew the perils of ineffective leadership, so he carefully selected his leaders to replace him while he was away.

Paul enquired among the church members for potential candidates. Euodia put herself forward as a potential eligible candidate. Paul prayerfully selected Euodia because of her faithfulness and great leadership ability. She was steadfast and consistent in her faith. Paul had no reservations when he entrusted the church in Philippi into her care.

Euodia was a great teacher, motivating the church members to develop their gifting, as a result the church in Philippi grew and expanded.

Not long after Euodia took over leadership, Syntyche, another church leader, challenged her over headship of the church. Conflict ensued over leadership, creating division and struggle for power within the church. The nature of this discord had the potential to completely destroy the church in Philippi, resulting in many of the believers being confused, discouraged, and attempting to leave the church.

One of the church elders contacted Paul, giving him insight into what was happening at the church in Philippi.

Paul:

- wrote a letter to the church, pleading with the two women, Euodia and Syntyche, to have the same thoughts and put away differences.
- instructed them to submit to each other as they would do to Christ.
- warned them that they should never seek their own interests or be involved in that which was destructive to the body of Christ.
- admonished them to agree with one another in Christ so that the church would be united.

The other leaders were instructed by Paul to support the work through such a difficult phase. Euodia was disappointed and hurt, but willing to step down from leadership, allowing her rival Syntyche to lead the church in Philippi. Euodia's example of true humility greatly impacted Syntyche, resulting in a complete change in her negative attitude to leadership. Syntyche no longer viewed leadership as power to be grasped or a position that she should compete for.

Leadership is God-given, God-designed, and God-ordained. It is God who establishes or demotes leaders.

Syntyche was embarrassed and apologised for her contentious behaviour, which caused a rift within the church. The two women were able to submit themselves to God and each other, their humility caused church members to unite once more. They independently resolved their conflict without Paul's physical intervention, and made a commitment to work together for the good of God's Kingdom.

Paul was proud of their conflict resolution and commended both women for their faithfulness in the ministry. He reminded them that their names are written in the book of life.

Euodia:

- characterised true Christ-likeness when she showed forgiveness and the fear of God, and a willingness to give up her rights and privileges to others.
- led by example as a humble servant of God, not invigorated by power, but willing to be demoted from her leadership role when conflict occurred.
- did not attempt to prove her innocence. She demonstrated self-sacrifice and purity of heart.
- became one of the most outstanding leaders in her time.
- knew while she was alive that her name was written in the book of life.

Euodia was distinguished, a woman of reputable status, accredited by the apostle Paul. In a society predominantly led by men, she was able to contend with them and secured a successful leadership role. Her humility, availability and willingness to take second place in the light of opposition became the elevating factors in her life and ministry.

Modern-Day Reality: Promotion comes from God.

CHAPTER 104

TRYPHENA AND TRYPHOSA

(Romans 16:12–16)

Their presence and work in the Roman church attracted many women,
and wealthy Romans to the gospel.

They lived in an era characterised by discrimination, since Jews and Gentiles alike viewed certain groups of people as insignificant. This indifference was prevalent in the life of Apostle Paul; being a minister to the Gentiles, he was disregarded by the Jews and was not originally welcomed by Christians. It was God's mercy that made him who he was. Women were another group of people discriminated against in the church by both Jews and Gentiles.

The Apostle Paul, though a Jew, he fully understood that all people are made one by the blood of Jesus. There is no emphasis on gender, class, ethnicity, and position. This preacher to the Gentiles saw the significance and worth in women.

Two of these women were Tryphena and Tryphosa, twin sisters; their names were uncommon in Rome. It was common practice in wealthy Roman households for their children to have names that depicted their character; this was not practiced among the poor and marginalised. It was believed that Tryphena and Tryphosa were no exception; their parents were wealthy Roman citizens, who called them *daintiness and delicacy*. The people of Rome were ethnocentric, boasting about their incredible wealth, unique culture, class, distinction, pride, and prejudice. Despite being born into a life of luxury, the girls were converted to the Christian faith and were involved in the ministry of the church. This was significant since the poor, the notorious, and the infamous readily accepted the Christian teachings, than their wealthy and influential counterparts.

Paul:

- knowing their wealthy background, chose to mention them with common slaves.
- emphasised that Christ makes all people one. Both wealthy and slaves are equal in His sight.
- commended these women for their hard work; they worked along with the men in proclaiming the good news of Christ.

Tryphena and Tryphosa:

- gave up their noble life of luxury, wealth, and security to become followers of Christ. They had a deep desire to share their faith in an era when the rich struggled with the idea of identifying with the Christian faith.
- focused on eternal treasures laid up in heaven; they knew what it was like to be born into earthly wealth.

- remained single women and totally committed to the cause of Christ, their presence and work in the Roman church attracted many women and wealthy Romans to the gospel, as a result the church grew.
- realised that even though people have great material wealth, they are poor without Christ. Their wealth cannot secure them a position in Christ.
- knew that Christ's purpose in redemption was not only to elevate the poor and the marginalized, but also to create unity.

Paul singled out Tryphena and Tryphosa for an expression of gratitude for their devotion and labour of love for God's people. They exemplified incessant, arduous labour in the church as deaconesses, using their material wealth and spiritual riches to impact the affluent in their society.

Modern-Day Reality: Material wealth cannot compare to eternal riches.

CHAPTER 105

Mother of the Prostitute: Great Babylon

(Revelation 17:1–18; 18:1–24; 19:1–4)

This Great Babylon Mother of Prostitutes usurped authority over the universe as if she created the world.

He was the only apostle who lived to a ripe old age and died a natural death; a man filled with wisdom. The fact that he outlived his contemporaries meant he saw and experienced more. God honoured him, allowing him to envision life in the future.

In his account, he recorded his vision of a powerful woman decked in the colours representing great strength and royalty (Daniel 5:16; 29, Esther 8:15; Mark 15:17). She wore an outfit complimenting her great power. She was adorned from head to toe in jewellery made from gold or pearls. This woman displayed superiority, elegance, and extreme wealth. Her horse was one, only the elite could ride. She intimidated all those around her with pomp and pride, displaying her despicable title on her forehead, **the Great Babylon Mother of Prostitutes**.

The Great Babylon Mother of Prostitutes:

- was anti-Christianity; she carried out her mission of persecuting and martyring the saints.
- gloated in the performance and the fulfilment of her purpose.
- shouted with joy and excitement as she became intoxicated from the blood of all the Christians who were killed.
- did not act on her own; her accomplice was the despicable beast with multiheads. This creature emerged from the bottomless pit as a terrifying sight, instilling great fear to all those within its vicinity.

The creature was a representation of people who lived and died and will live again. It signified people who never knew God and whose names were never recorded in heaven. There was a fierce war between those who represented the creature and those who acknowledged Christ as Lord and His unstoppable power on earth.

Christ and His followers nullified the power of the multiheaded beast, defeating the authority of the Babylonian figure. The process was painstaking, as Christians suffered at the hand of these hideous *monsters* who sought to frustrate the rule of Christ on earth. The strong Babylonian figure, with an air of superiority possessed powers greater than any other power on earth. Her power was no match to the power of God on earth.

They possessed great power, controlling government systems. They were unaware that this sphere of influence was given to them by God. Great Babylon Mother of Prostitutes usurped authority over the universe as if she created the world. She controlled and mastered seven powerful rulers in seven different eras. At the time John penned this account, five of her seven leaders have concluded their period of leadership. These five leaders had a common element: inflicting pain and hardship, and ensuring that the subsequent leader was crueller than his predecessor.

The sixth of seven world leaders managed the world during John's life time. He prophesied about the seventh and final leader, the Great Babylon Mother of Prostitutes. The book of Revelation was written thousands of years ago, it is safe to conclude, that we are in the era of the seventh and final ruler, the Great Babylon Mother of Prostitutes. It must be noted that the era characterised by global chaos, indifference and instability, a period of unprecedented natural and man-made disasters.

This period of her control marked the end of the end. Her fall culminated in the abrupt end of her evil rule, the disintegration of her kingdom. Then the kingdoms of this world will become the Kingdom of our God and of His Christ. He shall reign forever and ever.

Modern-Day Reality: Evil powers have a predicted end. Only God's reign is eternal.

CHAPTER 106

THE WOMAN AND THE DRAGON

(Revelations 12:1–17)

While in labour she was alert and attentive; she saw the dragon,
the enemy, and she knew his evil intention.

One of those spectacular moments in heaven was captured as the woman appeared, dressed in the radiance of the sun. It was quite evident that she was pregnant, and from the sound she was making it was also apparent that she was about to give birth to her baby.

Her luminance lit up the atmosphere, making it impossible to look upon her face. Her hair was neatly curled. Above the curls she wore a golden crown with many stars. She stood firmly on the moon.

She groaned with pain and her beautiful attire, including her crown, could no longer remain in its place as she agonised in her labour. She paced the moon in her pain, praying for the midwife to come.

Her labour was progressing rather well. However, as she tried to cope with the pain, she saw a very unusual sight. A red-hot dragon appeared from nowhere causing her pain to accelerate to excruciating heights. It was her moment as she gave birth instantly. The woman did not spare a moment to cuddle her baby. She felt strong, ready to fight and defeat her challenger.

The dragon:

- *had seven heads and was wearing a crown on each head.*
- *was gigantic with a very long tail.*
- *had great power in his tail and was able to do wonders.*
- *pulled millions upon millions of stars from heaven and they fell to the earth. The fallen stars caused devastation. They destroyed lives, both on land and in the sea.*

The dragon was silent as it came closer to the woman and stood in front of her. He was viciously waiting to snatch her baby immediately after birth. The dragon knew his time was up and he would be conquered by this healthy male child. The child was destined to be a mighty ruler of the world. However, his mother was not waiting for her son to be a grown man. She faced her opponent and was set to defeat him.

The woman:

- *knew the dragon had great power.*
- *was not afraid of the dragon.*
- *protected her son from the dragon.*
- *knew that her seed would totally destroy this wicked beast.*
- *knew she was fulfilling the purpose of God.*

The baby:

- *was taken to a secured place of honour and majesty.*
- *was destined to reign on the throne.*
- *had greater power than the dragon.*

The woman escaped the torture of the wicked dragon, into a place of peace and solitude.

The outrageous dragon:

- raged war and lost all the battles.
- was thrown out of heaven by his opponent.
- was angry.
- wanted people to be afraid of him.
- roamed the country in search of the woman. He got news that she was in a certain place and he went there to capture her.

As the furious beast got to the exact location where this woman and her baby hid, he opened his mouth, by his miraculous power a great river flowed out of his mouth. The woman was protected by God as the earth swallowed up all the water that came out of his mouth. The dragon's wrath intensified at the safety of the mother and baby. The disillusioned dragon, concluded his effort as defeat and stormed out in search of anyone who trusted and believed in God. Children of God always experienced majestic protection from the onslaughts of the enemy. The power that God's children possess is far greater than the powers of the enemy. Therefore, God's children must never accept defeat.

The dragon noted that all true believers in God were immune from his devious acts and he could not touch them or bring about ill effect on them. He stormed away in anger.

The account is a typology of four magnificent moments of the Christian faith.

(1) When Satan was cast out.
(2) It depicts the birth of Christ who came to rule, restore, and seize the power that Satan had.
(3) A futuristic description of the second coming of the Lord and Saviour Jesus Christ, who reigns Supreme as the King of kings and Lord of lords.
(4) It is a true likeness of what Christianity represents today, a life of victory against the enemy and a people who are unstoppable with power to completely defeat their enemy.

The citation of the female gender typified God's unique agent through whom reproduction occurs and new life is generated into the world. The woman giving birth denotes increase; God expects those who are called by Him to reach out to others and win them for Christ. Even though birth was imminent, she was alert and attentive; she saw the dragon, the enemy, knowing his evil intentions, she acted immediately. We are expected to be watchful, be alert and know the intentions of the devil. The woman represents all of God's chosen people who are fearless as they stand and withstand evil in this world. It was interesting that God chose a woman as the key feature in demonstrating His power of increase and watchfulness in this account. God chose her as one demonstrating love and protection.

In another sense, some aspect of the woman represents the 'motherhood' of God, the one who took it upon Himself to birth us into His Kingdom despite the cost. God fights for us and He is undefeated in battle. God also protects us from every cunning intention or action of the enemy. The description of her clothes, radiance, posture, and position; standing on the moon are a representation of God illuminating darkness. Her position on the moon is one of authority, being above all and over all.

Modern-Day Reality: Christians can anticipate some suffering for Christ, but we will overcome.

CHAPTER 107

The Chosen Lady

(2 John 1:1–12)

Femininity at its best is incomplete without the
acknowledgment of God-given order.

John was the only apostle who lived out his natural life to a very old age. He would have seen a lot in his lifetime and had more knowledge about the fate of those who confessed Christ and served Him to the end. He was excited about the elect woman and her children who followed the way of truth as they were instructed.

The elect or chosen woman typified the church, a called-out and special people. It is noteworthy that the church is viewed in the context of a female, a bride, an elect or chosen lady. To look carefully at the characteristics of the female through scripture meant as Eve was created out of Adam, so the elect woman was born out of Christ. This romantic story that commenced in Genesis with the first Adam and Eve in the garden of Eden rolled on through countless centuries and concluded as a marriage of the second Adam (Christ) to His bride the elect lady, '**the second Eve**'.

Mary (the female gender) carried the baby Jesus, and at the right time she gave birth to Him (Luke 1:35). She is a type of the elect woman, the one who bears life. However, femininity at its best is incomplete without the acknowledgment of God-given order and context. Scriptural balance is noted in Isaiah 45:10, where a father gives life and a mother gives birth to life. Both genders are inter-dependent on each other.

Gender analysis in the eyes of God is found in Ephesians 5:25–33: this inseparable love, demonstrated by Christ to the church is equivalent to the love displayed by husband and wife. This is the most valuable relationship in the mind of God; comparing His love for us to that of a husband for his wife. The husband ought to love his wife unconditionally even as Christ loves the church, which is His bride.

Often the Bride is the most distinguished character at a wedding. Jesus refers to the church as His bride.

Christ referred to His body, in terms of the female gender, His Bride. Femininity denotes growth and increase. In the natural a woman carries a pregnancy, travails in labour to bring forth new life. Equally the church brings forth new life with pain, agony and suffering.

The church supports people, until the new life of Christ is formed. The reference is made of the nurturing instinct of a woman who cradles and nurses her baby with love, patience, and discipline. In the same way, the church or the elect woman waits patiently for maturity of the body and exercise meekness and gentleness in the process of growing up.

The Old Testament account in 1 Samuel 6:7-14 bears reference of the female gender displaying strength of character and selflessness. The ark of God, a sacred emblem representing His power and glory among His people was transferred. The two female cows after giving birth were given the task to take the ark of God to another nation. Their young ones were taken away and locked up, yet these heifers did what was not normal. They went off to take the ark of God with their teats filled with milk for their calves, denying their young ones food. They took the ark of God without looking back. The heifer did not complain—a demonstration of the highest degree of sacrifice, self-denial, and commitment to doing the master's will.

Through the eyes of the reproductive scientists, a female infant is born with the ability to reproduce, and every ovum is present at birth. The church being born from Christ has the ability and power to multiply, as seen in the early church (Acts 2:40–41). One hundred and twenty (120) believers (represented the men, since women were not counted) became three thousand one hundred and twenty (3, 120) in less than a week after the manifestation of the Holy Spirit.

The Bible records the principle of producing after their kind, viewed through the eyes of the church. The church is known to attract a predominantly female audience in general. Could women find the church more attractive because of these female characteristics and similarities?

Though there are more women than men within the church overall, leadership within the church is predominantly male. The principle of producing after their kind does not seem to be applicable within this context. Male leadership seems to attract other male leaders, but males being predominantly attracted to the church, seem as a work in progress. It is believed that more work is needed, including a retrospective look at the biblical model.

John, as a senior leader, expressed his longing to meet face-to-face with the church, the elect woman. At that moment he was constrained by space, time, and distance; nevertheless, he was very happy to send a letter until the right time when he will be able to communicate verbally.

The elect lady and her children were commanded to demonstrate love for each other and to govern their lives by the law of love.

John:

- warned the chosen lady to safeguard herself against falsehood, whether in teachings or living.
- told the chosen lady that the hallmarks of false teachings are those who fail to acknowledge that Jesus was born of a virgin Mary or the humanity of Christ.
- concluded that the elect lady must avoid those teachers and embrace teachers who teach the truth about Christ.
- instructed them against losing their reward in Christ.

The chosen lady exemplified a godly life. She was encouraged by John to keep on reproducing new lives, to keep on birthing new ideas and new concepts. She was encouraged to continue to demonstrate love. Love creates unity and togetherness, which serves as a buffer against falsehood.

The unique role of men equates to the role of Christ, as protector, sacrifice, conqueror, and victor. Jesus Christ had accomplished all those roles. Therefore, the female role would be that which is required to bring about completeness and oneness whether we are male or female. God is the head and we serve as the body under His authority. Whether male or female, we are commanded to produce, increase, nurture and demonstrate the highest degree of love, God's love. We are to live a life of sacrifice to God as His Elect.

Modern-Day Reality: All Christians, whether male or female, qualify to be the elect lady/the church.

CONCLUSION

During the period of writing, I could not be oblivious to the fact that significant changes are occurring in some areas of the world where women struggle for rights to freedom and equity. On four separate occasions, British Broadcasting Corporation (BBC) highlighted areas of breakthrough regarding the rights of women. The first story was recognition of women drivers in Saudi Arabia who were allowed to obtain driver's licences for the first time. The second instant was a stewardess on a Turkish Airline who took legal action against the airline for being paid less than her male counterpart. The third story is about Malala Yousafzai (Noble Peace Prize Winner), who was shot in her head by the Taliban in Pakistan in 2012 for her role in campaigning for education among girls. She was fit to return to her home after six years.

The fourth was a major historical landmark, the unveiling of the first female statue in London. The statue honoured Millicent Farcet, a woman who campaigned for women's right to vote during the nineteenth century. She was memoralised in 2018, more than one hundred (100) years later. Amidst these breakthroughs, there are much more to be done globally for women and their right to freedom. I recently encountered cultures where puberty among boys is an occasion to kill the fattened cow and celebrate this milestone with the entire community, however, among the female gender, the said day in their lives is just a 'normal day'.

Within the context of the church, I was privileged to be part of a national gathering with a congregation of over five hundred (500) persons. During the congregational singing, two separate male figures stepped out of the audience and acted inappropriate. One of the men stood up in front of the congregation as though conducting an orchestral band. The other male proceeded to dance with one of the female minister on the pulpit during the service and no effort was made to constrain the duo's inappropriate behaviour. I often wonder what the reaction would have been if such inappropriateness originated from two females. It certainly would not have been tolerated.

Prejudice against women is an epidemic; despite cultural shift, changes seem to be slow. We cannot deny that change is nonexistent. It could be easily forgotten that what is considered to be basic human right in the Western world could be areas of prejudices and struggles among women in many other parts of the world.

One great encounter I had was in Kenya, Africa. I saw a baboon carrying her babies. The male baby was carried on her back exposed to the elements and must cling on to his mother for life while learning about danger and survival. However, the female, rather delicate, was carried in warm, comfortable style with more protection, a reminder of the distinct roles. More than any other time in history, many cultures are making adjustments in their attitude towards women and recognising and endorsing the unique contribution they make in our societies today.

In the book of Genesis, we learnt that Eve came out of Adam;

therefore, she possessed his Deoxyribonucleic acid (DNA). It can be noted in a scientific way that whatever is found in the man is also embodied within the woman. It draws out the sense of similarity within us and deserves to be acknowledged and respected. Undoubtedly, many women have influenced their husbands in remarkable ways, causing them to violate their own convictions and consciences—for example Eve, Sarah, Jezebel, and Sapphira. Therefore, as a result of such influences, it can be inferred, whatever was in the woman could not be found in the man.

Women exemplify Christ's authority as He submitted to God the Father; displaying such Christlike spirit and without uttering a word, they can lead others to Christ. Through the purity of their lives they show respect for God, not a mere exhibit of their external possession of gold jewellery, fancy hairstyles, makeup, and fine clothing. None of this depicts true inner beauty. Real beauty is gentle, of a quiet spirit, and permanent; it is God's definition of true beauty. Christian women long ago made themselves beautiful in that way. Sarah (a type of the church) obeyed Abraham (a type of Christ). Abraham followed God and sacrificed all that he had just as Christ sacrificed Himself. Women are true children of Sarah if they fearlessly do what is right.

Even Christ chose to identify with the female gender in such unique way as He refers to his body, as His bride (a woman). He also did more than any other in history to elevate women to a place of worth and self-esteem. The account of the woman caught in adultery on the verge of being stoned to death according to the law of Moses: she was restored to wholeness and continued to live in her society without guilt. The woman with the bleeding disorder was made completely whole, though she struggled in a predominantly male arena. She breached protocol to get to Jesus without being observed by the twelve disciples. How did she really do it? The Samaritan woman at the well conversed with Jesus, left the well with jubilance and a positive message even though she had lived a promiscuous life in the village.

In His effort to elevate the status of women, Christ who was never married while He was on earth, waits for the day when He takes the church as His bride (a woman). The only wedding proposed to take place at the end of the age. Christ chose to figuratively describe the joyous reunion at the end of the age as one of a relationship between a man and a woman on the most significant day of their lives. He chose to describe the church as a woman, His bride. I believe this is deliberate and not accidental.

Scriptural account of what was Jesus' most traumatic experience on earth, recorded that His twelve bosom partners (all male) deserted Him and hardly looked back during His crucifixion and death. Commendable that the women stayed, knew exactly where he was buried, lamented, suffered from palpitations and insomnia, prepared spices, woke very early, visited the tomb, and got the information firsthand. They heard that Jesus was alive and were the first to see Him after His resurrection. The men disappeared when the women were there. These characteristics of woman were significant and powerful. They represented the qualities, Christ chose as a replica for His own body. Regardless of gender whether male or female we are described as the body of Christ, His bride. Therefore, Christ's bride could not be a weak insignificant character.

Christ endorsed the uniqueness of those female characters and this is further highlighted in chapter 107 *The Chosen Lady*.

Amidst the plethora of social, societal, and cultural injustices, women have always succeeded because of their resilience. Some characters in this book have made claim to fame and success by developing an approach of optimism and possibility. Their success spans thousands of years, outstretching their longevity.

The root problem in numerous societies is the need for dignity, respect, and equity among the sexes. A rather simple solution of embracing and enhancing similarities while celebrating differences would be a key element for resolution. The mantra for living must be to treat others in the same way one expects to be treated. The dilemma we face is not one that will resolve overnight, but hopefully over time.

REFERENCES

Adams, D. et al. (1999). *Collins Concise Dictionary & Thesauru*s. Great Britain. Harper Collins Publishers.

Douglas, J.D. et al. (1982) *New Bible Dictionary Second Edition*. England. Inter Varsity Press.

Dow, J.L. (1992). *Collins Gem Dictionary of the Bible*. Great Britain. Harper Collins Publishers.

Schurer, E. (1995). *A history of the Jewish People in the time of Jesus Christ*. Division 1 Vol.1 & Vol.11. USA. Hendrickson Publishers, Inc.

Weller, B.F. et al. (1990). *Bailliere's Nurses Dictionary 21st Ed*. London. Bailliere Tindall.

INDEX

Index

www.ingramcontent.com/pod-product-compliance
Ingram Content Group UK Ltd.
Pitfield, Milton Keynes, MK11 3LW, UK
UKHW022341240325
456661UK00006B/21